NATIONAL GEOGRAPHIC
ANIMAL
ENCYCLOPEDIA

NATIONAL GEOGRAPHIC SOCIETY

Washington, D.C.

A Marshall Edition
Conceived, edited, and designed by
Marshall Editions
The Old Brewery
6 Blundell Street
London N7 9BH

First published in the United States by the
National Geographic Society
1145 17th Street N.W.
Washington, D.C. 20036-4688

Copyright © 1999, 2000 Marshall Editions

All rights reserved. Reproduction of the whole or any
part of the contents without written permission from the
National Geographic Society is prohibited.

Cataloging-in-Publication Data on page 264

Originated in Singapore by Master Image
Printed in China

Author: Jinny Johnson
Other contributors: Steve Setford, Roger Few,
Philip Whitfield
Consultants: *Mammals:* Ronald M. Nowak, author
of the fourth, fifth, and sixth editions of *Walker's
Mammals of the World;* Sara Churchfield,
King's College, University of London
Birds: Jon L. Dunn, chief consultant for *Field Guide
to the Birds of North America,* published by National
Geographic; Malcolm Ogilvie, formerly of the Wildfowl
and Wetlands Trust
Reptiles and Amphibians: Thomas A. Jenssen, Associate
Professor of Zoology, Virginia Polytechnic Institute and
State University; Barry Cox, formerly of King's College,
University of London
Fish: Valerie C. Chase, National Aquarium, Baltimore,
Md.; Philip Whitfield, Head of the Division of Life
Sciences, King's College, University of London
Insects, spiders, and other invertebrates:
Jerry Harasewych, Curator, Department of Invertebrate
Zoology, National Museum of Natural History,
Washington, D.C.; David W. Inouye, Department
of Biology, University of Maryland; Bryan Turner, King's
College, University of London

Contents

Introduction

The land, air, and waters of our world are filled with an astonishing variety of life, and more than 1.5 million kinds, or species, of animals have been named so far. All of these animals can be divided into two main groups—vertebrates and invertebrates.

Fishes, amphibians, reptiles, birds, and mammals are all vertebrates, which means they have a backbone in their body. Invertebrate animals, such as insects, spiders, and snails, do not have a backbone. Scientists believe that most species of vertebrates, such as mammals and birds, are already known, but there may be millions of species of insects and other small invertebrates that still await discovery. This illustrated encyclopedia provides an invaluable catalog of all the major types of animals from whales to fleas.

The Earth has a number of natural zones, or habitats, divided according to the climate and the plants and animals that live there. The habitats are shown on this **map**. The colors are the same as for the habitat symbols (see page 5).

Key to map (see page 5 for full key)

 Temperate grassland

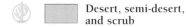 Tropical grassland

 Northern forest

 Deciduous forest and seasonal forest

Tropical evergreen forest

Desert, semi-desert, and scrub

Coral reef

Coast

High ground

Tundra and polar

Map of the world's main natural habitats

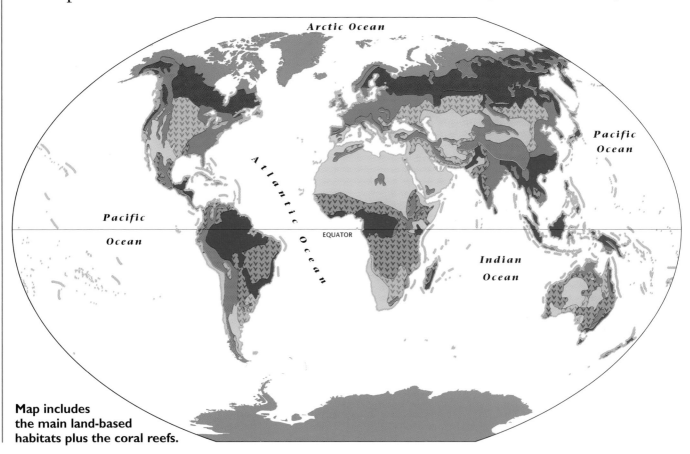

Map includes the main land-based habitats plus the coral reefs.

How to use this book

This encyclopedia of animals is divided into six chapters: mammals, birds, reptiles, amphibians, fish, and insects, spiders, and other invertebrates. Each chapter contains an introduction, pages that describe the features of each type of animal (such as a mammal), catalog pages that illustrate and give facts about many different species, and focus pages that look in more detail at particular animals. There are also five special essays featuring information on animal adaptation and behavior.

Habitat
Habitat symbols show where the species or insect family lives. The key is below.

Size
The approximate size of the animal is given in imperial and metric measurements. See page 263 for a list of the abbreviations in the book.

Range
This lists the areas of the world in which the species is found.

Scientific name
Most species of animals have a common name, such as long-nosed echidna, which can vary from place to place. All species have a scientific or Latin-based name, which always stays the same. It is shown in *italics*. In the insects and spiders section, the family name is usually given instead of the species name.
Number of species is the number in that family.

Long-nosed echidna

Status
A solid red dot means the species is almost extinct. A red semi-circle means the species is endangered, and a red ring means it is vulnerable, or nearly endangered.

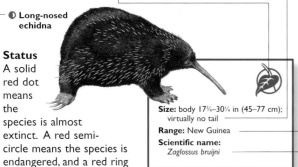

Size: body 17¾–30¼ in (45–77 cm); virtually no tail
Range: New Guinea
Scientific name: *Zaglossus bruijni*

Key to habitat symbols

Temperate grassland
includes steppe, prairie, pampas, bush, open country, moors, heaths, plains, and lowlands

Tropical grassland
also called savanna

Northern forest
includes taiga, northern (boreal), and coniferous forests

Deciduous forest and seasonal forest
includes temperate and tropical seasonal forests

Tropical evergreen forest
includes tropical and subtropical rain forests, bamboo, and mangroves

Desert
includes rocky areas, sandy areas, semi-desert, scrub, brushland, arid (dry) and semi-arid land

Fresh water
includes rivers, lakes, ponds, lagoons, streams, creeks, wetlands, marshes, swamps, inland waters, floodplains, springs, ditches, dams, riverbanks, and underground water in caves

Inhabited areas and agricultural land
includes gardens, orchards, parks, farmland, cultivated land, fields, plantations, pasture, towns and cities, hedgerows, and roadsides

Coast
includes mud flats, shores, cliffs, islands, and tidal areas

Coastal water
includes estuaries and the seafloor

Coral reef

Oceanic
includes open seas and oceans, top and middle layers of water

Deep sea

High ground
includes hills, foothills, plateaus, volcanoes, and mountains

Tundra and polar
includes Antarctic and Arctic regions, pack ice and ice floes

Worldwide
used for insects and spiders only

Temperate
used for insects and spiders only

Tropical
used for insects and spiders only

Mammals

Human beings are just 1 of about 4,800 mammal species. Mammals come in all shapes and sizes and are found in almost every part of the world, from the frozen Arctic to the hottest deserts, the densest forests, and the biggest oceans. There are many different kinds of mammals, each with its own way of life. The tiger, for example, hunts prey in the depths of the forest, whereas dolphins swim through the sea, moles burrow underground, bats fly through the air, horses gallop across the ground, and monkeys swing through the trees.

Fossils show that the first mammals evolved more than 200 million years ago from a group of mammal-like reptiles, when dinosaurs still roamed the Earth. The earliest mammals were small shrewlike animals that fed on insects and dinosaur eggs. When dinosaurs died out about 65 million years ago, mammals took their place as the dominant creatures. Their ability to adapt to very different habitats helped mammals spread throughout the globe.

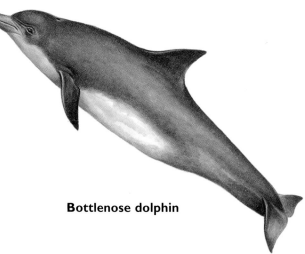

A female **polar bear** dozes with her cub in the sunshine on the Arctic ice. One of the reasons why mammals are so successful is that they take greater care of their young than other animals, protecting them until they are old enough to fend for themselves.

Bottlenose dolphin

What is a mammal?

Mammals are a very diverse group of animals, but they all have certain things in common. They are warm-blooded, have lungs to breathe in air, and have a bony frame called a skeleton to support their bodies and protect their internal organs. Most have relatively large brains, good senses, and hair or fur.

Indian elephant

Mammals are warm-blooded animals, meaning that they can keep their body temperature constant, whatever the temperature of their surroundings. When they are too hot, many mammals sweat to cool down. **Elephants** cannot sweat, so they keep cool by staying in the shade, bathing in water, and letting heat radiate from their huge ears.

Senses

Mammals generally have well-developed senses of sight, hearing, smell, taste, and touch. These senses help them locate food, avoid predators, find a mate, and much more. The sense organs are mostly found in the head, near the brain.

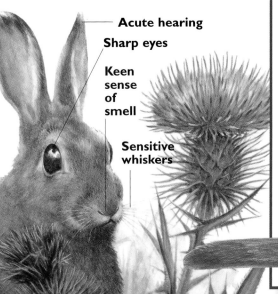

Acute hearing

Sharp eyes

Keen sense of smell

Sensitive whiskers

Types of mammals

Most mammals give birth to live young. In the majority of mammals, known as eutherians, the babies grow inside the mother's womb. They are supplied with food and oxygen by a special organ called the placenta and are well developed when they are born. The babies of some mammals, called marsupials, are very undeveloped at birth and crawl into a special pouch, where they can grow stronger in safety. Monotreme mammals are unusual in that they lay eggs, instead of producing live babies.

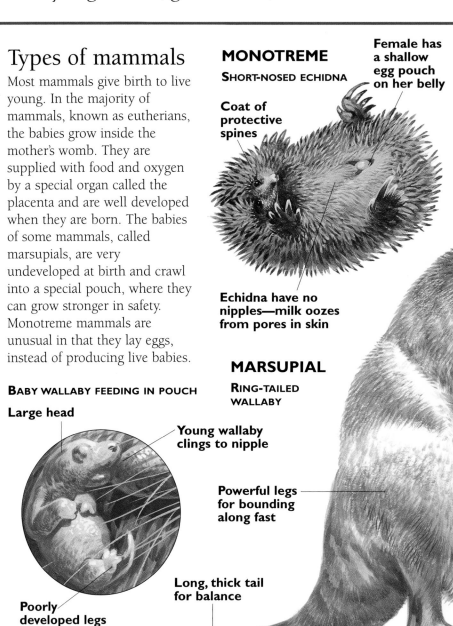

MONOTREME

SHORT-NOSED ECHIDNA

Female has a shallow egg pouch on her belly

Coat of protective spines

Echidna have no nipples—milk oozes from pores in skin

BABY WALLABY FEEDING IN POUCH

Large head

Young wallaby clings to nipple

Poorly developed legs

MARSUPIAL

RING-TAILED WALLABY

Powerful legs for bounding along fast

Long, thick tail for balance

Suckling

Instead of having to gather food for her babies like other animals, a female mammal is able to make her own baby food. She has special mammary glands (also called breasts or udders) that produce milk, which the babies suck from nipples. This is called suckling. The milk contains sugar, fat, proteins, and vitamins, which the babies need to grow and stay healthy.

Female wild boar with young

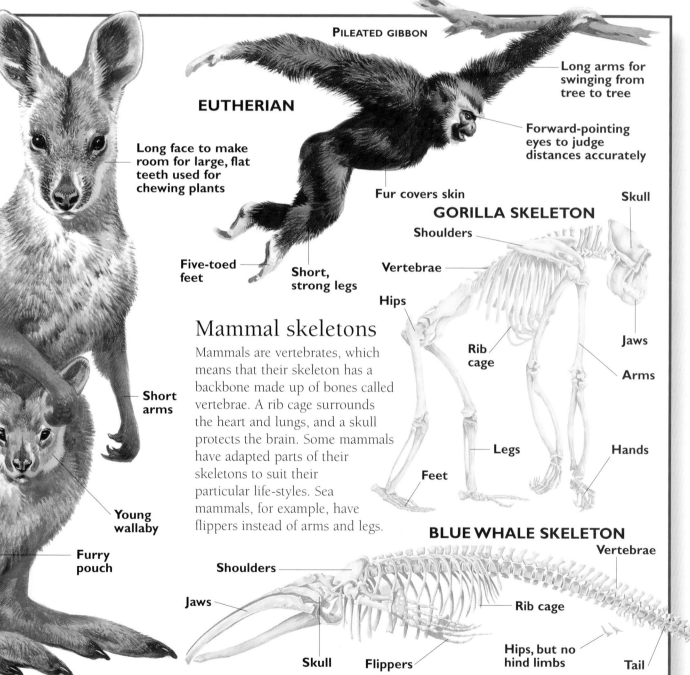

PILEATED GIBBON

EUTHERIAN

Long arms for swinging from tree to tree

Forward-pointing eyes to judge distances accurately

Long face to make room for large, flat teeth used for chewing plants

Fur covers skin

Five-toed feet

Short, strong legs

Short arms

Young wallaby

Furry pouch

Mammal skeletons

Mammals are vertebrates, which means that their skeleton has a backbone made up of bones called vertebrae. A rib cage surrounds the heart and lungs, and a skull protects the brain. Some mammals have adapted parts of their skeletons to suit their particular life-styles. Sea mammals, for example, have flippers instead of arms and legs.

GORILLA SKELETON

Shoulders

Vertebrae

Hips

Rib cage

Skull

Jaws

Arms

Legs

Hands

Feet

BLUE WHALE SKELETON

Shoulders

Jaws

Skull

Flippers

Vertebrae

Rib cage

Hips, but no hind limbs

Tail

9

Monotremes and marsupials

In most mammal species, the young develop inside their mother's body for a long time before they are born. But monotremes and marsupials are different. Just like their reptile ancestors, monotremes lay eggs. However, when the eggs hatch, the young feed on their mother's milk like other mammal babies. Milk oozes from enlarged skin pores (female monotremes have no nipples). Marsupials give birth to very undeveloped babies: Some are no bigger than a grain of rice, and all are hairless and blind. Once they are born, young marsupials develop in a furry pouch on the underside of their mother's body.

Monotremes

Monotremes consist of echidnas (sometimes called spiny anteaters) and platypuses. A female echidna lays a single soft-shelled egg and puts it in a shallow pouch on her belly. The egg is covered in a sticky substance for seven to ten days until it hatches. The platypus is one of the few venomous mammals: Males have a spur on each hind foot, which they use to inject poison into an enemy. A female platypus lays two or three eggs at the end of a long tunnel. The eggs take up to two weeks to hatch.

① Long-nosed echidna

Size: body 17¾–30¼ in (45–77 cm); virtually no tail
Range: New Guinea
Scientific name: *Zaglossus bruijni*

Long-nosed echidna

Echidnas have long, slender snouts. They have no teeth and weak jaws, so they grab insects with their rough, grooved tongues and crush them against the roofs of their mouths.

Platypus

The platypus spends most of the day in a riverside burrow. At dawn and dusk it comes out to feed on the riverbed, using its sensitive bill to probe the mud for insects, worms, grubs, crayfish, and frogs. Its bill is a skin-covered framework of bone.

Platypus

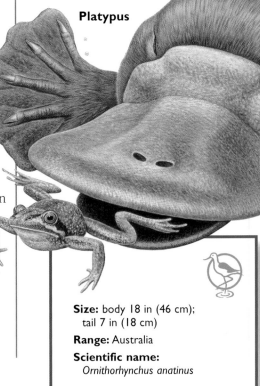

Short-nosed echidna

The echidna's spiny coat protects it from attackers. When threatened, it either curls into a ball or, if it is on soft soil, digs straight down so that only its spines are visible. In this way, its soft spineless face and underparts are protected.

Size: body 13¾–19¾ in (35–50 cm); tail 3½ in (9 cm)
Range: Australia, southeastern New Guinea
Scientific name: *Tachyglossus aculeatus*

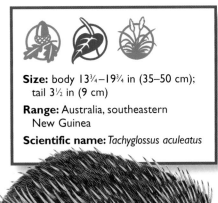

Short-nosed echidna

10

Size: body 18 in (46 cm); tail 7 in (18 cm)
Range: Australia
Scientific name: *Ornithorhynchus anatinus*

Marsupials

The word "marsupial" means "pouched mammal." A tiny marsupial baby has to wriggle its way through its mother's fur to reach her pouch. Once inside, it latches on to a nipple and drinks her milk. The nipple swells up inside the baby's mouth and keeps the baby fastened to its milk supply. The pouch gives the baby a safe place in which to grow and develop until it is ready to face the outside world. There are more than 250 marsupial species, most of which live in Australia and on neighboring islands, but a few species are found in the Americas.

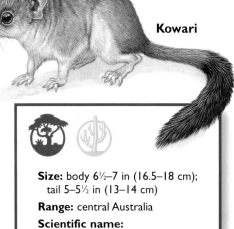

Kowari

Size: body 6½–7 in (16.5–18 cm);
tail 5–5½ in (13–14 cm)
Range: central Australia
Scientific name:
Dasyuroides byrnei

Water opossum

The water opossum is the only marsupial that lives in water. It emerges from its riverbank burrow to swim and search for fish, shellfish, and other small water creatures, which it carries back to the bank to eat. It swims with its webbed hind feet and steers with its long tail. Its oily fur repels water, keeping it dry.

Water opossum

Size: body 10½–13 in (27–33 cm);
tail 14¼–15¾ in (36–40 cm)
Range: Mexico, Central and
South America
Scientific name: *Chironectes minimus*

Kowari

At home in grasslands and deserts, these marsupials live alone or in small groups in an underground burrow. At night, they hunt among the tussock grass for insects, lizards, and birds to eat. Kowaris breed in winter and produce litters of five or six young.

Virginia opossum

This is the only marsupial native to Canada and the United States. It often scavenges for food in dumps and garbage bins. To escape a predator such as a dog, bobcat, or eagle, the opossum may "play dead," lying on its side with its tongue hanging out and its eyes shut or staring into space. Thinking it is dead, the predator may become less cautious, giving the opossum a chance to escape.

Virginia opossum

Size: body 12¾–19¾ in (32.5–50 cm);
tail 10–21 in (25.5–53.5 cm)
Range: southeastern Canada
through U.S.A. to Central America
Scientific name: *Didelphis virginiana*

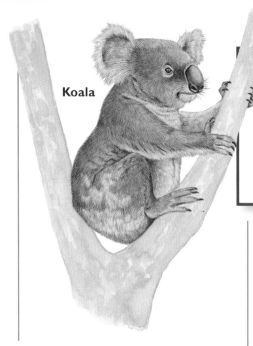

Koala

Size: body 23½–33½ in (60–85 cm);
virtually no tail

Range: eastern Australia

Scientific name:
Phascolarctos cinereus

Koala

The koala spends up to 18 hours each day asleep. The rest of the time it feeds on the leaves of eucalyptus trees. It has a long gut, which enables it to digest the tough leaves and deal with the leaves' poisonous chemicals. Special pouches in its cheeks store the leaves until it needs to eat them.

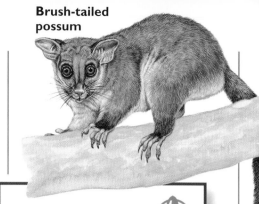

Brush-tailed possum

Size: body 12½–22¾ in (32–58 cm);
tail 9½–13¾ in (24–35 cm)

Range: Australia; introduced into
New Zealand

Scientific name:
Trichosurus vulpecula

Brush-tailed possum

In its natural woodland habitat, the brush-tailed possum feeds on flowers, leaves, fruit, insects, and young birds. In populated areas, it makes its home in eaves of buildings and feeds on garbage. It has one young once or twice a year.

Short-nosed bandicoot

The short-nosed bandicoot hunts by following the scent of its prey. It lives in areas of dense vegetation, where it can hide from larger predators such as eagles and foxes. It feeds on worms, insect larvae, and underground fungi.

Size: body 27½–47 in
(70–120 cm); virtually no tail

Range: eastern Australia,
Tasmania

Scientific name: *Vombatus ursinus*

Wombat

Wombat

The wombat feeds on grass in forests and scrubland and can go without water for months at a time. In high summer, this burly mammal spends the day in a long, deep burrow, sheltered from the heat. The female gives birth to a single young, which stays in her pouch for three months. Once out of the pouch, it forages with her for several months before leaving to live independently.

Tasmanian devil

About the size of a small dog, the Tasmanian devil has powerful jaws that enable it to crush the bones of its prey. This stocky marsupial moves slowly. It uses its keen sense of smell to locate prey in the dark. It feeds on reptiles, birds, fish, small mammals, and the remains of larger, dead animals.

Size: body 20½–31½ in (52–80 cm);
tail 9–11¾ in (23–30 cm)

Range: Tasmania

Scientific name:
Sarcophilus harrisii

Size: body 11¾–13 in (30–33 cm);
tail 3–7 in (7.5–18 cm)

Range: southern and eastern
Australia, Tasmania

Scientific name: *Isoodon obesulus*

Tasmanian devil

Short-nosed bandicoot

Greater glider

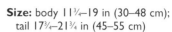

Red kangaroo

The red kangaroo is the largest marsupial. It usually bounds along on its back legs only, making huge leaps and reaching speeds of up to 35 mph (56 km/h). It lives in Australia's hot, dry deserts and in grasslands. The female gives birth to a single baby called a joey, which emerges from her pouch at the age of two months. Whenever danger threatens, the joey dives back into her pouch out of harm's way.

Size: body 3¼–5¼ ft (1–1.6 m); tail 35½–43½ in (90–110 cm)
Range: central Australia
Scientific name:
Macropus rufus

Red kangaroo

Musky rat-kangaroo

This tiny kangaroo is unusual because it regularly gives birth to twins. Unlike other kangaroos, it prefers to move around on all fours like a rabbit. In spite of its name, the musky rat-kangaroo does not have a bad, musky smell.

Musky rat-kangaroo

Size: body 9–13½ in (23–34 cm); tail 5–6¾ in (13–17 cm)
Range: northeastern Australia
Scientific name:
Hypsiprymnodon moschatus

Bridled nail-tail wallaby

The nail-tail gets its name because it has a small fingerlike nail hidden in thick hair at the tip of its tail. It has a strange way of hopping, moving its arms in circles as it bounces along. Heavy grazing by sheep and cattle has destroyed much of the scrubland where the nail-tail used to live and feed. It eats grass and roots.

Size: body 17¾–26¼ in (45–67 cm); tail 13–26 in (33–66 cm)
Range: eastern Australia
Scientific name:
Onychogalea fraenata

◑ **Bridled nail-tail wallaby**

Size: body 11¾–19 in (30–48 cm); tail 17¾–21¾ in (45–55 cm)
Range: eastern Australia
Scientific name:
Petauroides volans

Greater glider

The greater glider has flaps of skin running between its wrists and ankles. To get from tree to tree in the eucalyptus forests where it lives, it leaps into the air and spreads out its arms and legs. The skin flaps act like a kind of parachute, allowing it to glide to its destination.

Lumholtz's tree kangaroo

The tree kangaroo spends most of its time high up in the forest trees, where it eats leaves and fruit. It can even sleep up there, crouched on a thick branch. Its numbers are dwindling because logging is causing its rain forest habitat to shrink.

Lumholtz's tree kangaroo

Size: body 20½–31½ in (52–80 cm); tail 16½–36½ in (42–93 cm)
Range: northeastern Australia
Scientific name:
Dendrolagus lumholtzi

MONOTREMES AND MARSUPIALS

Insect eaters, sloths, and colugos

A lthough these animals are not all related to one another, many of them feed almost exclusively on insects, and they are perhaps among the oddest-looking mammals of all. The insect eaters include armadillos, anteaters, pangolins, aardvarks, moles, tenrecs, shrews, and hedgehogs. Sloths and colugos are plant eaters and spend most of their time in the trees.

Three-toed sloth

Size: body 19¾–23½ in (50–60 cm); tail 2½–2¾ in (6.5–7 cm)
Range: northern South America
Scientific name:
Bradypus tridactylus

Anteaters, armadillos, pangolins, aardvarks, and sloths

Anteaters and armadillos are edentate mammals. The word "edentate" means "toothless," which is misleading, as only the anteaters are truly toothless. In fact, some armadillos have up to a hundred teeth, although they are small and peglike. These mammals do not need big biting teeth because they feed on ants and termites, which they lick up with their tongues. Sloths are also edentates, but they feed on leaves instead of insects, chewing them very slowly. They eat, sleep, mate, and even give birth hanging upside down in trees. Pangolins and aardvarks have life-styles similar to those of armadillos and anteaters, even though they are not closely related to them.

Three-toed sloth

The three-toed sloth is the slowest living mammal, managing a top speed of just 6½ feet (2 m) per minute on the ground. The hairs of its fur have grooves in which tiny plants called algae live. The algae give the fur a greenish tinge, which camouflages the sloth, hiding it from eagles, jaguars, and other predators.

Giant anteater

This anteater sniffs out ant nests and termite mounds, breaks them open with its claws, and thrusts its long, sticky tongue inside. Ants and termites become glued to the tongue, which is covered with tiny spines. The anteater is careful never to destroy a nest or eat all the ants, so it can feed there in the future.

Size: body 3¼–4 ft (1–1.2 m); tail 25½–35½ in (65–90 cm)
Range: Central and South America to northern Argentina
Scientific name:
Myrmecophaga tridactyla

O **Giant anteater**

14

① Giant armadillo

Giant armadillo

Like other armadillos, the giant armadillo's body is covered with horny plates. It weighs up to 132 pounds (60 kg) and is very strong. It can burrow into ant nests or smash open termite mounds with its front limbs. Unlike the nine-banded armadillo, it can only partly roll into a ball—it runs from danger or digs a hole.

Size: body 29½–39½ in (75–100 cm); tail 19¾ in (50 cm)

Range: South America, from Venezuela to northern Argentina

Scientific name: *Priodontes maximus*

Aardvark

The aardvark looks as if it is made from parts of other animals, with its kangaroolike tail, piglike body, and rabbitlike ears. The aardvark feeds on termites at night. During the day, it sleeps in its burrow, which it digs with its strong feet. The burrow may be very long and complex, with numerous openings.

Aardvark

Size: body 3¼–5¼ ft (1–1.6 m); tail 17½–23½ in (44.5–60 cm)

Range: Africa south of the Sahara

Scientific name: *Orycteropus afer*

Northern tamandua

The tamandua is a tree-dwelling anteater. On the ground, it moves slowly and clumsily, but in the trees of the forest it is an agile climber. It uses its tail for gripping. If attacked, the tamandua strikes out with its sharp, powerful claws. The female gives birth to a single baby, which travels around the rain forest on her back.

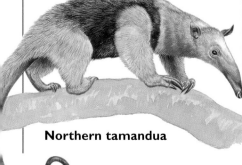

Northern tamandua

Size: body 21¼–22¾ in (54–58 cm); tail 21½–21¾ in (54.5–55.5 cm)

Range: from southern Mexico to northern South America

Scientific name: *Tamandua mexicana*

Nine-banded armadillo

When threatened, this armadillo rolls up into a ball so that its soft belly is protected by an armor-plated back. It spends most of the day asleep in a burrow, which it digs with its strong front claws. The hind legs kick away loose soil. Beetles and ants are the armadillo's main food.

Nine-banded armadillo

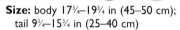

Size: body 17¾–19¾ in (45–50 cm); tail 9¾–15¾ in (25–40 cm)

Range: southern U.S.A., Mexico, Central and South America

Scientific name: *Dasypus novemcinctus*

Giant pangolin

The giant pangolin's body is covered with large, overlapping scales. When feeding on ant nests, thick eyelids protect the eyes from bites, and special muscles seal off the nostrils to keep out the ants. It can roll up into a ball if threatened or lash out with its tail, which is clad in razor-sharp scales.

Giant pangolin

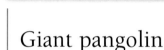

Size: body 29½–31½ in (75–80 cm); tail 19¾–25½ in (50–65 cm)

Range: eastern and central Africa

Scientific name: *Manis gigantea*

Moles, tenrecs, shrews, hedgehogs, colugos, and solenodons

Moles, tenrecs, shrews, and hedgehogs feed almost exclusively on insects and small creatures such as worms, centipedes, snails, and spiders. Many of these mammals have long, narrow snouts in order to reach into the small spaces where insects hide. They also have sharp teeth and claws and poor sight but a good sense of smell. Although elephant shrews and tree shrews are called shrews, they are classified differently from the other shews shown here. Colugos can glide through the trees using special flaps of skin. Solenodons have a poisonous bite— a very rare feature in mammals.

Streaked tenrec

The streaked tenrec is covered with protective spines. The female produces a litter of 7 to 11 babies. If she feels threatened, she raises a small patch of spines on her back and vibrates them rapidly. This makes a clicking noise to warn her young of approaching danger.

Streaked tenrec

Size: body 6¼–7½ in (16–19 cm); virtually no tail

Range: Madagascar

Scientific name: *Hemicentetes semispinosus*

European hedgehog

European hedgehog

Size: body 5¼–10½ in (13.5–27 cm); tail ⅓–2 in (1–5 cm)

Range: Europe; introduced into New Zealand

Scientific name: *Erinaceus europaeus*

The hedgehog roots around in hedges and undergrowth for small creatures to eat, making piglike grunts as it goes. If it is attacked, the hedgehog curls up into a ball, so that its prickly coat deters predators. In cold climates, it hibernates through the winter.

Giant golden mole

The giant golden mole hunts aboveground for beetles, small lizards, slugs, and worms. When disturbed, it heads straight for the safety of its burrow. Even though this mole is blind, it always knows exactly where the entrance is. No one knows quite how it does this.

◑ **Giant golden mole**

Size: body 7¾–9½ in (20–24 cm); no tail

Range: South Africa

Scientific name: *Chrysospalax trevelyani*

Star-nosed mole

The nose of this little mole is surrounded by a fringe of 22 sensitive, fingerlike tentacles, which help it find food on the bottom of ponds and streams. An excellent swimmer, this mole feeds mostly on worms, aquatic insects, and small fish.

Size: body 4½–5 in (11–12.5 cm); tail 3–3½ in (7.5–9 cm)

Range: southeastern Canada, northeastern U.S.A.

Scientific name: *Condylura cristata*

Star-nosed mole

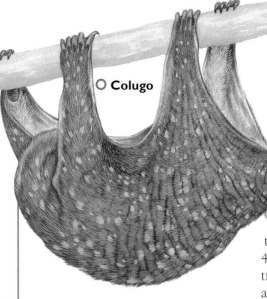
O **Colugo**

Size: body 15–16½ in (38–42 cm); tail 8¾–10½ in (22–27 cm)
Range: Philippines
Scientific name: *Cynocephalus volans*

Colugo

The forest-dwelling colugo, also known as the flying lemur, has flaps of skin running from its neck to the tip of its tail. By leaping into the air and stretching out its arms and legs to open the flaps, it can glide for 440 feet (135 m) between the trees. It is an agile climber but is almost helpless on the ground.

Common tree shrew

This squirrel-like creature is an excellent climber. It normally lives alone or with its mate and feeds on ants, spiders, seeds, buds, and probably small birds and mice. It nests in holes in trees or among tree roots, where the female gives birth to a litter of one to three young.

Common tree shrew

Size: body 5½–9 in (14–23 cm); tail 4¾–8¼ in (12–21 cm)
Range: southern Asia
Scientific name: *Tupaia glis*

O **Short-eared elephant shrew**

Size: body 3¾–5 in (9.5–12.5 cm); tail 3¾–5½ in (9.5–14 cm)
Range: southern Africa
Scientific name: *Macroscelides proboscideus*

Short-eared elephant shrew

Elephant shrews are named for their extraordinary, trunklike noses. They walk on all fours, but when they need to move fast, they hop on their back legs like miniature kangaroos. They live in dry, open country. They feed on termites, seeds, fruit, and berries in the daytime but find shelter from the midday sun in burrows.

Armored shrew

The armored shrew has an incredibly strong backbone and is said to be able to support the weight of a grown man without being crushed! It lives in forests, where it feeds on insects and other small creatures.

Size: body 11–12½ in (28–32 cm); tail 6¾–9¾ in (17–25 cm)
Range: Cuba
Scientific name: *Solenodon cubanus*

Cuban solenodon

The solenodon probes the forest floor at night in search of food such as insects, fungi, and roots. It can also climb trees to reach fruit, berries, and buds. It kills lizards, frogs, and small birds with a venomous bite. The venom is produced by glands in its lower jaw.

Size: body 4¾–6 in (12–15 cm); tail 2¾–3¾ in (7–9.5 cm)
Range: central Africa
Scientific name: *Scutisorex somereni*

① Cuban solenodon

Armored shrew

17

Bats

Bats are the only flying mammals. They power themselves through the air on smooth wings of skin, making sudden midair turns and spectacular twists. Most bats spend the day asleep, hanging upside down, out of reach of predators. At night, they are ready to launch themselves into the air to hunt for food. Some bats use echolocation to find their food and navigate in the dark. They make high-pitched sounds that bounce, or echo, off nearby objects and are picked up by the bats' ears. The bats use the echoes to locate their prey and avoid obstacles.

Linnaeus's false vampire bat

Size: body 5–5¼ in (12.5–13.5 cm); no tail; wingspan 30–39 in (76–100 cm)

Range: southern Mexico to Peru and Brazil; Trinidad

Scientific name: *Vampyrum spectrum*

Spear-nosed bat

The spear-nosed bat will eat insects and fruit but prefers the flesh of mice, birds, and small bats. The spear-nosed bat, in turn, is preyed upon by false vampire bats. It has a broad spear-shaped flap of skin sticking up from its nose. Huge flocks of these heavy-bodied bats like to live in buildings and caves. Flocks emerge at dusk to fly to their feeding grounds. The female gives birth to a single baby once or twice a year.

Spear-nosed bat

Size: body 4–5¼ in (10–13 cm); tail 1 in (2.5 cm); wingspan 17¼–18½ in (44–47 cm)

Range: Central America and northern South America

Scientific name: *Phyllostomus hastatus*

Linnaeus's false vampire bat

The largest bat in North and South America, this species does not drink blood like a true vampire bat. It hunts for prey such as birds, rodents, and other bats and may also eat some fruit and insects. Using its feet and wing claws, it moves well on all fours and can stalk mice and other prey on the ground. It then makes a final pounce, killing its victim by breaking its neck. The bats breed once a year and take great care of their young. The young are suckled by the mother at first and then fed pieces of chewed mouse flesh.

Ghost bat

The ghost bat, a type of false vampire bat, gets its name from the eerie color of its pale fur at night. It flies over all kinds of terrain, from forest to desert, and feeds on mice, birds, geckos, and other bats. By day, it roosts in caves, cracks in rocks, and old mine shafts, but it is easily disturbed by people. It is now rare because quarrying (removing stone) has destroyed some of its most important roosts.

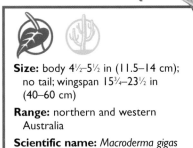

Size: body 4½–5½ in (11.5–14 cm); no tail; wingspan 15¾–23½ in (40–60 cm)

Range: northern and western Australia

Scientific name: *Macroderma gigas*

○ **Ghost bat**

Greater fruit bat

The largest wings in the bat world belong to the greater fruit bat. By day, these bats roost in trees in flocks of several thousand, taking flight at dusk to find juicy fruit to eat or sweet flower nectar to lap up. They help fruit trees reproduce by carrying pollen, which sticks to the bats' fur, from flower to flower. Fruit seeds the bats spit out or pass in their droppings take root and grow into new fruit trees.

Size: body 13¾–15¾ in (35–40 cm); no tail; wingspan 5 ft (1.5 m)
Range: southern and southeastern Asia
Scientific name: *Pteropus giganteus*

Greater fruit bat

Greater horseshoe bat

The greater horseshoe bat feeds on beetles, swooping down to snatch them off the ground with pinpoint accuracy. It roosts in caves, trees, and the roofs of old buildings. But as caves are explored, trees cut down, and buildings leveled, it is harder and harder for the bat to find suitable homes. It is now almost extinct in northwestern Europe.

Size: body 4¼–5 in (11–13 cm); tail 1–1½ in (2.5–4 cm); wingspan 13–13¾ in (33–35 cm)
Range: Europe, Asia, northern Africa
Scientific name: *Rhinolophus ferrumequinum*

Greater horseshoe bat

Tube-nosed fruit bat

The scroll-shaped nostrils of this bat stick out on each side of its head like a pair of snorkel tubes. They probably help the bat find ripe fruit such as guavas, figs, and even young coconuts. Using its sharp teeth, the bat chews the fruit to extract the juice. It drops the unwanted pulp on the ground.

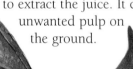

Tube-nosed fruit bat

Size: body 2¾–4¾ in (7–12 cm); tail ⅝–1 in (1.5–2.5 cm); wingspan 7¾–11 in (20–28 cm)
Range: Pacific islands near New Guinea
Scientific name: *Nyctimene major*

American long-eared bat

This bat's ears are nearly as long as its head and body combined. The bat uses its sensitive ears to detect the calls and movements of insect prey and to find its way by echolocation. The long-eared bat hibernates in caves during winter. In summer, it roosts in colonies of 50 to 100 bats in buildings and trees, feeding at night mainly on moths.

Size: body 1½–2 in (4–5 cm); tail 1¼–1¾ in (3–4.5 cm); wingspan 9–11 in (23–28 cm)
Range: southwestern Canada, U.S.A., Mexico
Scientific name: *Plecotus townsendii*

American long-eared bat

19

Roosting bats

The common vampire bat is a cave dweller, clinging to cave roofs and roosting in total darkness in colonies of up to 1,000 bats, but most commonly about 100. It is a wary bat and usually only emerges on very dark, moonless nights.

The body of the **common vampire bat** is 3½ in (9 cm) long, and its wingspan is 7 in (18 cm). It has no tail, a snub nose, and short pointed ears. It has fewer teeth than most bats because it has no need to chew or grind up food.

Vampire bats

The only mammals to feed entirely on blood are vampire bats, which live in the tropics of Mexico, Central America, and South America. The common vampire bat, *Desmodus rotundus*, preys on sleeping animals—usually cattle and horses—and sometimes even people. The two other vampire species, *Diaemus youngi* and *Diphylla ecuadata*, prey on large birds such as chickens. The common vampire bat feeds on its victim for about 30 minutes. The victim does not lose a dangerous amount of blood, but the bat's bite can spread disease and infection. Over the course of a year, a colony of 100 bats drinks a volume equal to the blood of 25 cows or 14,000 chickens.

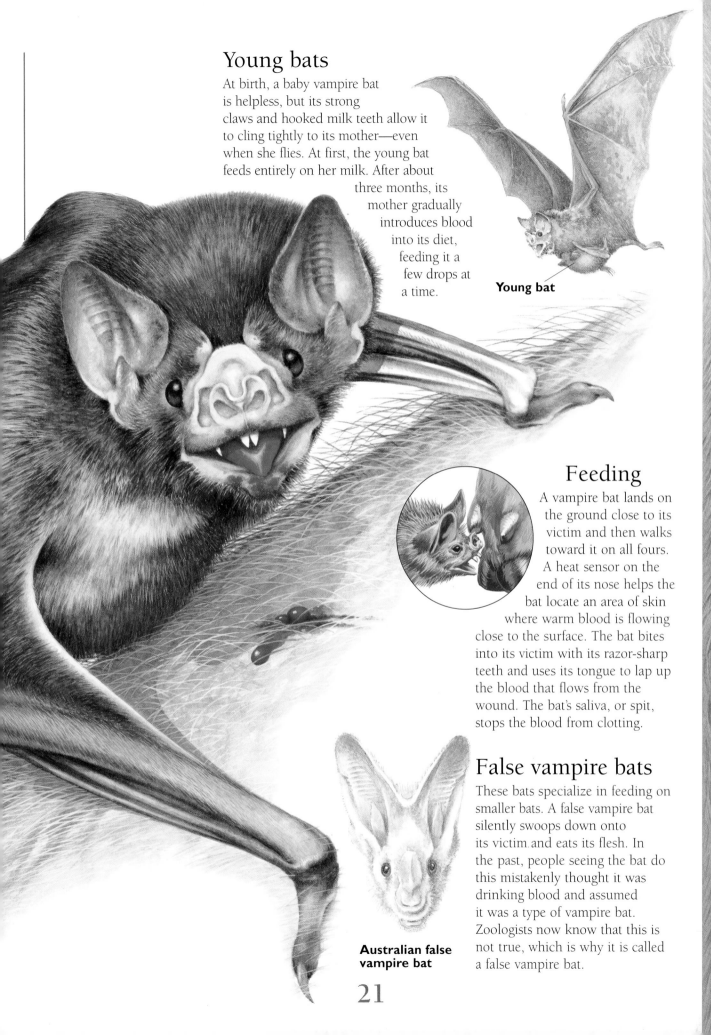

Young bats

At birth, a baby vampire bat is helpless, but its strong claws and hooked milk teeth allow it to cling tightly to its mother—even when she flies. At first, the young bat feeds entirely on her milk. After about three months, its mother gradually introduces blood into its diet, feeding it a few drops at a time.

Young bat

Feeding

A vampire bat lands on the ground close to its victim and then walks toward it on all fours. A heat sensor on the end of its nose helps the bat locate an area of skin where warm blood is flowing close to the surface. The bat bites into its victim with its razor-sharp teeth and uses its tongue to lap up the blood that flows from the wound. The bat's saliva, or spit, stops the blood from clotting.

False vampire bats

These bats specialize in feeding on smaller bats. A false vampire bat silently swoops down onto its victim and eats its flesh. In the past, people seeing the bat do this mistakenly thought it was drinking blood and assumed it was a type of vampire bat. Zoologists now know that this is not true, which is why it is called a false vampire bat.

Australian false vampire bat

21

Primates

Pygmy marmoset

Humans, monkeys, apes, lorises, tarsiers, and lemurs all belong to a group of about 250 species called primates. These mammals tend to have relatively large brains, making them intelligent and quick to learn new skills. Many primates have opposable thumbs, which means that their thumbs can move across their palms to press against their fingers, allowing them to grasp objects firmly. Some also have opposable big toes. Most primates live in trees, and they have forward-pointing eyes to help them judge the distance between branches.

Size: body 5½–6¼ in (14–16 cm); tail 6–7¾ in (15–20 cm)

Range: South America: upper reaches of Amazon River area

Scientific name: *Cebuella pygmaea*

Pygmy marmoset

The pygmy marmoset, one of the smallest primates, eats tree gum, spiders, and insects. It is often attacked by large birds, so it tries to keep out of sight. It moves in short dashes or by creeping along very slowly, sometimes staying quite still to keep from being spotted.

Lemurs, aye-ayes, lorises, bush babies, tarsiers, marmosets, and tamarins

Lemurs, aye-ayes, bush babies, lorises, and tarsiers are found in parts of Africa and southern Asia. They have smaller brains than monkeys and apes, and their skeletons resemble those of small, tree-dwelling, shrewlike animals, which were probably the first primates to evolve. The marmosets and tamarins of the South American rain forests are close relatives of the New World monkeys. They are among the most attractive primates, with colorful fur and unusual "hairstyles."

Slender loris

This creature's opposable thumbs and big toes enable it to grip branches tightly as it moves slowly and carefully through the trees on its long, thin legs. It feeds on insects, lizards, birds, and eggs, creeping up on its prey and then snatching it with both hands.

Size: body 7–10¼ in (18–26 cm); virtually no tail

Range: southern India, Sri Lanka

Scientific name: *Loris tardigradus*

Ring-tailed lemur

The ring-tailed lemur climbs to the tops of trees to bathe in the early morning sunshine after a cold night. It marks its territory with smelly secretions from scent glands. In the mating season, two rival males will rub their tails with this scent and have a "stink fight" by wafting their smelly tails in the air.

Size: body 17¾ in (45 cm); tail 21¾ in (55 cm)

Range: Madagascar

Scientific name: *Lemur catta*

○ **Ring-tailed lemur**

○ **Slender loris**

Golden lion tamarin

This beautiful primate gets its name from the silky lionlike mane that covers its head and shoulders. It lives in family groups and sleeps in hollows of old trees at night. It is a nimble creature that leaps from branch to branch searching for insects, lizards, and birds to eat.

● **Golden lion tamarin**

Size: body 7½–8¾ in (19–22 cm);
tail 10¼–13½ in (26–34 cm)
Range: southeastern Brazil
Scientific name:
Leontopithecus rosalia

Emperor tamarin

The emperor tamarin is easily recognized by its long drooping "mustache." Small troops of these tamarins dart through the trees looking for insects, fruit, tender leaves, and even flowers to eat. They will also lap up sap flowing from damaged parts of trees and steal bird eggs.

Emperor tamarin

Size: body 7–8¼ in (18–21 cm);
tail 9¾–12½ in (25–32 cm)
Range: western Brazil, Peru, Bolivia
Scientific name:
Saguinus imperator

Greater bush baby

The bush baby gets its name from its call, which sounds like a child crying. It eats plants and tree gum but also preys on reptiles and birds, pouncing and killing its victims with one bite. The bush baby hunts at night, and its keen eyes can see prey in the moonlight.

Greater bush baby

Size: body 10½–18½ in (27–47 cm);
tail 13–20½ in (33–52 cm)
Range: central and southern Africa
Scientific name:
Otolemur crassicaudatus

Western tarsier

The tarsier's huge eyes make it a ruthless night-time hunter, but the eyeballs are so big that they cannot move in their sockets. To make up for this, the tarsier can turn its head all the way around. It also has large batlike ears to detect the sounds of its small prey.

Western tarsier

Size: body 3¼–6¼ in (8.5–16 cm);
tail 5¼–10½ in (13.5–27 cm)
Range: Sumatra and Borneo
Scientific name: *Tarsius bancanus*

Size: body 14¼–17¼ in (36–44 cm);
tail 19¾–23½ in (50–60 cm)
Range: Madagascar
Scientific name:
Daubentonia madagascariensis

Aye-aye

The aye-aye taps on trees with its long middle finger, listens for the sound of insects moving under the bark, and then uses the same finger to pull the insects out. Because local tradition says that seeing this strange-looking animal brings bad luck, it is often killed.

❿ **Aye-aye**

23

New World monkeys

The monkeys that live in the lush rain forests of Central and South America are known as New World monkeys. Their long tails help them balance when they are high up in the trees. Many—such as the capuchin, howler, and spider monkeys—have prehensile (gripping) tails, which they can wrap around branches and use like an extra limb. They have long fingers, strong feet that grip well, and are excellent runners and leapers. Unlike their Old World relatives, they have broad nostrils that open to the sides, and they have no sitting pads on their buttocks.

Woolly spider monkey

This monkey moves around the rain forest by using its long arms and prehensile tail to swing from branch to branch. Numbers are decreasing because their rain forest home is being destroyed, leaving them little refuge from hunters, who kill them for meat.

❶ Woolly spider monkey

Size: body 24 in (61 cm); tail about 26¼ in (67 cm)

Range: southeastern Brazil

Scientific name: *Brachyteles arachnoides*

Red howler

Red howler

Red howler monkeys live in the rain forest in troops of as many as 30. Sometimes, all the males in a troop join together in a dawn chorus of howling that can be heard up to 3 miles (5 km) away. The howling tells other monkeys to stay away from their territory. The male howler monkey has a large throat with a special chamber that amplifies its call.

Size: body 31½–35½ in (80–90 cm); tail 31½–35½ in (80–90 cm)

Range: South America

Scientific name: *Alouatta seniculus*

White-fronted capuchin

This intelligent monkey is always picking up things, hoping that they will be edible. It feeds on a very wide variety of plants and small creatures. It soaks its hands and feet in urine and uses the scent to mark its territory as it moves through the trees.

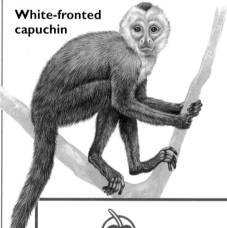
White-fronted capuchin

Size: body 11¾–15 in (30–38 cm); tail 15–19¾ in (38–50 cm)

Range: South America

Scientific name: *Cebus albifrons*

Monk saki

Monk saki

The monk saki has long, shaggy hair around its face and on its neck, and a thick, bushy tail. This shy, wary monkey lives high in the trees and never ventures down to the ground. It usually moves on all fours but may sometimes walk upright on a large branch. It can make huge leaps between branches. These monkeys spend their time in pairs or small family groups.

Size: body 13¾–19 in (35–48 cm); tail 12¼–20 in (31–51 cm)

Range: South America

Scientific name: *Pithecia monachus*

Old World monkeys

There are about 80 species of monkeys in Asia and Africa. These monkeys are known as Old World monkeys. They have close-set, downward-pointing nostrils. On their buttocks are pads of hard skin that allow them to rest their weight on their bottoms comfortably while they sleep sitting upright. They tend to be larger than the New World monkeys of the Americas. Unlike the New World monkeys, they do not have prehensile (gripping) tails. Most Old World monkeys are active in the daytime and sleep at night. They have excellent eyesight, hearing, and sense of smell.

Size: body 15¾–22½ in (40–57 cm); tail 19¾–29½ in (50–75 cm)

Range: western Africa

Scientific name:
Cercopithecus diana

O Diana monkey

Diana monkey

This elegant, colorful monkey is an excellent climber and spends almost all its time high up in the trees of the rain forest. Troops of up to 30 monkeys live together, led by an old male. They feed mainly on plants but also eat insects and the eggs and young of birds.

Mandrill

The forest-dwelling mandrill is unmistakable, with its flaming red nose and blue cheeks. A female mandrill gives birth to a single baby, which she carries about with her, either on her back or clinging to her belly. One male guards a group of females and young as they forage for fruit, nuts, worms, and mushrooms.

Size: body 21¾–37½ in (55–95 cm); tail 2¾–4 in (7–10 cm)

Range: western central Africa

Scientific name:
Mandrillus sphinx

Mandrill

Japanese macaque

Japan's mountain forests are home to macaque monkeys. In cold winters, these monkeys warm themselves in volcanic springs, where water heated deep below ground bubbles up to the surface to form steaming pools. They eat fruit, leaves, insects, and small animals.

❶ Japanese macaque

Size: body 19¾–29½ in (50–75 cm); tail 2½–4½ in (7–12 cm)

Range: Japan

Scientific name:
Macaca fuscata

Proboscis monkey

The male proboscis monkey has a long, fleshy nose, which straightens out when he makes his loud honking call. The nose probably acts like a loudspeaker, amplifying his call to warn other monkeys of danger. It also turns red or swells when he is angry or excited. The female has a much smaller nose and a quieter cry. The proboscis monkey lives in mangrove swamp jungles, where it climbs nimbly through the trees using its long fingers and toes to grip the branches.

○ **Proboscis monkey**

Size: body 20¾–30 in (53–76 cm); tail 21¾–30 in (55–76 cm)
Range: Borneo
Scientific name: *Nasalis larvatus*

Olive baboon

Orderly troops of up to 150 olive baboons move around Africa's savanna, eating leaves, shoots, seeds, roots, bark, fruit, insects, eggs, and lizards. These large, heavily built baboons also hunt small mammals, such as young antelopes. They spend much of their time grooming each other's fur, removing dirt, parasites, and dead skin to keep clean. They mainly live on the ground but sleep at night in trees or on rocks.

Size: body 18–27½ in (46–70 cm); tail 16½–31½ in (42–80 cm)
Range: western, central, and eastern Africa
Scientific name: *Procolobus badius*

Red colobus

This monkey lives in troops of 50 to 100 animals. The troop contains many small family groups, each consisting of a male and several females with their young. The red colobus makes spectacular leaps between the branches of trees as it searches for fruit, leaves, and flowers to eat. Chimpanzees sometimes band together in hunting parties to prey on the red colobus.

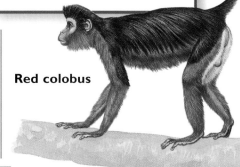

Red colobus

Size: body up to 3¼ ft (1 m); tail 17¾–29½ in (45–75 cm)
Range: western, central, and eastern Africa
Scientific name: *Papio anubis*

Olive baboon

Allen's swamp monkey

This little-known monkey lives near rivers and in swamps. Though it eats mainly leaves and fruit, it also goes into the water to snatch crabs and even fish. It, in turn, is hunted by local people for meat and because it sometimes raids farmers' crops. This monkey is becoming increasingly scarce.

Size: body 15¾–19¾ in (40–50 cm); tail 17¾–21¾ in (45–55 cm)
Range: Congo and Democratic Republic of the Congo
Scientific name: *Allenopithecus nigroviridis*

Allen's swamp monkey

Apes

Gorillas, chimpanzees, and orangutans are called great apes. They are our closest living relatives. After humans, they are the most intelligent of all the primates and can even be trained to use simple sign language. Gibbons are tree-dwelling apes of southern Asia. They are smaller than great apes, so they are known as lesser apes. Apes live in family-based groups. They usually walk on all fours, putting their weight on their feet and on the knuckles of their hands, but they can walk upright. They have no tails.

O Orangutan

Size: height standing 4–5 ft (1.2–1.5 m); no tail
Range: Borneo and Sumatra
Scientific name: *Pongo pygmaeus*

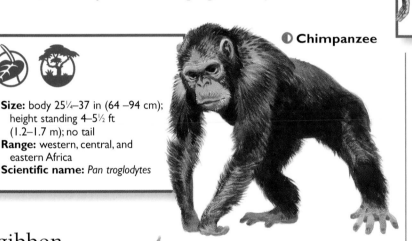

◑ Chimpanzee

Size: body 25¼–37 in (64–94 cm); height standing 4–5½ ft (1.2–1.7 m); no tail
Range: western, central, and eastern Africa
Scientific name: *Pan troglodytes*

Orangutan

After the gorilla, the orangutan is the second largest primate. It builds a platform of sticks to form a tree nest in which it sleeps, building a new one as often as every night. A female orangutan gives birth to a single baby, which clings to her fur as she moves around in the treetops.

Lar gibbon

The lar gibbon lives in trees and rarely descends to the ground. It swings through the trees and runs upright along branches. At dawn, the gibbons start calling, or singing, with males and females alternating in duets. They live in small family groups.

Lar gibbon

Size: body 16½–22¾ in (42–58 cm); no tail
Range: Southeast Asia
Scientific name: *Hylobates lar*

Chimpanzee

The chimpanzee mainly eats plants, but occasionally insects and meat. It makes many noises, gestures, and facial expressions. It has learned to use everyday objects as simple tools. For example, stones are used to smash open nuts, wads of leaves to mop up drinking water, and sticks to pry grubs out of rotten wood and to extract ants and termites from their nests.

Size: height standing 4½–6 ft (1.4–1.8 m); no tail
Range: western central Africa
Scientific name: *Gorilla gorilla*

Gorilla

Gorillas spend most of their time on the ground. They feed on leaves, buds, stalks, berries, bark, and ferns. They live in troops of as many as 30 animals, made up of a leading adult male, a few young males, and several females and their young. Young gorillas travel on their mother's back until they are two or three years old.

◑ Gorilla

27

Carnivores

The carnivorous, or flesh-eating, mammals include dogs, bears, raccoons, mustelids, mongooses, civets, hyenas, and cats. Most carnivores have finely tuned senses of sight, hearing, and smell, so they can find their prey before it detects them. Their agile bodies enable them to catch prey using very little energy. The main difference between carnivores and other mammals is that carnivores have special teeth that can shear flesh from bone, the way scissors cut paper. Some carnivores have adapted their diet to include other food, such as seeds, fruit, roots, and insects.

Dogs

All domestic dogs are descended from wolves. Wolves and other wild dogs have long legs for chasing prey and sharp teeth for killing it. A dog's most important sensory organ is its nose, which it uses to detect the scent of prey, find a mate, and identify other animals. They can even tell whether another animal is afraid or relaxed. Wild dogs hunt animals as small as mice and as large as moose. Some wild dogs, such as foxes, live on their own, whereas others, such as wolves and hunting dogs, live, travel, and hunt in groups called packs. Pack members share their food and defend each other.

Maned wolf

Size: body 4 ft (1.2 m); tail about 11¾ in (30 cm)
Range: South America
Scientific name:
Chrysocyon brachyurus

Maned wolf

The maned wolf is similar to the red fox in appearance, but with longer legs and a longer muzzle. A wary creature, the maned wolf lives in remote areas and hunts mainly at night. It eats large rodents, birds, reptiles, frogs, fruit, and plants.

Bush dog

With its stocky legs, short tail, squat body, and broad face, the bush dog looks more like a small bear than a dog. It inhabits grasslands and open forests, hunting in packs by day for rodents. It spends most of the night underground in a den that may have been stolen from another animal, such as an armadillo.

African hunting dog

Hunting dogs hunt together as a pack. The pack chases a group of animals, such as wildebeest, separates one from the fleeing herd, and then moves in for the kill. These dogs once hunted throughout the African savanna. But because so many were shot by farmers who thought they would attack their cattle, today the dogs are found only in a few scattered places.

Size: body 31½–43½ in (80–110 cm); tail 11¾–15¾ in (30–40 cm)
Range: Africa south of the Sahara to South Africa
Scientific name: Lycaon pictus

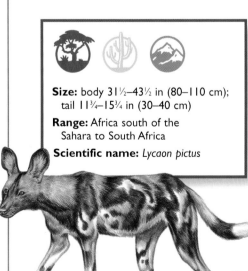

❶ **African hunting dog**

Size: body 22¾–29½ in (57.5–75 cm); tail 5–6 in (12.5–15 cm)
Range: Central and South America
Scientific name:
Speothos venaticus

❍ **Bush dog**

Arctic fox

Arctic fox

The arctic fox can withstand temperatures as low as -58°F (-50°C) on the icy, windswept tundra. It feeds on ground-dwelling birds, lemmings and other small rodents, and the leftovers from polar bear kills. In winter, its white coat acts as a camouflage against the snow and ice, so the fox can creep up unseen on its prey. When the snow melts, its coat turns brown or gray, blending with the rocks and plants.

Size: body 18–26¾ in (46–68 cm); tail up to 13¾ in (35 cm)
Range: Arctic regions of Europe, Asia, and North America
Scientific name: *Alopex lagopus*

Fennec fox

The fennec is the smallest fox. Its large ears, up to 6 inches (15 cm) long, allow heat to escape from its body, keeping the fox cool in the hot deserts where it lives. It hunts at night for small rodents, birds, insects, and lizards. During the day it finds shelter in burrows in the sand.

Fennec fox

Size: body 14½–16¼ in (37–41 cm); tail 7½–8¼ in (19–21 cm)
Range: northern Africa, southwestern Asia
Scientific name: *Fennecus zerda*

Red fox

Size: body 18–33¾ in (46–86 cm); tail 12–21¾ in (30.5–55.5 cm)
Range: North America, Europe, northern Africa, northern Asia
Scientific name: *Vulpes vulpes*

Red fox

The red fox has adapted to many different environments, from forests and grasslands to mountains, deserts, and even towns and cities. Red foxes live and hunt alone and only come together to breed and rear their young. They usually prey on rodents, rabbits, and other small animals, but they will also eat fruit, vegetables, earthworms, and fish.

Gray wolf

The largest of all the wild dogs, the gray wolf preys on hoofed mammals, such as bison, moose, and musk-oxen. Packs vary in size from 5 to 20 dogs, led by the strongest male. Each pack has its own hunting territory of up to 386 square miles (1,000 km²) or more. The wolves howl loudly to warn other packs to stay away.

Gray wolf

Size: body 3¼–4½ ft (1–1.4 m); tail 11¾–19 in (30–48 cm)
Range: Canada, northern U.S.A., eastern Europe, Asia
Scientific name: *Canis lupus*

CARNIVORES

29

Raccoons, bears, and pandas

Both the bear and raccoon families developed from doglike ancestors millions of years ago. Bears are the largest flesh-eating land mammals, but they will eat almost anything, including plants and insects. Raccoons—and their relatives the coatis and olingos—are long-tailed carnivores that like to spend much of their time in trees. There are two different types of pandas: The giant panda is sometimes classified with the bear, and the red panda with the raccoon. Some zoologists think that each kind of panda should be classified in a separate family of its own.

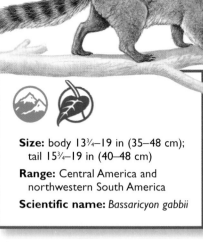

Olingo

Size: body 13¾–19 in (35–48 cm); tail 15¾–19 in (40–48 cm)
Range: Central America and northwestern South America
Scientific name: *Bassaricyon gabbii*

Olingo

The olingo lives mostly in the trees, using its long tail to help it balance as it runs along branches and leaps from tree to tree. It lives alone or in pairs but joins up with other olingos to look for food. It mostly eats fruit but also feeds on insects, small mammals, and birds.

Coati

With its long nose, the coati probes into holes and cracks in the ground, searching for insects, spiders, and other small animals. Groups of up to 40 animals hunt both day and night, resting during the hottest part of the day. After mating, the female goes off alone to give birth to a litter of between two and seven young in a cave or a tree nest.

Size: body 17–26¼ in (43–67 cm); tail 17–26¾ in (43–68 cm)
Range: southeastern U.S.A., Central and South America
Scientific name: *Nasua nasua*

Raccoon

The raccoon runs and climbs well and swims if necessary. It is most active at night. As well as catching prey such as frogs, fish, mice, and birds, it often raids garbage cans, searching for edible items with its long, sensitive fingers. It has a peculiar habit of washing food before eating it. Its thick fur keeps it warm during winter.

Raccoon

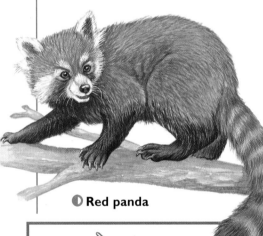

◐ Red panda

Size: body 20–25 in (51–63.5 cm); tail 11–19 in (28–48 cm)
Range: Nepal to Myanmar; southwestern China
Scientific name: *Ailurus fulgens*

Red panda

The red panda looks more like a raccoon than a giant panda. It sleeps during the day, curled up on a branch with its tail over its eyes or its head tucked into its chest. It feeds during the night, mainly on bamboo shoots, although it will also eat grass, roots, fruit, acorns, mice, birds, and bird eggs.

Size: body 16¼–23½ in (41–60 cm); tail 7¾–15¾ in (20–40 cm)
Range: southern Canada, U.S.A., Central America
Scientific name: *Procyon lotor*

Coati

Polar bear

Size: body 7¼–8 ft (2.2–2.5 m); tail 3–5 in (7.5–12.5 cm)

Range: ice sheets and coastal waters of Arctic Ocean

Scientific name: *Ursus maritimus*

Polar bear

With a thick layer of specially insulated fur to keep it warm, a polar bear is perfectly comfortable roaming across the Arctic ice in freezing temperatures. Cubs are born in dens dug by their mother in deep snow. They stay with her for about 28 months, learning how to hunt seals and fight.

Brown bear

Also known as the grizzly, the brown bear eats mostly leaves, berries, fruit, nuts, and roots and sometimes insects, rodents, and fish. It also hunts large mammals such as moose and musk-oxen. The bear may hide the dead prey under dirt and leaves until it is ready to eat it.

Brown bear

Size: body 5–8 ft (1.5–2.5 m); small tail

Range: Europe, Asia, North America

Scientific name: *Ursus arctos*

Sun bear

The sun bear spends the day sleeping and sunbathing. It searches for food at night, using its long tongue to lick honey out of bees' nests and termites from their mounds. With its curved claws it hooks fruit from branches and tears off tree bark to uncover tasty grubs.

Size: body 3½–4½ ft (1.1–1.4 m); no tail

Range: Southeast Asia

Scientific name: *Helarctos malayanus*

Sun bear

◑ Giant panda

Size: body 4–5 ft (1.2–1.5 m); tail 5 in (12.5 cm)

Range: central China

Scientific name: *Ailuropoda melanoleuca*

Giant panda

The giant panda has to feed for up to 12 hours each day to survive. During that time it consumes up to 28 pounds (12.5 kg) of bamboo. The panda has a thumblike bone in each hand that allows it to grip its food. There are only about 1,000 giant pandas left in the wild.

Spectacled bear

This mountain bear has light rings around its eyes and across its muzzle, making it look as if it is wearing glasses, or spectacles. It makes a tree nest by building a platform of branches. It forages for food at night and spends the day in its nest.

○ Spectacled bear

Size: body 5–6 ft (1.5–1.8 m); tail 2¾ in (7 cm)

Range: western South America

Scientific name: *Tremarctos ornatus*

31

Mustelids, civets, and mongooses

All of these mammals are small to medium-size carnivores. Most of the mustelids, which include ermines, badgers, otters, skunks, and wolverines, have a long, supple body, short legs, and a long tail. There are about 65 species of mustelids living in every part of the world except Australia, Madagascar, and Antarctica. The 34 or so species of civets are tree-dwelling hunters that are active at night. They live in southwestern Europe, Africa, and Asia. There are 39 species of mongooses. These fast-moving ground dwellers live in Africa and Asia.

Size: body 21¾–31½ in (55–80 cm); tail 11¾–19¾ in (30–50 cm)

Range: Alaska, Canada, contiguous U.S.A.

Scientific name: *Lutra canadensis*

North American river otter

The otter moves quickly both in water and on land. It uses its tail to push itself along in water, and its short, thick fur keeps its skin warm and dry. Its nostrils and ears can be closed off when it is in water. The otter lives in a burrow in the riverbank. Rarely seen during the day, it comes out at night to find various water creatures to eat.

Ermine

Ermine

The agile ermine is a skilled hunter. It kills with a powerful bite to the back of the prey's neck. Rodents and rabbits are its main victims, but it also kills other mammals as well as birds, fish, and insects. In the northern part of its range the ermine loses its dark fur at the beginning of winter and grows a pure white coat. Only the tail tip stays black.

Size: body 9–11 in (23–28 cm); tail 3¼–4¾ in (8–12 cm)

Range: Europe, Asia, North America

Scientific name: *Mustela erminea*

American badger

With its short legs, strong claws, and long, flattened body, the badger is designed for life underground. During the day it usually stays in its burrow, coming out at dusk to hunt for prey such as rodents, birds, and snakes. It normally lives alone except during the breeding season, when the female cares for her litter of one to five young for several months.

○ **Wolverine**

Wolverine

A powerful, heavily built animal, the wolverine is extremely strong for its size and can kill prey larger than itself. It spends most of its life on the ground, but it will climb trees to find bird eggs and berries. Young are born in spring. They suckle for approximately two months and remain with their mother until they are about two years old. Then she drives them away to find their own territory.

Size: body 25½–33¾ in (65–86 cm); tail 6¾–10¼ in (17–26 cm)

Range: Siberia, Scandinavia, North America

Scientific name: *Gulo gulo*

Size: body 20–28 in (50–71 cm); tail 4–6 in (10–15 cm)

Range: southwestern Canada to Mexico

Scientific name: *Taxidea taxus*

African palm civet

Sea otter

This otter feeds on shellfish and uses rocks as tools to help it open the hard shells. The otter lies on its back in the water and places a rock on its chest. It bangs its prey against the rock until the shell breaks, revealing the soft flesh inside.

Sea otter

Size: body 3¼–4 ft (1–1.2 m); tail 9¾–14¼ in (25–37 cm)
Range: Bering Sea, California
Scientific name: *Enhydra lutris*

African palm civet

This civet has short legs and a long, thick tail. It is a skilled climber and spends much of its life in trees, where it rests during the day. It usually hunts at night, catching insects and small animals such as lizards and birds. It also eats many kinds of fruit and leaves. The female gives birth to litters of two or three young at any time of year.

Size: body 17–23½ in (43–60 cm); tail 19–24½ in (48–62 cm)
Range: central Africa
Scientific name: *Nandinia binotata*

Size: body 13¾ in (35 cm); tail 9¾ in (25 cm)
Range: Iraq to Southeast Asia; introduced into West Indies, Hawaii, Fiji
Scientific name: *Herpestes auropunctatus*

Indian mongoose

The mongoose eats almost any food it can catch, including snakes, scorpions, and insects. It is popular among humans because it hunts pests such as rats and mice. As a result, the mongoose has been introduced into areas outside its normal range.

Indian mongoose

Meerkat

Meerkats are a type of mongoose. They are sociable animals, and several families may live together. During the day, while most of the group forages for food such as insects, lizards, birds, and fruit, some meerkats watch out for birds of prey. They give a shrill call to alert the others to any danger.

Meerkat

Size: body 9¾–11¾ in (25–30 cm); tail 7½–9½ in (19–24 cm)
Range: southern Africa
Scientific name: *Suricata suricatta*

Striped skunk

Skunks are well known for the foul-smelling fluid they spray when threatened. The fluid comes from glands near the tail. The strong smell makes it difficult for an enemy to breathe and irritates its eyes. This skunk searches for insects, worms, fruit, and other food at night.

Size: body 11–15 in (28–38 cm); tail 7–9¾ in (18–25 cm)
Range: North America
Scientific name: *Mephitis mephitis*

Striped skunk

33

Cats and hyenas

Cats are ruthless hunters. Their strong legs enable them to catch their prey in a brief, rapid chase or with a lightning-quick pounce. They have flexible backbones that allow them to twist and turn easily when chasing prey. When they pounce, their claws extend and grip their victim's flesh, but when the cat is walking or running, the claws retract into the toes so they are not damaged. Most cats have coats patterned with spots or stripes to camouflage them as they stalk prey. There are 36 species of wild cats, from big cats such as lions and tigers to smaller ones such as lynxes.

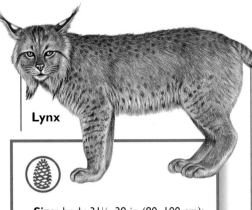

Lynx

Size: body 31½–39 in (80–100 cm); tail 1½–3¼ in (4–8 cm)

Range: northern North America

Scientific name: *Lynx canadensis*

Lynx

The lynx lives alone in forests and woodlands and hunts hares, rabbits, rodents, small deer, and birds such as grouse. The tufts on its ears help it hear in dense forests, where sound does not travel well. The lynx has excellent eyesight—it can spot a mouse 250 feet (75 m) away.

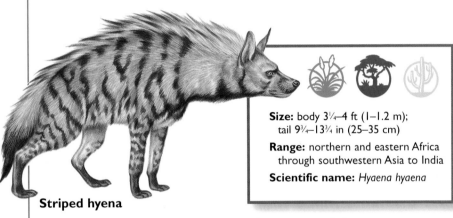

Striped hyena

Size: body 3¼–4 ft (1–1.2 m); tail 9¾–13¾ in (25–35 cm)

Range: northern and eastern Africa through southwestern Asia to India

Scientific name: *Hyaena hyaena*

Wild cat

The wild cat looks similar to a domestic cat but is larger and has a shorter, thicker tail. It is a good tree climber but stalks most of its prey on the ground, catching small rodents and ground-dwelling birds. In courtship, males howl and screech to attract a mate.

Mountain lion

Deer are the main prey of this hunter. Having stalked its victim, the mountain lion pounces and kills it with a swift bite to the neck. It then drags the carcass to a sheltered place, where it can feed undisturbed. It lives in lowland swamps, forests, and grasslands and also on mountain slopes up to 15,750 feet (4,500 m).

Striped hyena

Although hyenas have a doglike body, they are actually related to cats. They specialize in feeding on carrion (dead animals), especially the leftovers of kills made by big cats such as lions. Striped hyenas also prey on young sheep and goats, small mammals, birds, lizards, snakes, and insects.

Wild cat

Mountain lion

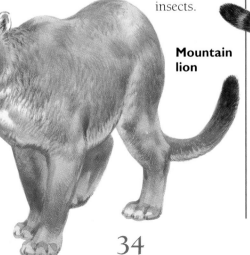

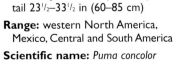

Size: body 3¼–5¼ ft (1–1.6 m); tail 23½–33½ in (60–85 cm)

Range: western North America, Mexico, Central and South America

Scientific name: *Puma concolor*

Size: body 19¾–25½ in (50–65 cm); tail 9¾–15 in (25–38 cm)

Range: Europe, Africa, southwestern Asia, India

Scientific name: *Felis silvestris*

Leopard

The leopard hauls the bodies of large prey up into trees, out of reach of scavenging hyenas and jackals. Its stunning coat is dappled with spots to camouflage it among the leaves of the trees and the long grass below. It will sometimes leap straight out of a tree onto passing prey.

Leopard

Size: body 4¼–6¼ ft (1.3–1.9 m); tail 3½–4½ ft (1.1–1.4 m)

Range: Africa south of the Sahara, southwestern and southern Asia

Scientific name: *Panthera pardus*

Size: body 4½–6½ ft (1.4–2 m); tail 26¼–39½ in (67–100 cm)

Range: Africa south of the Sahara, northwestern India

Scientific name: *Panthera leo*

Male

Snow leopard

The solitary snow leopard feeds mainly on wild sheep and goats. Its broad, furry feet stop it from sinking in the snow on high mountain slopes. It can make huge leaps between rocky crags, using its tail for balance.

Size: body 4–5 ft (1.2–1.5 m); tail about 36 in (91 cm)

Range: central Asia

Scientific name: *Uncia uncia*

◐ Snow leopard

Lion

Lions live in grassland or scrub country in family groups called prides. A pride normally contains up to 3 males, 15 females, and their young. The females do most of the hunting, often stalking antelopes and zebras in pairs or larger groups. The males' role is to defend the pride's territory.

○ Lion

Jaguar

Female

Cheetah

The cheetah is the fastest land mammal, able to accelerate from 0 to 60 mph (96 km/h) in just three seconds. Having selected its prey when in hiding, the cheetah stalks its victim and then attacks with a short, rapid chase. Small antelope are its main prey.

Jaguar

The largest South American cat, the powerful jaguar is a good swimmer and hunts fish and turtles as well as peccaries, deer, and other land animals. It also climbs trees, where it may lie in wait for prey. The female has litters of one to four cubs and defends them fiercely from any intruder, including the father.

Size: body 5–6 ft (1.5–1.8 m); tail 27½–36 in (70–91 cm)

Range: southern U.S.A., Central and South America

Scientific name: *Panthera onca*

○ Cheetah

Size: body 3½–4½ ft (1.1–1.4 m); tail 25½–31½ in (65–80 cm)

Range: Africa south of the Sahara, southwestern to central Asia

Scientific name: *Acinonyx jubatus*

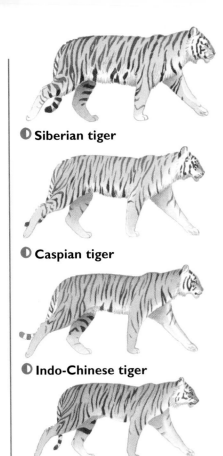

● **Siberian tiger**

● **Caspian tiger**

● **Indo-Chinese tiger**

● **Sumatran tiger**

Tiger types

The coloration and size of these animals vary according to where they live. Tigers from northern areas, such as Siberia, are larger and paler than those from tropical areas, such as Sumatra. The largest of all is the Siberian tiger. All tigers are now rare, including the Siberian, Indo-Chinese, and Sumatran, and some, such as the Caspian, have not been seen for many years.

Hunting

At dusk, tigers set out to hunt buffalo, deer, wild pigs, and other forest animals. They can only run fast for short distances, so they rely on their cunning and stealth to catch their prey. Their striped coats camouflage them against the background of trees and long grass, enabling them to sneak up on their victims without being seen. When they are close enough, they sprint forward and pounce on the unsuspecting animal.

Tigers

The tiger is the biggest and strongest of all the wild cats. At the beginning of the 20th century there were hundreds of thousands of tigers living throughout the forests of Asia. Hunting and the destruction of forests have had such a devastating effect on their numbers that there are now just 5,000 to 7,000 wild tigers left, living mainly in parts of India, Southeast Asia, and Siberia.

Tigers live alone, roaring loudly to tell other tigers to keep away from their territory, which they mark with scent, droppings, and scratches on tree trunks. They hunt large mammals, usually at night, and sometimes travel up to 12 miles (20 km) in search of food. As few as one in every ten hunts is successful, so when tigers do make a kill, they gorge themselves on as much meat as they can eat. Tigers try to avoid people. Only a few have become man-eaters.

Tiger cubs

Tigers can be born any time of the year in litters ranging from two to six cubs. They are blind for the first ten days. A mother suckles her cubs for three to six months. Not until they are about 18 months old do they hunt for themselves, and they stay with their mother for two to three years. The father takes no part in their rearing. Cubs are sometimes killed when another male tiger takes over their father's territory. If the cubs are killed, the female mates again.

Unlike domestic cats, **tigers** like to be near water and will take a dip to cool off on a hot day. They are good swimmers and may cross rivers or swim between islands in search of their prey. Tigers can occasionally be seen climbing trees.

Seals, whales, and dolphins

Millions of years ago, the ancestors of seals, whales, and dolphins left the land to live in the sea. Their bodies adapted to life in the water, becoming sleek and streamlined, and their limbs developed into paddle-shaped flippers. Under their skin, these marine mammals have a thick layer of fat called blubber to keep them warm. They spend much of their time underwater, often diving to great depths in search of food. But because they have lungs, not gills like fish, they have to surface regularly to breathe air.

Seals, sea lions, and walruses

With their torpedo-like bodies, these marine mammals are skillful swimmers and divers. They can slow down their heartbeat during dives to enable them to stay underwater for long periods. Unlike whales and dolphins, which give birth underwater, seals, sea lions, and walruses come ashore to have their babies. Seals and walruses swim by propelling themselves through the water with their tail-like hind flippers, but sea lions use their long front flippers.

California sea lion

This is the fastest swimmer of all the seals and sea lions, capable of speeds of 25 mph (40 km/h). It can also move fast on land by turning its back flippers forward and lifting its body. In the breeding season, huge colonies gather on the rocky southwestern shores of the United States.

California sea lion

Size: 5½–7¼ ft (1.7–2.2 m)

Range: Pacific coasts from Canada to Mexico

Scientific name: *Zalophus californianus*

Size: 4½–6 ft (1.4–1.8 m)

Range: Pacific and Atlantic coasts of South America

Scientific name: *Arctocephalus australis*

South American fur seal

South American fur seal

This seal eats fish, squid, penguins, and small marine creatures. The female gives birth to a single pup. She stays with it for 12 days, then goes off to sea to feed, returning regularly to suckle her young pup.

Size: 7¼–11½ ft (2.2–3.5 m)

Range: Arctic, North Atlantic, and North Pacific Oceans

Scientific name: *Odobenus rosmarus*

Walrus

Walrus

Walruses live in the Arctic, where they feed on shellfish. They have sharp tusks, which they use to drag themselves out of the water and also for fighting. Their four flat flippers make them excellent swimmers. On land, walruses move with great difficulty. They spend much of their time sleeping on the ice in large groups.

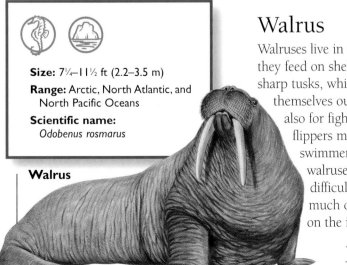

Leopard seal

Size: 10–11½ ft (3–3.5 m)
Range: seas surrounding Antarctica
Scientific name:
Hydrurga leptonyx

Leopard seal

The leopard seal is the fiercest hunter of all seals, with large tooth-studded jaws for grasping prey and tearing it apart. The leopard seal preys on penguins by catching them underwater just after they launch themselves off the ice. It also hunts smaller seals as well as fish, squid, and shellfish.

Harp seal

The harp seal feeds on fish and crustaceans. In the breeding season, rival males fight over females, using their teeth and flippers. After mating, the females form groups on the ice to give birth. The pups grow rapidly as they feed on their mother's nourishing fat-rich milk.

Size: 5¼–6¼ ft (1.6–1.9 m)
Range: North Atlantic and Arctic Oceans
Scientific name:
Pagophilus groenlandicus

Harp seal

Size: 7¾–9¼ ft (2.4–2.8 m)
Range: North Pacific Ocean
Scientific name:
Eumetopias jubatus

❶ Steller sea lion

Steller sea lion

This is the largest of the sea lions, and it catches fish, squid, and octopus. A large male may even eat smaller seals such as fur seals. The beaches where the Steller sea lion breeds are sometimes so crowded that young pups are crushed as males hurry across them to mate with females. A sea lion mother often goes to sea to find food. When she comes back, she makes a warbling sound to attract nearby pups and then smells and touches them until she finds the one that belongs to her.

Harbor seal

Like all seals, the harbor seal spends most of its life in the ocean, coming to land only to mate and give birth. Harbor seal pups are well developed when they are born. They can swim from birth and can dive for up to two minutes when just two or three days old. The harbor seal feeds on fish and squid.

Size: 4½–6 ft (1.4–1.8 m)
Range: North Atlantic and Pacific Oceans
Scientific name:
Phoca vitulina

Harbor seal

39

Whales, dolphins, porpoises, and sea cows

Whales are the largest sea mammals. There are two kinds of whales: toothed and baleen. Dolphins and porpoises are small, toothed whales. Baleen whales have bristly plates instead of teeth in their mouths. When they feed, they take gulps of water. Baleen plates act like filters, so the water drains out but the fish and plankton, including krill, stay in the whale's mouth. Toothed whales can locate other sea creatures by echolocation. They send out high-pitched clicking sounds and detect the echoes as they bounce back from objects. Sea cows (dugongs and manatees) are more closely related to elephants than to whales!

Dall's porpoise

These porpoises are larger and heavier than most porpoises and inhabit deeper waters. They live in groups of up to 15. Schools of 100 or more porpoises may gather to migrate north in summer and south in winter. Mothers suckle their calves for as long as two years.

Dall's porpoise

Size: 6–7½ ft (1.8–2.3 m)
Range: warm northern Pacific waters
Scientific name: *Phocoenoides dalli*

Killer whale

The largest of the dolphin family, the killer whale, or orca, is a fierce hunter that feeds on fish, squid, sea lions, seabirds, and even other whales. It sometimes snatches seals from the shore or tips them off floating ice into its mouth. It lives and hunts in family groups of up to 40 animals.

Size: 23–32 ft (7–9.7 m)
Range: worldwide, especially cooler seas
Scientific name: *Orcinus orca*

Harbor porpoise

These porpoises feed on fish such as herring and mackerel. They dive for up to six minutes when hunting prey, which they pinpoint using echolocation clicks. Before breeding, they perform long courtship rituals, caressing each other as they swim side by side. Calves are born 10 to 11 months after mating. While a mother suckles her calf, she lies on her side on the water surface, so the calf can breathe easily.

○ **Harbor porpoise**

Size: 4½–6 ft (1.4–1.8 m)
Range: northern Atlantic and Pacific Oceans, Black and Mediterranean Seas
Scientific name: *Phocoena phocoena*

Killer whale

Ganges dolphin

Common dolphin

This beautifully marked dolphin has pointed flippers, a curved fin, and a long beak. It lives in groups of between 20 and 100 dolphins. Several dolphins will join together to help injured or sick companions. These curious, playful sea mammals are often seen swimming alongside ships, leaping and rolling in the waves. They feed on fish and squid.

Common dolphin

Size: 5–7¾ ft (1.5–2.4 m)
Range: India and Bangladesh
Scientific name:
Platanista gangetica

Ganges dolphin

One of only five species of freshwater dolphin, the Ganges dolphin lives in muddy rivers in South Asia. It is blind—its eyes have no lenses in them—and uses echolocation to find its food: fish and shrimp.

Bottlenose dolphin

The curving line of this dolphin's mouth makes it look as if it is always smiling. It feeds mainly on bottom-dwelling fish and is a skillful echolocator, producing up to 1,000 clicking sounds a second. The bottlenose dolphin is often taught to perform tricks in aquariums.

Size: 7–8½ ft (2.1–2.6 m)
Range: warm and tropical oceans worldwide
Scientific name:
Delphinus delphis

Size: 10–14 ft (3–4.2 m)
Range: warm and tropical oceans worldwide
Scientific name:
Tursiops truncatus

Bottlenose dolphin

Blue whale

The world's largest mammal, the blue whale can weigh up to 215 tons (tonnes). This giant baleen whale feeds on huge quantities of tiny shrimplike creatures called krill, consuming 4 to 8 tons (tonnes) each day in the summer. The blue whale is in danger of extinction. There are only a few thousand left in the world's oceans.

Blue whale

Size: 82–105 ft (25–32 m)
Range: all oceans
Scientific name:
Balaenoptera musculus

○ **White whale**   ○ **Sperm whale**

Size: 13–20 ft (4–6.1 m)
Range: Arctic Ocean and subarctic waters
Scientific name:
  Delphinapterus leucas

White whale

White whales, also called belugas, often live together in small groups called pods. They communicate with a variety of sounds, such as whistles, clicks, clangs, twitters, and moos. Polar bears prey on belugas that get trapped by the Arctic ice. In winter, big herds of belugas migrate south.

Goose-beaked whale

This is one of 18 toothed whale species with a distinct beak. It has a tapering, scarred body marked by oval patches where parasitic lampreys have fed on it. It dives for up to 30 minutes to feed on squid and deep-water fish.

Size: 36–66 ft (11–20 m)
Range: all oceans
Scientific name:
  Physeter catodon

Gray whale

This whale stirs up the seabed with its snout and uses its baleen to filter out tiny creatures to eat. It makes a round trip of 12,430 miles (20,000 km) between its summer feeding waters off Alaska and the warmer, shallower waters off the coast of Mexico, where it breeds during winter.

Goose-beaked whale

Size: 21–23 ft (6.4–7 m)
Range: all oceans, temperate and tropical waters
Scientific name:
  Ziphius cavirostris

Narwhal

The narwhal is related to the white whale but has only two teeth. One of the male's teeth grows into a spiral tusk up to 8¾ feet (2.7 m) long, which sticks through its top lip. The tusk is probably used to impress females and fight rivals in the breeding season. Females sometimes have a short tusk.

Size: 40–50 ft (12.2–15.3 m)
Range: northeastern and northwestern Pacific Ocean
Scientific name: *Eschrichtius robustus*

Gray whale

Narwhal

Size: 13–20 ft (4–6.1 m)
Range: Arctic Ocean
Scientific name:
  Monodon monoceros

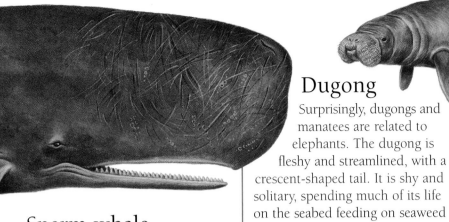

 O **Dugong**

Dugong

Surprisingly, dugongs and manatees are related to elephants. The dugong is fleshy and streamlined, with a crescent-shaped tail. It is shy and solitary, spending much of its life on the seabed feeding on seaweed and seagrass. A female dugong gives birth to a single baby and helps it to the surface to breathe.

Size: up to 10 ft (3 m)
Range: Red Sea, Indian Ocean, and waters off northern Australia
Scientific name: *Dugong dugon*

Sperm whale

This toothed whale has a huge head filled with a waxy substance called spermaceti. This may help the sperm whale alter its buoyancy—its ability to float. This enables it to reach depths of more than 3,280 feet (1,000 m) in search of squid to eat.

O **American manatee**

American manatee

Manatees live in estuaries, bays, and shallow coastal waters. They are fine swimmers and can reach speeds of 16 mph (25 km/h). They use their flattened tails as paddles and sometimes walk along the bottom of the ocean on their flippers, grazing on seagrass.

Size: up to 10 ft (3 m)
Range: Atlantic and Caribbean coastal waters from southeastern U.S.A. to Brazil
Scientific name: *Trichechus manatus*

Size: 26–33 ft (8–10 m)
Range: temperate and polar areas of all oceans
Scientific name: *Baleanoptera acutorostrata*

Minke whale

Minke whale

This baleen whale is a pint-size relative of the humpback and blue whales. Like them, the minke has distinctive grooves along its throat. In polar regions, the minke feeds mainly on krill, but in warmer waters it eats fish and squid as well.

Humpback whale

The humpback whale is famous for the amazingly complex songs it sings to keep in touch with other whales and to attract mates. This baleen whale often sings for hours on end, pausing only to breathe. These songs travel great distances through the water.

Size: 48–62½ ft (14.6–19 m)
Range: all oceans
Scientific name: *Megaptera novaeangliae*

O **Humpback whale**

45

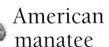

Hoofed mammals

Some mammals have toes that end in hard coverings called hoofs. Hoofs are made of keratin, as are nails and claws. Long ago, all hoofed mammals had five toes. As they evolved, they lost the use of some toes to enable them to run faster. Hoofed mammals are classified according to whether their feet have an odd (one or three) or an even (two or four) number of working toes. Elephants are the only hoofed mammals that still have five working toes.

Pigs, peccaries, and hippopotamuses

A pig is easily recognized by its long, muscular snout, which ends in a round, flat disk. The piglike peccary lives only in the Americas, whereas the hippo, the larger cousin of pigs and peccaries, is found in Africa. Pigs, peccaries, and hippos are even-toed hoofed mammals, with four toes on their feet (peccaries have only three on their hind feet). They have simpler stomachs than other even-toed hoofed mammals.

Wild boar

Wild boar

The wild boar is the ancestor of the farmyard pig. With its long snout it roots around the woodland floor for plants and insects to eat. It also digs up bulbs and tubers. Young boars have striped coats that blend in with the trees and hide them from predators.

Size: body 3½–4¼ ft (1.1–1.3 m); tail 6–7¾ in (15–20 cm)
Range: southern and central Europe, northern Africa, Asia
Scientific name: *Sus scrofa*

Size: body 9¼–14 ft (2.8–4.2 m); tail 13¾–19¾ in (35–50 cm)
Range: Africa south of the Sahara
Scientific name: *Hippopotamus amphibius*

Warthog

The warthog is not a pretty sight. It has long legs, curving tusks, and a long, broad head with two pairs of large, wartlike protuberances. It lives in small family groups on the African savanna and on treeless plains, where it feeds on short grasses and herbs. In the hottest part of the day, it rests in its burrow, which is often the abandoned home of an aardvark. Its main enemies are lions and leopards.

Size: body 3½–4½ ft (1.1–1.4 m); tail 13¾–19¾ in (35–50 cm)
Range: central and southern Africa
Scientific name: *Phacochoerus aethiopicus*

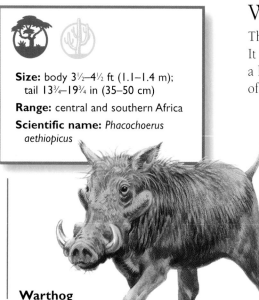

Warthog

Size: body 29½–35½ in (75–90 cm);
tail ⅝–1¼ in (1.5–3 cm)
Range: southwestern U.S.A., Mexico,
Central and South America
Scientific name: *Tayassu tajacu*

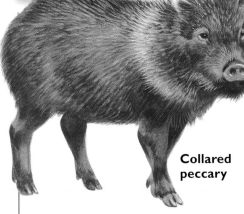

Collared peccary

**Pygmy
hippopotamus**

Collared peccary

A light neckband gives collared peccaries their name. They live in groups of up to 15 animals, marking their territory with scent produced by musk glands on their backs. They eat roots, herbs, grass, fruit, worms, and insect larvae. They can run fast enough to escape from predators such as jaguars and mountain lions.

Size: body 5½–6¼ ft
(1.7–1.9 m); tail 6–8¼ in (15–21 cm)
Range: western Africa from
Guinea to Nigeria
Scientific name:
Hexaprotodon liberiensis

Pygmy hippopotamus

This small hippopotamus lives around swamps but spends most of its time on dry land. The pygmy hippo is in danger of becoming extinct because its forest habitat is being cut down. It is also at risk from hunters, who kill the animal for its meat.

Bearded pig

The bearded pig has a long body and narrow head. It gets its name from the whiskers on its face. It lives in rain forests, scrubland, and mangrove swamps. Fallen fruit, rats, and insect larvae are this pig's main food. It often follows monkeys to pick up any fruit that they might have dropped. Females give birth to two or three piglets.

**Bearded
pig**

Hippopotamus

Hippopotamus

The hippo is one of the world's largest land mammals, with only the rhino and the elephant weighing more. It lives near rivers and lakes and spends up to 16 hours each day submerged in the water to keep cool. It emerges at sunset to graze on riverside plants and eat fallen fruit. It can swim well but often prefers to walk along the river bottom. A hippo can hold its breath underwater for up to five minutes.

Size: body 5¼–6 ft (1.6–1.8 m);
tail 7¾–11¾ in (20–30 cm)
Range: Malaysia, Sumatra,
Borneo
Scientific name: *Sus barbatus*

47

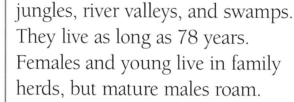

African

Asian

Elephants

Weighing as much as 13,000 pounds (5,900 kg) and standing up to 13 feet (4 m) tall at the shoulder, the elephant is the largest land mammal. There are two elephant species: One lives in Africa, the other in India and Southeast Asia. An elephant's trunk—a long nose attached to the upper lip—contains up to 100,000 muscles and is used for smelling, feeling, breathing, grasping food, and making loud trumpeting calls. The elephant uses its tusks for fighting, stripping bark off trees, and digging for water. Elephants live on grassy plains and desert scrublands and in tropical jungles, river valleys, and swamps. They live as long as 78 years. Females and young live in family herds, but mature males roam.

Two species

The African elephant is larger and heavier than its Asian cousin, with bigger, more rounded ears. It has two fingerlike projections on the end of its trunk, whereas the Asian has one. Both male and female African elephants have tusks, but only Asian males do.

Elephants at work

For thousands of years, humans have trained elephants to lift, push, and drag heavy objects. In forestry work, elephants are sometimes taught to use their tusks to lift heavy logs.

Big appetite

An African elephant eats about 330 pounds (150 kg) of grass, leaves, twigs, bark, roots, and fruit every day. In order to consume such a large amount, it has to spend three-quarters of its time feeding.

A **baby elephant** does not need to forage for food because it drinks its mother's milk for at least two years. Sometimes other adult females in the herd also suckle it.

Showers and mud baths

As well as releasing heat through their large, floppy ears, elephants keep cool by giving themselves a shower. They suck up water with their trunks and spray it over their bodies. With practice, an elephant can reach every part of its body by swinging its trunk and blowing at just the right moment. Elephants sometimes wallow in mud or throw dust over themselves. The mud and dust coat the skin, protecting it against insects and sunburn and stopping the evaporation of moisture from it.

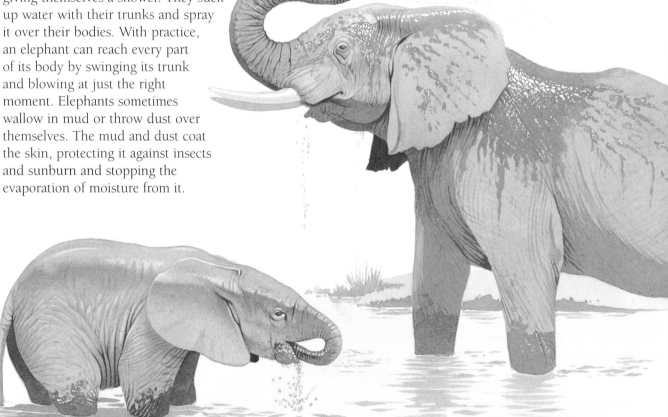

Camels

The camel family includes the Arabian and the Bactrian camels, the vicuña, and the guanaco. They are cud-chewing animals, and their feet have just two toes. The desert-dwelling Arabian and Bactrian camels have broad, flat pads under each foot to help them walk over sandy or rocky soil. Vicuñas and guanacos can breathe the thin air on mountain pastures, and their thick, woolly coats enable them to endure chilly temperatures at high altitudes.

Vicuña

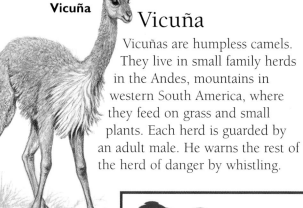

Vicuña

Vicuñas are humpless camels. They live in small family herds in the Andes, mountains in western South America, where they feed on grass and small plants. Each herd is guarded by an adult male. He warns the rest of the herd of danger by whistling.

Size: body 4½–5¼ ft (1.4–1.6 m); tail 6 in (15 cm)
Range: Peru to northern Chile
Scientific name: *Vicugna vicugna*

Arabian camel

Size:
  body 7¼–11 ft (2.2–3.4 m); tail 19¾ in (50 cm)
Range: northern Africa, southwestern Asia; introduced into Australia
Scientific name: *Camelus dromedarius*

Arabian camel

Arabian, or dromedary, camels are well suited to life in the desert. Their nostrils can close to keep out sand, and their tough lips enable them to eat thorny desert plants. They use their single hump to store fat, which their bodies break down into water and energy when food and drink become scarce.

Deer, giraffes, pronghorns, and bovids

These even-toed hoofed animals all chew the cud, which means that they have complex stomachs. When they eat, they briefly chew leaves and grasses and swallow them. The animal then brings the partly digested food, or a cud, back up into its mouth and chews it again. Giraffes, pronghorns, and bovids (cattle, antelope, sheep, and goats) have horns on their heads, whereas deer have antlers. Horns are permanent growths, but antlers drop off and grow again each year.

Water chevrotain

Water chevrotain

The tiny water chevrotain is about the size of a terrier. It has a hunched back, small head, and thin legs. It lives in forests near water and spends the day resting in thick undergrowth. At night it comes out to forage for fruit that has fallen to the ground, grass, leaves, and other delicacies. If danger threatens, it dives deep into the water to escape.

Size: body 29½–33½ in (75–85 cm); tail 4–6 in (10–15 cm)
Range: western and central Africa
Scientific name: *Hyemoschus aquaticus*

50

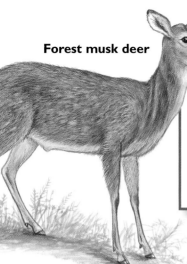

Forest musk deer

Size: body about 3¼ ft (1 m);
tail 1½–2 in (4–5 cm)

Range: Himalaya to central China

Scientific name:
Moschus chrysogaster

Forest musk deer

The male musk deer has a scent gland on the underside of its body. This oozes a strong-smelling liquid called musk, which the deer uses to send signals to females in the breeding season. The musk deer has a coat of long, thick, bristly hairs and two tusklike teeth on its upper jaw. It feeds on lichens, buds, shoots, grass, moss, and twigs.

Size: body 5¼–8 ft (1.6–2.5 m);
tail 4¾–9¾ in (12–25 cm)

Range: North America, northern Africa, Europe, Asia; introduced into New Zealand

Scientific name: *Cervus elaphus*

Wapiti

Male and female wapiti, or elk, live in separate herds. In spring, males lose their antlers and grow new ones. In the breeding season, rival males take part in fierce, antler-clashing fights to win the right to mate with females. The older males with bigger antlers usually win.

Wapiti

Caribou

The caribou, or reindeer, is the only deer species in which both males and females have antlers. Usually only males have them. It feeds mainly on lichens in winter. In summer many herds travel north to feed on the rich grass and plants of the tundra. Females and young live in herds, but males often live separately.

Caribou

Moose

Male

Moose

The moose is the largest of all the deer species. It has massive antlers, a broad overhanging muzzle, and a flap of skin that dangles from its throat. In winter the moose eats shrubs and pine cones and scrapes away the snow with its hoofs to find mosses and lichens. It swims well, and in summer it will often wade into lakes and rivers to feed on water plants. Males bellow to attract females.

Size: body 8–10 ft (2.5–3 m);
tail 2–4¾ in (5–12 cm)

Range: northern Europe, Asia, and North America

Scientific name: *Alces alces*

Size: body 4–7¼ ft (1.2–2.2 m);
tail 4–8¼ in (10–21 cm)

Range: Greenland, northern Europe, Asia, and North America

Scientific name: *Rangifer tarandus*

Size: body 10–13 ft (3–4 m); tail 35½–43½ in (90–110 cm)
Range: Africa south of the Sahara
Scientific name: *Giraffa camelopardalis*

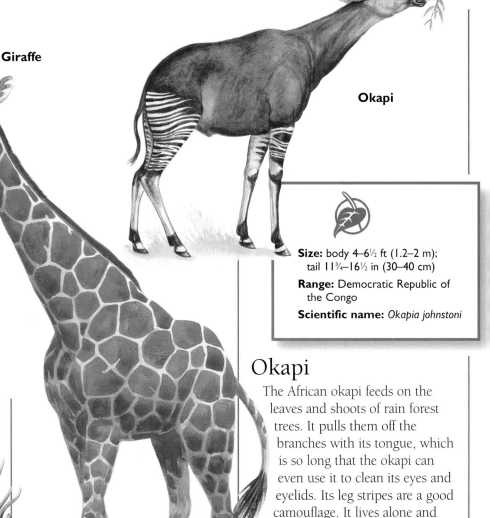

Giraffe

Okapi

Giraffe

The giraffe lives on Africa's savanna. With its amazingly long legs and neck, it stands nearly 19½ feet (6 m) tall, making it the tallest living mammal. Its great height enables it to feed on leaves and buds at the tops of trees and to spot approaching danger.

Size: body 4–6½ ft (1.2–2 m); tail 11¾–16½ in (30–40 cm)
Range: Democratic Republic of the Congo
Scientific name: *Okapia johnstoni*

Okapi

The African okapi feeds on the leaves and shoots of rain forest trees. It pulls them off the branches with its tongue, which is so long that the okapi can even use it to clean its eyes and eyelids. Its leg stripes are a good camouflage. It lives alone and meets other okapis only during the breeding season. Males have short horns, like those of a giraffe.

Size: body 3½–4¼ ft (1.1–1.3 m); tail 4–6 in (10–15 cm)
Range: South America south of the Amazon
Scientific name: *Ozotoceros bezoarticus*

Pampas deer

Pampas deer

This deer is found mostly in tall pampas grass, but much of its original habitat has been disturbed by farming. It has become rare in many places. It rests during the day and feeds on grass and shrubs at dusk. The young are born mostly from September to November.

Pronghorn

One of North America's fastest mammals, the pronghorn can run as fast as 40 miles per hour (65 km/h). Both sexes have horns, but only males have short forward-pointing prongs. It is now rare because of hunting and the destruction of its habitat.

Pronghorn

Size: body 3¼–5 ft (1–1.5 m); tail 3–4 in (7.5–10 cm)
Range: central Canada, western U.S.A., Mexico
Scientific name: *Antilocapra americana*

Blue wildebeest

In the dry season, huge herds of these large, cowlike antelopes walk great distances across the African savanna in search of fresh grass and watering holes. Young wildebeest calves are born during the wet season, when the herds split up and food is more plentiful.

Size: body 5½–7¾ ft (1.7–2.4 m); tail 23½–35½ in (60–100 cm)
Range: southern and eastern Africa
Scientific name:
Connochaetes taurinus

Blue wildebeest

Asian water buffalo

Water buffalo feed early and late in the day on grass and other vegetation growing near lakes and rivers. They spend much of the rest of the time wallowing in mud or submerged in water with only their muzzles and horns showing. They use their long, curved horns to defend themselves against tigers.

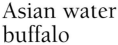

Size: body 8¼–10 ft (2.5–3 m); tail 23½–35½ in (60–100 cm)
Range: India, Southeast Asia
Scientific name: Bubalus arnee

Asian water buffalo

 Wild yak

Bongo

The shy, forest-dwelling bongo hides among the bushes and trees during the daytime. At dawn and dusk it comes out to feed on leaves, bark, and fruit. When it runs, the bongo tilts its head so that its horns lie along its back. This keeps them from catching on branches.

Size: body 5½–8¼ ft (1.7–2.5 m); tail 17¾–25½ in (45–65 cm)
Range: central Africa
Scientific name:
Tragelaphus eurycerus

Bongo

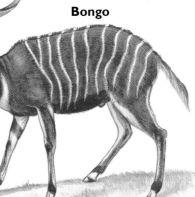

Size: body up to 10½ ft (3.25 m); tail 19¾–31½ in (50–80 cm)
Range: central Asia
Scientific name: Bos grunniens

Wild yak

Despite its size, the yak is surprisingly surefooted as it grazes on remote mountain slopes. Its long, thick, ragged hair reaches almost to the ground. It also has a woolly undercoat to help protect it against freezing temperatures.

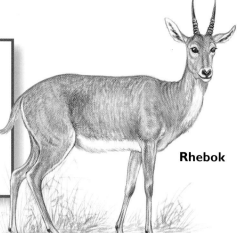

Size: body 3¼–4 ft (1–1.2 m); tail 4–7¾ in (10–20 cm)
Range: South Africa, Lesotho, Swaziland
Scientific name: *Pelea capreolus*

Rhebok

Size: body 7–11½ ft (2.1–3.5 m); tail 19¾–23½ in (50–60 cm)
Range: North America
Scientific name: *Bison bison*

Rhebok

The rhebok is a small, graceful antelope with a soft woolly coat. It lives on grassy hills and high plains with low bushes and scattered trees. This wary animal bounces away with a jerky run if it is disturbed. In the breeding season, the males stage fierce mock battles but rarely harm each other.

ⓘ European bison

American bison

Lechwe

The lechwe lives around lakes, swamps, and floodplains. It spends much of its time wading in shallow water, where it feeds on grasses and water plants. Its long, wide hoofs are ideal for plodding through mud but prevent it from moving quickly on dry land. When threatened by lions, hyenas, or other predators, it tries to hide in deep water, with just its nostrils showing.

American bison

There were once 60 million bison roaming the Great Plains of North America, but so many were killed by settlers in the 19th century that only about 200,000 remain today. They live in herds and feed on grass. Bison are now also raised for their meat.

Size: body 7–11½ ft (2.1–3.5 m); tail 19¾–23½ in (50–60 cm)
Range: eastern Europe
Scientific name: *Bison bonasus*

European bison

The European bison feeds on leaves, ferns, twigs, bark, and acorns found in the forest. In 1919 the species died out in the wild, due to hunting and deforestation. Six European bison were bred in captivity, and their offspring were released into the wild. There are now more than 500 European bison in the wild.

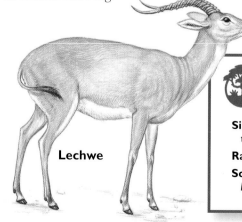

Lechwe

Size: body 4¼–5½ ft (1.3–1.7 m); tail 11¾–17¾ in (30–45 cm)
Range: southern Africa
Scientific name: *Kobus leche*

Arabian oryx

The desert-dwelling oryx can endure long periods without water. It gets all the moisture it needs from the grass and other vegetation it eats.

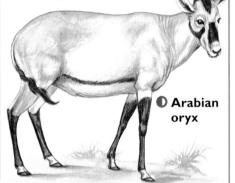

❶ Arabian oryx

Size: body 5¼ ft (1.6 m); tail 17¾ in (45 cm)
Range: Saudi Arabia
Scientific name: *Oryx leucoryx*

Addax

The addax is one of the few large animals that live in the Sahara. It feeds on desert plants. Its wide hoofs stop its feet from sinking into the desert sand. It is now extremely rare because it has been hunted for sport and for its horns and skin.

❶ Addax

Size: body 4¼ ft (1.3 m); tail 9¾–13¾ in (25–35 cm)
Range: northern Africa
Scientific name: *Addax nasomaculatus*

Impala

At home in light woodland or on the African savanna, the glossy-coated impala has long, elegant, spiral-shaped horns. When running, it can make leaps of up to 33 feet (10 m) in order to escape predators. It also seems to do this just for fun.

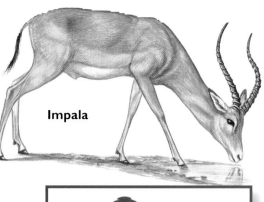

Impala

Size: body 4–5¼ ft (1.2–1.6 m); tail 11¾–17¾ in (30–45 cm)
Range: southern Africa
Scientific name: *Aepyceros melampus*

Saiga

The saiga lives on high grassy plains called steppes. Its nose has special hairs to filter dust from the air. They may help warm the air it breathes. In winter it grows a thick coat to protect it from icy steppe winds.

○ Saiga

Size: body 4–5½ ft (1.2–1.7 m); tail 3–4 in (7.5–10 cm)
Range: central Asia
Scientific name: *Saiga tatarica*

Chamois

In summer the nimble chamois grazes on mountaintops, often leaping between rocky crags to find food. It has sturdy legs and hoofs with special spongy pads underneath to help grip slippery surfaces. In winter it moves farther down the mountainside to feed on lichens, mosses, and shoots.

Size: body 35½–51 in (90–130 cm); tail 1¼–1½ in (3–4 cm)
Range: Europe to southwestern Asia
Scientific name: *Rupicapra rupicapra*

Chamois

55

Musk-ox

Size: body 6¼–7½ ft (1.9–2.3 m); tail 3½–4 in (9–10 cm)

Range: northern Canada, Greenland, and Alaska

Scientific name: *Ovibos moschatus*

Musk-ox

On the freezing tundra of the Arctic, musk-oxen dig through snow and ice with their hoofs to reach mosses, lichens, and roots. If attacked by wolves, they form a defensive circle around their young, with their horns pointing outward.

Horses, tapirs, and rhinos

Horses, tapirs, and rhinoceroses make up a group of odd-toed hoofed mammals. Animals in the horse family, including zebras and donkeys, live in herds and feed mainly on grass. Their feet have only one toe with a single hoof on the end. This enables them to run fast. Tapirs are short, stocky creatures with four toes on their front feet and three on the hind feet. Rhinoceroses have three toes on each foot, short legs, large heads, and one or two nose horns.

Size: body 4 ft (1.2 m); tail 2¾ in (7 cm)

Range: southern Europe, central and southern Asia

Scientific name: *Ovis orientalis*

Mouflon

Mouflon

The mouflon has long, inward-curving horns. In order to survive in the rugged mountains where it lives, it eats virtually any vegetation it can find—including poisonous plants, such as deadly nightshade.

Grevy's zebra

This species has the narrowest stripes of all zebras and lives in drier regions than most. It eats tough grasses and migrates in search of water holes.

Size: body 8½ ft (2.6 m); tail 27½–29½ in (70–75 cm)

Range: eastern Africa

Scientific name: *Equus grevyi*

Grevy's zebra

○ **Malayan tapir**

Size: body 8 ft (2.5 m);
tail 2–4 in (5–10 cm)
Range: Southeast Asia
Scientific name:
Tapirus indicus

Black rhinoceros

The black rhino's hooklike upper lip helps it grab leaves, buds, and shoots from small trees and bushes. It makes up for its poor eyesight with good senses of hearing and smell. If it feels threatened, it will charge. Despite its size, it can reach a speed of 30 miles per hour (48 km/h).

● **Black rhinoceros**

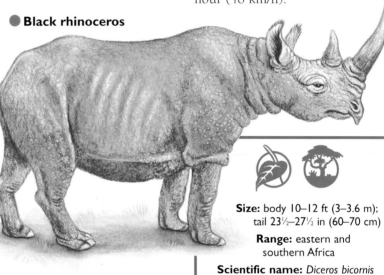

Size: body 10–12 ft (3–3.6 m);
tail 23½–27½ in (60–70 cm)
Range: eastern and
southern Africa
Scientific name: *Diceros bicornis*

Malayan tapir

The Malayan tapir is a shy, solitary animal that lives in humid, swampy forests. It swims well and rushes into the water to hide when it feels threatened. The Malayan tapir prefers to feed on aquatic vegetation but also eats the leaves, buds, and fruit of some land plants.

Przewalski's horse

This short, sturdy horse is the only true wild horse living today. It was once common on the dry plains of Mongolia, where it grazed on grass and leaves. It has not been seen in the wild since 1968 and now lives only in captivity.

Przewalski's horse

Size: body 6–6½ ft (1.8–2 m);
tail 35½ in (90 cm)
Range: Native to Mongolia and
western China, but now found
only in captivity
Scientific name: *Equus przewalskii*

Size: body 8–9¼ ft (2.5–2.8 m);
tail about 23½ in (60 cm)
Range: Southeast Asia
Scientific name:
Dicerorhinus sumatrensis

Sumatran rhinoceros

This is the smallest and hairiest member of the rhinoceros family. There are only a few hundred wild Sumatran rhinos left. It is hunted for its horns, which are used in traditional medicines, and the forests where it lives are being chopped down.

● **Sumatran rhinoceros**

Rodents and rabbits

Rodents are a large group of small to medium-size mammals that include such creatures as squirrels, rats, and beavers. There are at least 2,000 species of rodents, and they are found all over the world in every kind of habitat. Most feed on plants, and they have a pair of sharp incisor teeth in each jaw that allow them to chew through the toughest food. Pikas, rabbits, and hares are another successful group of plant-eating mammals called lagomorphs. They also have sharp incisors for chewing plant food.

Pikas, rabbits, and hares

Pikas are smaller than rabbits and have short, rounded ears and no tail. There are about 26 species, most of which live in north and central Asia, although 2 species also live in North America. Rabbits and hares are common in the Americas, Europe, Asia, and Africa and have been successfully introduced into Australia and New Zealand—about 55 species in all. Most of the fast-moving rabbits and hares have long, narrow ears, small, fluffy tails, and well-developed back legs.

European rabbit

European rabbits live together in a complex system of burrows called a warren. There may be a couple hundred rabbits in a colony. Grass and leafy plants are their main food, but they also eat grain and can damage young trees. Females have several litters a year.

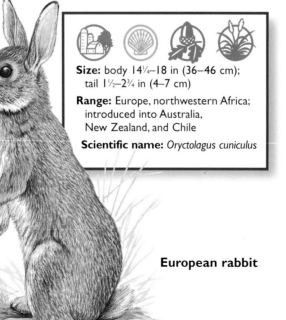

European rabbit

Size: body 14¼–18 in (36–46 cm); tail 1½–2¾ in (4–7 cm)
Range: Europe, northwestern Africa; introduced into Australia, New Zealand, and Chile
Scientific name: *Oryctolagus cuniculus*

American pika

Pikas live in family groups, which make homes in dens among rocks. Grass and juicy plant stems are their main food. In summer they gather extra food, which they pile up in little haystacks to keep for the winter months. Pikas can tunnel through snow to reach their food stores.

American pika

Size: body 7¾–9¾ in (20–25 cm)
Range: southwestern Canada, western contiguous U.S.A.
Scientific name: *Ochotona princeps*

Snowshoe hare

The snowshoe hare is dark brown in summer but turns white in winter. Only the tips of its ears remain dark. This seasonal change of hair color helps this hare hide from enemies. Usually active at night and in the early morning, the snowshoe hare eats grass in summer and twigs and buds in winter.

Snowshoe hare

Size: body 14¼–20½ in (36–52 cm); tail 1–2 in (2.5–5 cm)
Range: Canada, Alaska, northern contiguous U.S.A.
Scientific name: *Lepus americanus*

Squirrels, pocket gophers, pocket mice, springhares, and beavers

These animals are all rodents. The squirrel family includes animals such as woodchucks, prairie dogs, and chipmunks. Pocket gophers live in North America and spend most of their lives underground. Pocket mice are found in North and South America. Some are mouselike and live in dense forests. Others bound across arid plains on long hind legs. The single species of springhare can leap like a kangaroo. The two species of beavers spend much of their lives in water.

Size: body 4½–7 in (11.5–18 cm); tail 4½–7 in (11.5–18 cm)
Range: India, Sri Lanka
Scientific name: *Funambulus palmarum*

Indian striped palm squirrel

Indian striped palm squirrel

These active little squirrels leap about in palm trees during the day, feeding on palm nuts, flowers, and buds. Rival males fight for females but after mating have nothing further to do with them or the young. The females produce about three litters a year, each containing about three babies.

Woodchuck

The woodchuck, or groundhog as it is sometimes known, eats plenty of plant food in summer and gets fat. At the first sign of frost it goes into its burrow and sleeps through the winter, living on its store of body fat.

Size: body 17¾–24 in (45–61 cm); tail 7–9¾ in (18–25 cm)
Range: North America
Scientific name: *Marmota monax*

Woodchuck

Black-tailed prairie dog

Size: body 11–13 in (28–33 cm); tail 3–4 in (7.5–10 cm)
Range: central U.S.A. and Canada
Scientific name: *Cynomys ludovicianus*

Black-tailed prairie dog

Prairie dogs live in huge underground burrows called towns. A town may house several thousand animals. They come out during the day to feed on grass and other plants, and warn each other of any danger with sharp, doglike barks.

Gray squirrel

The gray squirrel is often seen in parks and gardens, but its natural home is oak and hickory forests, where it feeds on seeds, acorns, and nuts. It also eats fruit, insects, and tree sap. Gray squirrels nest in a tree or tree hole and breed twice a year in spring and summer.

Size: body 8–10 in (20–25 cm); tail 8–10 in (20–25 cm)
Range: eastern U.S.A. and Canada; introduced in Great Britain and South Africa
Scientific name: *Sciurus carolinensis*

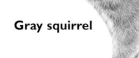

Gray squirrel

Plains pocket gopher

Plains pocket gopher

This gopher's name comes from its two deep, fur-lined cheek pouches. These can be crammed full of food (mostly roots) to carry back to the nest. Gophers spend most of their lives underground in burrows that they dig with their sharp front teeth and strong paws.

Size: body 7–9½ in (18–24 cm); tail 4–5 in (10–12.5 cm)
Range: central U.S.A.
Scientific name: *Geomys bursarius*

Desert kangaroo rat

Kangaroo rats belong to the pocket mouse family. This desert species spends the day in a burrow and comes out at night to find food, such as seeds, that it carries in cheek pouches to its burrow. It gets moisture from its food and may live its whole life without drinking water.

Size: body 4¾–6½ in (12–16.5 cm); tail 7–7¾ in (18–20 cm)
Range: southwestern U.S.A.
Scientific name: *Dipodomys deserti*

Desert kangaroo rat

Size: body 23–31 in (60–80 cm); tail 7¾–12 in (20–30.5 cm)
Range: North America
Scientific name: *Castor canadensis*

American beaver

One of the largest rodents, this beaver weighs up to 60 pounds (27 kg). Beavers eat leaves, bark, and twigs and live near water. They build dams across shallow streams with branches and mud to create ponds. A shelter, or lodge, is made of branches and mud, with underwater entrances.

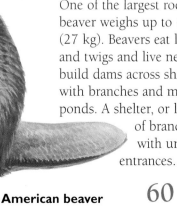

American beaver

Eastern chipmunk

The lively little chipmunk belongs to the squirrel family. It lives in burrows it digs under logs and boulders and comes out in the morning to forage for nuts, berries, and seeds. During autumn, chipmunks store food for the winter. They do not hibernate, but they become less active in winter.

Eastern chipmunk

Size: body 5¼–7¾ in (13.5–20 cm); tail 3–4½ in (7.5–11.5 cm)
Range: eastern North America
Scientific name: *Tamias striatus*

○ **Springhare**

Size: body 13¾–17 in (35–43 cm); tail 14¼–18½ in (36–47cm)
Range: southern Africa
Scientific name: *Pedetes capensis*

Springhare

When alarmed or traveling a long way, the springhare bounces along on its long hind legs like a kangaroo. When feeding, it moves on all fours. The springhare spends much of the day in its burrow and comes out at night to forage for bulbs, roots, and grain, as well as some insects.

New World rats and mice

There are at least 400 species in this group of rodents, found in all kinds of habitats, from the northern woodlands of Canada to the deserts and forests of South America. They adapt well to different conditions—fish-eating rats that live near rivers and lakes even have partially webbed feet. Most New World rats and mice are small—the largest, the giant water rat, measures 11¾ inches (30 cm) long. Plant material is their main food, although some also feed on insects.

Size: body 4¾–7 in (12–18 cm); tail 3¼–7 in (8–18 cm)
Range: Canada to Mexico
Scientific name: *Peromyscus maniculatus*

Deer mouse

Arizona cotton rat

Cotton rats sometimes occur in such numbers that they are considered pests. They feed on plants and small insects but may also take the eggs and chicks of bobwhite quails and eat crayfish and crabs. The female has her first litter of up to 12 young when just 10 weeks old.

◑ **Arizona cotton rat**

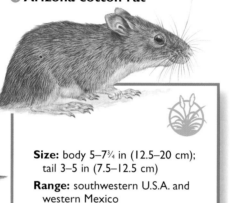

Size: body 5–7¾ in (12.5–20 cm); tail 3–5 in (7.5–12.5 cm)
Range: southwestern U.S.A. and western Mexico
Scientific name: *Sigmodon arizonae*

Deer mouse

Like the animal they are named after, deer mice run and hop through grass and dense vegetation. They build nests underground or in tree holes and feed on insects as well as seeds, nuts, and acorns. Young deer mice start to breed when only seven weeks old. They may have several litters a year, each containing up to nine young.

Hamsters and mole rats

Hamsters and mole rats are burrowing rodents. Hamsters are found from Europe all the way to eastern Asia. There are about 18 species, all of which have a rounded body and short tail. They have large cheek pouches, which they use for carrying food back to the burrow. There are many kinds of mole rats living in parts of Europe, Asia, and Africa. All spend most of their lives underground, usually alone or in small groups. Most feed on plants but may also eat insects. The most unusual is the virtually hairless naked mole rat, which lives in Africa in large colonies.

Common hamster

The hamster lives in a burrow with separate areas for sleeping and storing food. It feeds mainly on seeds, grain, roots, green plants, and insect larvae. In late summer it gathers extra food to store for the winter. From October to March or April, the hamster hibernates, waking from time to time to feed on its food stores.

Size: body 8¾–11¾ in (22–30 cm); tail 1¼–2¼ in (3–6 cm)
Range: from western Europe across central Asia
Scientific name: *Cricetus cricetus*

Common hamster

Naked mole rat

Size: body 3¼–3½ in (8–9 cm); tail 1½ in (4 cm)

Range: eastern Africa

Scientific name: *Heterocephalus glaber*

Size: body 14¼–19 in (36–48 cm); tail 4–6 in (10–15 cm)

Range: Southeast Asia

Scientific name: *Rhizomys sumatrensis*

Bamboo rat

This rat has a heavy body, short legs, and a short, almost hairless tail. Its front teeth are large and strong, and it uses these and its claws for digging. It burrows underground near clumps of bamboo—the roots of this plant are its main food. It also eats other plants, seeds, and fruit.

Bamboo rat

Naked mole rat

This little rodent has a life-style more like that of an insect than a mammal. It lives in groups of up to 30 animals, ruled by one female, or queen. She is the only one to breed. Worker mole rats dig burrows and gather food such as roots for the whole colony to eat. A few nonworkers tend the queen.

Swamp rats, gerbils, lemmings, and voles

There are nine species of African swamp rats. They do not always live near water or swampy areas, but they are all good swimmers. Lemmings and voles are plump-bodied rodents that live in North America, Europe, and Asia. All feed mainly on plants, and they usually live in large groups or colonies. Combined there are about 140 species. Gerbils live in dry parts of Africa and central and southwestern Asia. All are well adapted to desert conditions and are able to survive with very little water. Their long hind legs and feet help them run fast over hot sand.

Norway lemming

The Norway lemming is busy around the clock, feeding on grass, leaves, and moss. In winter it clears pathways under the snow so it can still run around foraging for food. Lemmings start to breed in spring under the snow and may produce as many as eight litters of six young each during the summer.

Norway lemming

Size: body 5–6 in (13–15 cm); tail ¾ in (2 cm)

Range: Scandinavia

Scientific name: *Lemmus lemmus*

Swamp rat

Swamp rat

This plump, active rat feeds on seeds, berries, plant shoots, and grasses. It often goes into water and even dives to escape enemies—many larger creatures feed on these rats. It usually makes a nest of leaves and twigs aboveground but may sometimes take over a burrow left by another animal.

Size: body 5–7¾ in (13–20 cm); tail 2–6¾ in (5–17 cm)

Range: southern Africa

Scientific name: *Otomys irroratus*

Great gerbil

This desert animal manages to survive in the Gobi, a desert with hot summers and icy winters. During the summer, it builds up stores of 130 pounds (60 kg) or more of plant material in its burrow so that it has plenty of food for the winter months.

Meadow vole

Size: body 6¼–7¾ in (16–20 cm); tail 5–6¼ in (13–16 cm)
Range: central Asia
Scientific name:
  Rhombomys opimus

Great gerbil

Size: body 3½–5 in (9–12.5 cm); tail 1¼–2½ in (3.5–6.5 cm)
Range: North America
Scientific name:
  Microtus pennsylvanicus

Meadow vole

The meadow vole manages to live in many kinds of habitats. Grass, seeds, roots, and bark are its main food, and it moves in the grass along runways that it clears and keeps trimmed. It makes a nest on the ground or in a burrow under a runway.

Old World rats and mice

This large group of more than 500 species of rodents contains some of the world's most common and widespread mammals. Rodents such as the brown rat and house mouse have adapted to life all over the world in many different kinds of conditions and will eat a wide range of foods. Many of this group are considered pests by humans because they damage grain and root crops as well as stored food. Some, such as the brown rat, also carry salmonella and other diseases.

Size: body 9¾–11¾ in (25–30 cm); tail 9¾–12½ in (25–32 cm)
Range: worldwide
Scientific name:
  Rattus norvegicus

Brown rat

Wood mouse

The wood mouse is one of Europe's most common small rodents. It comes out of its nest under the roots of trees in the evening and forages for seeds, insects, and berries. The female usually produces young between April and November but may breed through the winter if there is plenty of food.

Size: body 3¼–5 in (8–13 cm); tail 2¾–3¾ in (7–9.5 cm)
Range: Europe, Asia
Scientific name:
  Apodemus sylvaticus

Brown rat

The brown rat is a serious pest. It has followed humans all over the world and lives wherever people settle. An extremely adaptable animal, it eats any scraps of waste food. It breeds all year round and produces about eight litters a year of 8 to 10 young each.

Wood mouse

63

Dormice and jerboas

There are about 28 species of dormice living in Africa, Europe, and Asia. In autumn most dormice eat extra food to build up reserves of fat in the body. They then hibernate—sleep through the winter—living on their fat but waking from time to time to feed on stored food. Jerboas are small rodents with long back legs used for jumping. There are some 50 species of jerboas living in North America, eastern Europe, northern Africa, and Asia.

Great jerboa

This lively rodent leaps through the desert on its long back legs. At night it searches for seeds and insects to eat, which it finds by combing through the sand with the long, slender claws on its front feet. During the day the jerboa stays in a burrow.

Great jerboa

Desert dormouse

This dormouse is active at night, catching insects to eat. It is nomadic and feeds on plants during the summer. In winter it digs a burrow where it hibernates. This rodent was first discovered in 1938.

Size: body 2¾–3¼ in (7–8.5 cm); tail 2¾–3¾ in (7–9.5 cm)
Range: Kazakhstan
Scientific name: *Selevinia betpakdalaensis*

Size: body 6¼–10 in (16–26 cm); tail 6¼–8¾ in (16–22 cm)
Range: central Asia
Scientific name: *Allactaga major*

◑ **Desert dormouse**

Porcupines, chinchillas, guinea pigs, capybaras, and hutias

These widely varied animals all belong to small families of medium-size to large rodents. Porcupines are instantly recognized by the long, sharp spines covering parts of the body and tail. There are two families: One occurs in Africa and Asia, and the other in North and South America. Chinchillas and guinea pigs are rodents that live in South America. The capybara also lives in South America and is the only species in its family. The 12 species of hutias all live on islands in the West Indies.

○ **Chinchilla**

Size: body 8¾–15 in (22–38 cm); tail 3–6 in (7.5–15 cm)
Range: northern Chile
Scientific name: *Chinchilla laniger*

Chinchilla

The chinchilla lives among the rocks in the high Andes and is prized for its thick fur. A colony may have 100 animals. Chinchillas feed on plants and usually sit up to eat, holding their food in their front paws. Females are larger than males. They breed in winter and have two litters of up to six young.

Crested porcupine

Size: body 28–33 in (71–84 cm);
tail up to 1 in (2.5 cm)
Range: Africa
Scientific name:
Hystrix africaeaustralis

Crested porcupine

The spines on the back of the crested porcupine are up to 11¾ inches (30 cm) long. If threatened, the porcupine charges backward, driving these sharp spines, which detach easily from its body, into its enemy. This porcupine lives in a burrow during the day and comes out at night to feed.

Tree porcupine

The body of the tree porcupine is covered with short, thick spines. Its tail is prehensile, which means it has special muscles that grip easily, acting like an extra limb. Tree porcupines usually feed at night on leaves, plant stems, and fruit.

Size: body 11¾–24 in (30–61 cm);
tail 13–17¾ in (33–45 cm)
Range: Bolivia, Brazil, Venezuela
Scientific name:
Coendou prehensilis

Tree porcupine

Bahamian hutia

The hutia feeds mostly on fruit and leaves, but it also eats some insects and small reptiles. It is a good climber and may search for food in trees. Active during the day, it rests in a burrow or rock crevice at night. Unfortunately, hutias are now rare because they are preyed on by mongooses and dogs introduced into the West Indies by people.

○ **Bahamian hutia**

Size: body 11¾–19¾ in (30–50 cm);
tail 2 in (5 cm)
Range: Bahamas
Scientific name:
Geocapromys ingrahami

Guinea pig

Guinea pig

Also known as the cavy, the wild guinea pig—though not related to a pig—squeals like one when excited. Guinea pigs live in family groups, which may form colonies of up to 40 animals. At dawn and dusk guinea pigs come out of their burrows to eat grass and leaves.

Size: body 7¾–15¾ in (20–40 cm);
no visible tail
Range: Peru to Argentina
Scientific name:
Cavia tschudii

Capybara

The largest living rodent, the capybara has a strong body and large head. It spends much of its time in water and is an expert swimmer and diver. Its feet are partially webbed, and when swimming only its eyes, ears, and nostrils show above the water. It eats mainly plants, including water plants, and is usually active at dawn and dusk.

Capybara

Size: body 3¼–4¼ ft (1–1.3 m)
Range: Panama to eastern Argentina
Scientific name:
Hydrochoerus hydrochaeris

Why do zebras have stripes?

A zebra's stripes, the humps on a camel's back, the "fishing rod" on the head of an angler fish, and the leaflike wings of an insect may seem extraordinary features, but they all make the animals that have them better able to survive in their environments. These types of features are called adaptations and include the special markings or colors, known as camouflage, that allow creatures to hide from predators or prey. Other features help animals survive in extreme conditions such as hot deserts or freezing polar lands.

Some insects look remarkably like the leaves of the trees and bushes they live among, making it very hard for their enemies to spot them. The bright green wings of this **leaf insect** are leaf shaped and have veinlike markings. The edges even look as if they have been nibbled by insects.

The **Bactrian camel** is one of the biggest animals in the desert, and special features help it cope with life there. Wide, flat feet stop it from sinking into soft sand. Large humps store fat to help it survive food shortages. When it gets the chance, the camel can drink a huge quantity of water at one time.

66

The bold black and white stripes of the **zebra** are probably not used for camouflage, since they make the animal very obvious in the grasslands of Africa. Because the pattern of the stripes is slightly different in each individual, experts think that patterns help the zebras to recognize their own family group. This helps keep them together and therefore safer from predators.

The flap of skin that looks like a fishing rod on the **angler fish's** head is a special structure for catching prey. Other fish come near to investigate what could be a morsel of food. The angler opens its huge mouth and swallows the prey.

Birds

Birds are among the most successful of all the world's animals and have conquered air, land, and water. They are found all over the world, including the icy lands of Antarctica and the remotest islands. They have been sighted at heights of more than 26,250 feet (8,000 m) in the Himalaya and at 130 feet (40 m) below sea level around the shores of the Dead Sea.

There are more than 10,000 different species of birds, ranging in size from tiny hummingbirds, weighing only a few ounces (grams), to huge eagles and fast-running ostriches. Despite their differences, all birds lay eggs. The baby bird is protected inside a hard-shelled egg, which is usually kept warm, or incubated, by the parents in a nest. The incubation period—the time taken for a chick to grow inside the egg and break out of the shell—varies from about 10 to 12 days in small birds, such as warblers and wrens, to as many as 84 days in albatrosses.

These **western gulls** are in flight off the coasts of California's Channel Islands. Coastal birds such as gulls do not spend much time actually in the water, but they do depend on the sea for most of their food. Gulls eat fish and are the scavengers of the shore. They eat scraps from fishing boats and take food from garbage dumps.

The **royal flycatcher** lives in tropical rain forests

69

What is a bird?

A typical bird has a strong but light body, two legs, and a pair of wings. The wings are, in fact, modified forelimbs. All birds are covered with feathers—and are the only creatures that have feathers. The feathers are made of keratin, a protein that also makes up the scales on reptiles and the hair and nails of humans and other mammals.

Not all birds fly. The world's largest bird, the **ostrich**, is too heavy to take to the air. Instead it runs fast on its long legs.

Wings

A bird's wings are shaped for different kinds of flight (note: the drawings are not in proportion to the birds' actual sizes). The long, broad wings of hawks and vultures allow these birds to soar on air currents over land. The long wings of the albatross are suited to the wind conditions over oceans. Fast-flying birds such as swifts and swallows have slender pointed wings. The pheasant's wings are for slow, flapping flight.

Albatross

Swift

Swallow

Hawk

Vulture

Pheasant

Bird anatomy

Here is a powerful martial eagle poised to snatch its prey. Strong wings keep the body in the air, and its tail feathers are spread to help it steer during flight. Strong talons are held ready to crush prey, which will be torn apart with the hooked beak. All birds have wings, beaks, and claws that are shaped for their particular life-style.

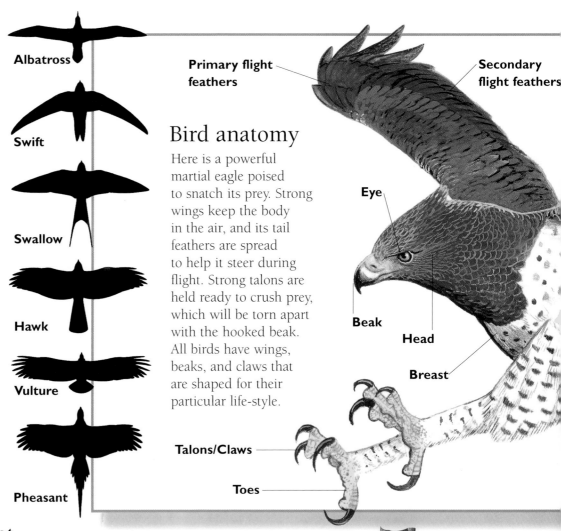

Primary flight feathers

Secondary flight feathers

Eye

Beak

Head

Breast

Talons/Claws

Toes

All types of feet

Perching birds, such as crows, all have four-toed feet, three toes facing forward and one backward. Seabirds, such as cormorants, have webbed feet. The ostrich's two-toed feet are suited to running, and the eagle's strong toes and claws are used for killing prey.

Carrion crow

Harpy eagle

Ostrich

Great cormorant

Growth region

Yolk

Egg white (albumen)

Embryo (baby bird)

Shell

Yolk

A baby bird grows inside an **egg**. The yolk is its food supply, and the layers of egg white protect it from sudden movements or changes in temperature. The hard shell protects the whole structure.

Warbler

Red-breasted merganser

Giant hummingbird

Common redshank

Mallard

Beaks

Bird beaks can pick up food, break open nuts and hard seeds, and tear apart flesh, though not every beak does all of these things. Beaks vary widely in shape depending on a bird's diet. The needle-sharp beaks of warblers are ideal for picking up insects, whereas birds of prey, such as eagles, have large, hooked beaks. Parrots have strong beaks for cracking hard nuts. Waders such as the redshank use their long beaks for probing in the sand for small creatures to eat. The toucan's beak allows the bird to reach fruit at the end of slender branches that would not support the bird's weight. Most ducks use their wedge-shaped beaks for cropping grass at the water's edge and for dabbling in mud for plant seeds, but the merganser's long beak is adapted for catching fish. Hummingbirds plunge their long, slender beaks right into flowers to reach the sweet nectar deep inside. And the strong beaks of finches are perfectly designed for feeding on tough seeds.

Toucan

Parrot

Finch

Wing coverts (small feathers)

Wing

Rump

Tail feathers

Flight feather

Bristle feather

Contour feather

Feathers

Feathers keep a bird warm and also streamline its body. They are windproof and sometimes waterproof. For many birds colorful or specially shaped feathers, such as filoplumes and bristles, help them attract mates. The largest, strongest feathers are usually the flight feathers on the wings and the tail feathers. Softer contour feathers cover the body, and down feathers beneath them add warmth.

Filoplume

Golden eagle

71

Greater prairie-chicken

Prairie-chickens feed mainly on leaves, fruit, and grain. In the summer they also catch insects, particularly grasshoppers. In the breeding season, male birds blow out their orange neck pouches and raise their crests to attract females. They give booming calls and stamp their feet as they display. Females lay 10 to 12 eggs.

Size: 16½–18 in (42–46 cm)
Range: North America
Scientific name:
  Tympanuchus cupido

Greater prairie-chicken

Size: 15½–17½ in (40–45 cm)
Range: northern Europe, northern Asia
Scientific name:
  Tetrao tetrix

Black grouse

In spring, male black grouse perform a group display, called a lek, to attract female birds. Every morning they gather at a special place to dance, call, and spread their beautiful tails before the watching females. The females mate with the dominant males and lay clutches of 6 to 11 eggs.

Black grouse

Wild turkey

The wild turkey has a lighter, slimmer body and longer legs than domestic farm turkeys. It has bare skin on its head and neck. The turkey can fly well for short distances. It rests in trees but finds most of its food on the ground. It eats seeds, nuts, and berries and also catches small creatures such as insects and lizards.

Capercaillie

This magnificent turkeylike bird is the biggest of all the grouse. It feeds mainly on pine needles and pine seeds in winter. Its diet changes in summer, when it eats the leaves, stems, and juicy fruit of cranberry, bilberry, and other forest plants.

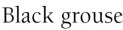

Size: male 33¾ in (86 cm); female 22¾ in (58 cm)
Range: Europe and northern Asia
Scientific name:
  Tetrao urogallus

Female

Wild turkey

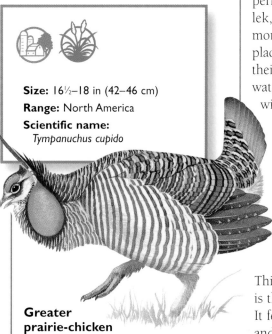

Capercaillie

Male

Size: 36–48 in (91–122 cm)
Range: U.S.A., Mexico
Scientific name:
  Meleagris gallopavo

Ground birds

The long-legged running birds, such as ostriches, rheas, cassowaries, and emus, live in dry grasslands and semi-desert areas. They cannot fly and often have to travel far to find food, so it is important for them to be fast runners. They also rely on running to escape from danger. Kiwis have shorter legs and move more slowly on the ground. They cannot fly either. Also included in this section are ground-living birds from other families, such as the curassow, tinamou, great bustard, satin bowerbird, and Pallas's sandgrouse. All of these birds can fly but spend most of their lives on the ground.

Satin bowerbird

The male bowerbird builds a bower, or chamber, on the ground to attract females. The bower is made of sticks and decorated with bright blue flowers and berries. If a female comes near, the male dances in his bower, flapping his wings and puffing up his feathers.

Satin bowerbird

Size: 10½–13 in (27–33 cm)
Range: eastern Australia
Scientific name:
  Ptilonorhynchus violaceus

Great curassow

Brown kiwi

Using its long, sensitive beak, the brown kiwi probes in the undergrowth for insects, worms, and berries. Females lay one enormous egg per nest. Like other kiwis, this bird has tiny wings under its hairlike body feathers and cannot fly.

○ Brown kiwi

Great curassow

The great curassow finds food, such as fruit and leaves, on the ground but flies up into the trees to roost. If in danger, it runs away rather than flies. The male has a loud booming call.

Size: 37 in (94 cm)
Range: Mexico to Ecuador
Scientific name:
  Crax rubra

Great tinamou

Dense rain forest is the home of the great tinamou. This bird can fly but is weak and clumsy in the air. If in danger it usually remains still, relying on its brownish coloring to keep it hidden. It spends most of its time on the ground, eating berries, seeds, and insects. Females lay up to 12 greenish blue or violet eggs, which are among the most beautiful of all bird eggs.

Size: 27½ in (70 cm)
Range: New Zealand
Scientific name:
  Apteryx australis

Size: 18 in (46 cm)
Range: Mexico to South America
Scientific name:
  Tinamus major

Great tinamou

Size: 13¾–15¾ in (35–40 cm)

Range: Europe, central Asia to Mongolia and China

Scientific name: *Syrrhaptes paradoxus*

Pallas's sandgrouse

Pallas's sandgrouse

The male sandgrouse often flies long distances to find water for his chicks. On his belly are special feathers that soak up water like sponges. Once he finds a water hole, the sandgrouse wades in to soak his belly feathers. He then flies back to the nest, where the chicks eagerly drink the water.

Great bustard

The great bustard is one of the world's heaviest flying birds. A large male weighs up to 40 pounds (18 kg) but can still fly. Females are much lighter—up to 11 pounds (5 kg)—and do not have bristly "whiskers." Great bustards move in flocks as they search for plants, seeds, and insects to eat. They have strong legs and can run fast.

○ **Great bustard**

Size: male up to 41 in (104 cm); female 29½ in (75 cm)

Range: Europe and Asia

Scientific name: *Otis tarda*

Size: 6½ ft (2 m) tall

Range: Australia

Scientific name: *Dromaius novaehollandiae*

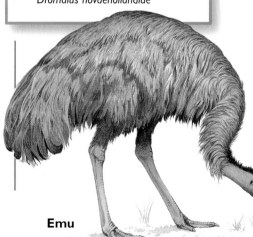

Emu

Emu

The emu is the second largest bird in the world, and, like the ostrich, it cannot fly. It runs at speeds of up to 30 mph (48 km/h) on its long legs as it looks for food in the Australian bush. Fruit, berries, and insects are its main foods, but it also eats green plants and crops. The female lays 9 to 20 eggs, which the male keeps warm (incubates).

Common cassowary

The common cassowary lives in the tropical rain forest. It cannot fly, and scientists think it may use the large horn casque, located on the top of its head, to help it break through the undergrowth as it searches for fallen fruit to eat. Males and females look similar, but females are slightly larger and have brighter plumage. They have extremely strong legs with very sharp-toed feet, which they use as weapons if attacked.

○ **Common cassowary**

Size: 5 ft (1.5 m) tall

Range: New Guinea, northern Australia

Scientific name: *Casuarius casuarius*

Size: 42 in (107 cm)

Range: parts of Africa, mostly south of the Equator

Scientific name: *Bucorvus cafer*

Greater roadrunner

True to its name, the greater roadrunner runs at speeds of up to 19 mph (30 km/h) on its big, strong feet. It can fly but does not often do so. This speedy bird eats ground-living insects as well as bird eggs, lizards, and even snakes.

Size: 19¾–23½ in (50–60 cm)
Range: southwestern U.S.A., Mexico
Scientific name: *Geococcyx californianus*

Red-legged seriema

The graceful seriema rarely flies but runs fast to escape from any danger. It kills snakes and lizards with its sharp bill and also feeds on seeds, leaves, and insects. The nest, made from sticks, is built on the ground. The female lays two or three eggs, which the pair take turns incubating.

Size: 27½ in (70 cm)
Range: central South America
Scientific name: *Cariama cristata*

Southern ground hornbill

Most hornbills live in trees, but this species spends much of its life on the ground. It wanders around in pairs or family groups, searching for insects, reptiles, and other small animals to eat.

Greater rhea

Size: 5 ft (1.5 m) tall
Range: South America
Scientific name: *Rhea americana*

Greater rhea

The largest birds in South America, greater rheas are fast runners but cannot fly. They usually live in groups of up to 30 birds. At breeding time the male rhea mates with several females. He makes a shallow nest on the ground and incubates all their eggs together.

Ostrich

The ostrich, the world's largest living bird, is too big and heavy to fly. Instead it runs fast and can reach speeds of up to 43 miles per hour (70 km/h). Ostriches feed mainly on plants and seeds but also catch small reptiles. Ostrich eggs are larger than any other bird eggs. One egg weighs about 3¼ pounds (1.5 kg).

Size: 5¾–9 ft (1.75–2.75 m) tall
Range: Africa
Scientific name: *Struthio camelus*

Southern ground hornbill

Ostrich

Waders, waterbirds, cranes, and seabirds

A huge variety of birds live in and around water. Wading birds, such as sandpipers, plovers, and jacanas, spend much of their lives on seacoasts or by rivers and lakes farther inland. Waterbirds, such as herons, flamingos, and ducks, spend more time actually in the water, and many are excellent swimmers. Lakes, ponds, rivers, and marshlands provide plenty of plant and animal foods, and birds can nest among bankside reeds. Seabirds depend on the ocean for their food, and many can swim and dive to perfection.

Common redshank

This bird lives near almost any kind of water. It breeds on moorland and marshes but spends the winter on shores, mud flats, meadows, and estuaries. Insects are its main food, but it also eats other small creatures such as crabs and snails. It lays eggs in a grass-lined nest on the ground.

Common redshank

Size: 11 in (28 cm)

Range: Europe, Asia, northern Africa

Scientific name: *Tringa totanus*

Waders

Most wading birds, or shorebirds, are small to medium size, ranging from the smallest plovers, only 6 inches (15 cm) long, to curlews measuring almost 23½ inches (60 cm) in length. Wading birds usually feed on the ground, and most are fast runners. Their beaks are various lengths and shapes for probing to different depths in mud and sand looking for food. All are strong fliers, and many perform long migrations every year between winter feeding areas and the place where they lay eggs and rear young in spring and summer.

Pied avocet

The avocet has an unusual beak that curves upward. It catches insects and small water creatures by holding its long beak slightly open and sweeping it from side to side on the surface of mud or in shallow water. In deeper water it dips its head below the surface to find food.

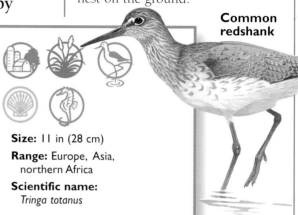

Pied avocet

Size: 16½ in (42 cm)

Range: Europe, Asia, Africa

Scientific name: *Recurvirostra avosetta*

American golden-plover

This golden-plover is a champion long-distance traveler. It breeds on the Arctic tundra of North America. After breeding, it flies about 8,000 miles (13,000 km) south to spend the winter months in South America. It feeds mainly on insects and other small creatures such as snails.

American golden-plover

Size: 9–11 in (23–28 cm)

Range: Arctic North America; winters in South America

Scientific name: *Pluvialis dominica*

Northern jacana

Northern jacana

The jacana has amazing feet. The toes and claws are very long so that the bird's weight is spread over a large area. This allows the jacana to walk on unsteady surfaces, such as floating lily pads, as it looks for insects, fish, and mollusks.

Size: 9¾ in (25 cm)
Range: southern U.S.A., Mexico, Central America
Scientific name: *Jacana spinosa*

Northern lapwing

Northern lapwing

The lapwing is also known as the pewit because of the shrill call it makes during its display flight. A common bird of farmland and other open areas, it eats insects, worms, snails, and some seeds.

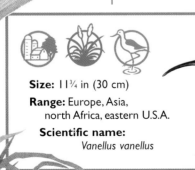

Size: 11¾ in (30 cm)
Range: Europe, Asia, north Africa, eastern U.S.A.
Scientific name: *Vanellus vanellus*

Eurasian oystercatcher

The oystercatcher has a long, blunt beak, which it uses to pry shellfish such as cockles and mussels off seashore rocks and to chisel open their hard shells. It also eats insects and worms, which it finds on farmland.

Eurasian oystercatcher

Size: 18 in (46 cm)
Range: coastal Europe, coastal Siberia, central Russia
Scientific name: *Haematopus ostralegus*

American woodcock

Although it is similar to the sandpiper, the American woodcock spends more time inland than other wading birds. It feeds mainly on earthworms, which it finds by probing the soil with its long beak. Females make their nests under trees or bushes and lay up to four eggs.

American woodcock

Size: 11 in (28 cm)
Range: North America
Scientific name: *Scolopax minor*

Eskimo curlew

Huge flocks of eskimo curlews used to migrate every year from the northern tundra to South America, where they spent the winter months. Today, the bird is either extinct or almost extinct because so many have been shot by hunters. No eskimo curlews have been seen since the 1960s.

● **Eskimo curlew**

Size: 11–13 in (28–33 cm)
Range: Alaska and northern Canada to South America
Scientific name: *Numenius borealis*

Waterbirds and cranes

Waterbirds such as egrets, storks, ibises, and flamingos are all large birds with long necks and legs. They stand in water while feeding and pick up food with their beaks. Ducks, geese, and swans swim on the water as they look for food, and some even dive beneath the surface. They have strong legs and webbed feet to help them swim. Other birds found in fresh water include cranes, grebes, and loons. Cranes are long-legged birds that wade in shallow water to find food. Fast-swimming grebes and loons feed mainly on fish, which they chase and catch under the water with their pointed beaks.

Tundra swan

This swan lays eggs and rears its young on the Arctic tundra. In autumn it flies south, usually returning to the same place year after year. Tundra swans feed on plants in shallow water.

Tundra swan

Size: 3½–4½ ft (1.1–1.4 m)
Range: North America, northern Europe, Asia
Scientific name: *Cygnus columbianus*

Canada goose

This goose breeds in the north and migrates south in autumn. Birds use the same routes year after year and tend to return to their birthplace to breed. The female lays about five eggs in a shallow nest scraped on the ground. Her mate stays nearby while she incubates the eggs for 28 to 30 days. Canada geese feed on water- and land plants.

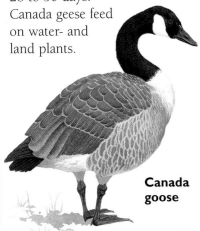

Canada goose

Size: 25–45 in (64–114 cm)
Range: North America; introduced into Europe and New Zealand
Scientific name: *Branta canadensis*

Glossy ibis

The beautiful glossy ibis is the most widespread member of its family. It lives around lakes and marshy areas and eats insects and water creatures, which it picks from the mud with its long bill. Glossy ibises breed in colonies, sometimes of thousands of birds. The female lays three or four eggs in a nest in a tree or reed bed. Both parents incubate the eggs and care for the young once they hatch.

Size: 21½–25½ in (55–65 cm)
Range: West Indies, Africa, southern Europe, Asia, Australia, southern U.S.A.
Scientific name: *Plegadis falcinellus*

Glossy ibis

Mallard

The mallard is the ancestor of most domestic ducks. It has been introduced into Australia and New Zealand and is often seen on ponds in city areas. It eats plants as well as insects and other small creatures and is often seen feeding tail-up in shallow water.

Mallard

Size: 16¼–26 in (41–66 cm)
Range: Northern Hemisphere; introduced into Australia and New Zealand
Scientific name: *Anas platyrhynchos*

Sun bittern

In its courtship display, the sun bittern spreads its wings and fans its tail to reveal colorful feathers. It spends most of its life searching shallow water for prey, such as insects and fish, which it seizes in its sharp beak.

Size: 18–20 in (46–51 cm)
Range: Europe, Asia, Africa, Australia, New Zealand
Scientific name: *Podiceps cristatus*

Great crested grebe

This beautiful bird does not often fly and is rarely seen on land, where it moves awkwardly. Before mating, great crested grebes perform an elegant courtship dance on the water. During the dance they wag their heads and present each other with pieces of weed.

Great crested grebe

Size: 18 in (46 cm)
Range: southern Mexico to Bolivia and Brazil
Scientific name: *Eurypyga helias*

Sun bittern

Mandarin duck

Mandarin duck

The colorful mandarin duck is most active at dawn and dusk, when it feeds on seeds, acorns, and rice as well as insects, snails, and small fish. Mated pairs stay together year after year. They perform elaborate courtship displays using the sail-like feathers on their sides.

Common crane

Size: 16–20 in (41–51 cm)
Range: eastern Asia, including Japan; introduced worldwide
Scientific name: *Aix galericulata*

Size: 13–14 in (33–36 cm)
Range: almost worldwide
Scientific name: *Gallinula chloropus*

Common moorhen

Common crane

The common crane is famous for its dancing display. The birds walk in circles, bowing, bobbing, and tossing small objects over their heads. Cranes nest on the ground or in shallow water. After the breeding season they fly south. They eat roots, stems, leaves, frogs, and shrews.

Size: 3½–4 ft (1.1–1.2 m)
Range: Europe, Asia, midwestern U.S.A., Africa
Scientific name: *Grus grus*

Common moorhen

A lively bird, the moorhen lives on fresh water almost anywhere, including city parks. Pond weeds, fallen fruit, and berries are its main food, and it also catches insects. It makes its nest in reeds or in bushes at the water's edge.

Red-throated loon

This graceful bird has a slender beak and a red patch on its throat. It flies well and can take off easily from small areas of water. An expert swimmer, it feeds on fish that it catches underwater. It makes a variety of calls, including growling sounds and high-pitched wails. The female lays two eggs in a nest on the ground or in shallow water.

Red-throated loon

Size: 20¾–27¼ in (53–69 cm)
Range: North America, northern Asia, northern Europe
Scientific name: *Gavia stellata*

Great egret

This egret, also known as the common egret, lives in marshy areas and eats fish, insects, and other small creatures. It finds its food either by waiting in the water until it spots something or by slowly stalking its prey. In the breeding season adults have a mostly black beak. The rest of the year it is yellow. Breeding pairs make a nest in a tree or clump of reeds. The female lays two to five eggs, and the parents take turns incubating the clutch.

Size: 28–36 in (71–91 cm)
Range: Colombia, Venezuela
Scientific name: *Chauna chavaria*

Northern screamer

Great egret

Size: 33½–40 in (85–102 cm)
Range: worldwide, except much of Europe and North Africa
Scientific name: *Ardea alba*

Northern screamer

Although related to ducks and geese, the northern screamer does not have webbed feet and seldom swims in open water. It has a loud trumpeting call, which it uses as an alarm signal to warn others of danger. This noisy bird lives in the rivers and swamps of a small area in northern South America. It walks on top of floating leaves, its long toes helping to spread its weight. Females lay two to seven eggs in a nest made of plants.

Common eider

Size: 22–28 in (56–71 cm)
Range: the far north of Europe and North America
Scientific name: *Somateria mollissima*

Common eider

Like most ducks, the common eider lines her nest with downy feathers plucked from her breast. The down of the eider is particularly warm and soft. It has long been collected by people for making items such as comforters and sleeping bags. Eiders live mainly on shellfish and other small creatures.

Limpkin

This long-legged waterbird uses its curved beak to probe for snails and mussels in muddy swamps. It also eats seeds, insects, and even reptiles. It is called the limpkin because it seems to limp when it walks. Limpkins can fly but spend most of their lives on the ground.

Limpkin

Size: 23¼–28 in (59–71 cm)
Range: southeastern U.S.A., Mexico, West Indies, Central and South America
Scientific name: *Aramus guarauna*

Bald ibis

This bald-headed bird used to be much more widespread, but because of changes in its habitat and food supply caused by farming, it now breeds only in Morocco, in a dry, rocky area where there is not much farming. Its diet includes crickets, frogs, and berries.

● **Bald ibis**

Size: 28–31 in (71–79 cm)
Range: Morocco
Scientific name:
Geronticus eremita

Size: 4–4½ ft (1.2–1.4 m)
Range: northern Canada, southern U.S.A.
Scientific name:
Grus americana

◑ **Whooping crane**

Whooping crane

These cranes are very rare in the wild and are now strictly protected. To increase numbers, birds are being bred in captivity for release into the wild. Whooping cranes eat grain and plants as well as insects, frogs, and other small animals.

Greater flamingo

The flamingo's long legs allow it to wade into deeper water than most other birds when looking for food. It feeds by sucking water and mud in at the front of its beak and then pumping it out again at the sides, where bristly plates trap small plants and animals. The flamingo builds a nest of mud, where it usually lays only one egg.

Greater flamingo

Size: 3½–4¾ ft (1.1–1.45 m)
Range: southern Europe, parts of Asia and Africa, Mexico, West Indies, Central and South America
Scientific name: *Phoenicopterus ruber*

WADERS, WATERBIRDS, CRANES, AND SEABIRDS

Little penguin

Galápagos penguin

This is the only penguin that lives near the Equator. The Galápagos Islands are bathed by a cool current, making the area suitable for a cold-loving penguin. The Galápagos penguin feeds mainly on small fish. It nests in small groups, and females lay two eggs in a cave or a hole in volcanic rock.

Red-tailed tropicbird

Red-tailed tropicbird

This elegant seabird is an expert in the air but moves awkwardly on land. It usually nests on ledges or cliffs in a position that allows for easy takeoff. Fish and squid are its main food. Females lay a single egg on the ground. Both parents incubate the egg and care for the chick.

Size: 15¾ in (40 cm) tall
Range: New Zealand and southern Australia
Scientific name: *Eudyptula minor*

Size: 19¾ in (50 cm) tall
Range: Galápagos Islands
Scientific name: *Spheniscus mendiculus*

 Galápagos penguin

Little penguin

The smallest of all the penguins, this penguin lives around coasts and islands, looking for small fish and other food in shallow waters. It nests in a crevice or burrow. The female lays two eggs, which both parents take turns incubating for between 33 and 40 days.

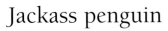 **Wandering albatross**

Jackass penguin

This penguin lives in a warmer climate than most other penguins but keeps cool in the cold offshore current. It breeds on land and nests in a burrow or under rocks. It is active on land only at night.

Size: 3½–4½ ft (1.1–1.35 m)
Range: southern oceans
Scientific name: *Diomedea exulans*

Size: 27¼ in (69 cm) tall
Range: South Africa
Scientific name: *Spheniscus demersus*

Jackass penguin

Wandering albatross

This seabird has the longest wingspan of any bird—up to 11 feet (3.4 m). It spends most of its life soaring over the open ocean, sometimes flying up to 300 miles (500 km) in a day.

Size: 35½–39½ in (90–100 cm) including tail
Range: Indian and tropical Pacific Oceans
Scientific name: *Phaethon rubricauda*

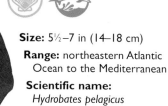

Size: 5½–7 in (14–18 cm)
Range: northeastern Atlantic Ocean to the Mediterranean
Scientific name: *Hydrobates pelagicus*

European storm-petrel

This seabird eats fish and squid, which it catches as it swoops low over the water. It also eats food scraps thrown from ships. The storm-petrel spends most of its life at sea but comes ashore in the breeding season to nest in a burrow or rock crevice.

European storm-petrel

Size: 11½–14¼ in (29–36 cm)
Range: North Atlantic Ocean
Scientific name: *Fratercula arctica*

Atlantic puffin

Atlantic puffin

This puffin uses its colorful beak to catch fish and can hold as many as a dozen fish at a time. An expert swimmer and diver, the puffin can also fly well. Its short legs are set well back on the body, so it waddles clumsily when it comes on land to nest. The female puffin lays one egg, sometimes two, in an old burrow or in a new hole.

Northern gannet

A sturdily built seabird with a strong beak, the northern gannet soars over the ocean, searching for fish and squid. When it spots prey, the gannet plunges 100 feet (30 m) or more into the water to seize the catch and bring it to the surface.

Size: 34¼–39½ in (87–100 cm)
Range: North Atlantic Ocean to the Gulf of Mexico
Scientific name: *Morus bassanus*

Northern gannet

Great frigatebird

Great frigatebird

This large seabird has a wingspan of more than 6 feet (1.8 m) and a big, hooked beak. It spends most of its life in the air. It catches food by snatching prey from the surface of the water or by threatening other seabirds until they drop their meals. Large colonies nest together on oceanic islands.

Size: 33¾–39½ in (86–100 cm)
Range: Indian and Pacific Oceans
Scientific name: *Fregata minor*

WADERS, WATERBIRDS, CRANES, AND SEABIRDS

Penguins

Penguins are better suited to life in the sea than any other bird. Expert swimmers and divers, they use their strong flippers to push themselves through the water. On land, penguins walk upright and have an awkward gait. They cannot fly.

Most penguins live around the Antarctic and on islands near the Antarctic Circle and have to survive in freezing conditions. They have a dense covering of glossy waterproof feathers, which keep them both warm and dry. A thick layer of fat beneath the feathers also helps to keep out the cold.

There are 17 species of penguins. The smallest is the little, or fairy, penguin, which measures about 15 inches (39 cm). The biggest is the emperor penguin, which stands about 3¾ feet (1.15 m) tall. All have similar coloring, with black or gray feathers on the back and white ones on the belly.

Friendly behavior

Penguins are sociable birds and usually live in huge colonies on land and in the sea. Penguins usually keep the same mate for several years. When a breeding pair meets, they rub their heads in greeting. They also preen each other's feathers.

Penguin prey

Squid and fish are the main food of the king penguin and other large penguins, such as the emperor. Smaller penguins, such as the gentoos and chinstraps, catch shrimplike krill and other small sea animals.

Underwater hunter

The king penguin dives deep to catch prey, often plunging to 150 feet (45 m) or more. The deepest recorded dive for this bird is 820 feet (250 m). The penguin uses its tail and webbed feet for steering as it dives.

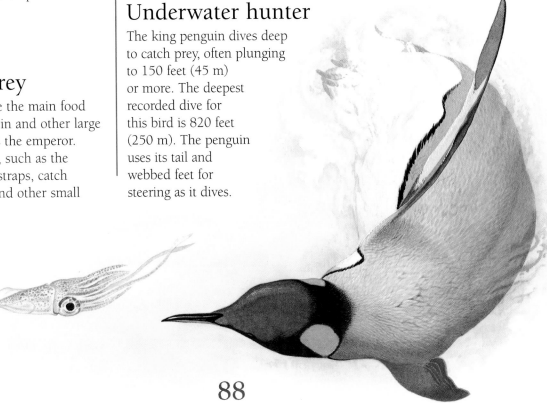

Tobogganing

Not at their best on land, penguins slip and slide as they waddle on webbed feet over the frozen ground. Often the birds lie down on their bellies and toboggan over the ice—an easier way to move. Once in the water, most penguins swim at speeds of 3 to 6 miles per hour (5 to 10 km/h).

Taking care of young

At the beginning of winter the female emperor penguin lays one egg on land. Her partner then incubates the egg on top of his feet for about 64 days. When the chick hatches he keeps it warm on his feet, tucked under a fold of skin.

Adélie penguins nest in large colonies along the Antarctic coasts. Eggs are laid in late November (the Antarctic spring) and incubated first by the male and then by the female for a total of 35 days.

Owls and birds of prey

Long-eared owl

Most birds of prey hunt and kill other creatures to eat. Although this is a varied group of birds, ranging from tiny falcons to huge condors, they all have features in common. These include keen vision to spot food from the air, strong feet with sharp claws, and a hooked beak for tearing prey apart. Eagles, hawks, and buzzards are all birds of prey. Owls, too, kill other animals to eat, but, unlike hawks and eagles, they usually hunt at night.

Long-eared owl

The long tufts on the head of this owl are feathers, not ears. But this bird does have excellent hearing, which helps it catch prey such as voles and mice. This owl lays its eggs in a nest abandoned by a crow or another bird.

Size: 13–16 in (33–40.5 cm)
Range: North America, Europe, northwestern Africa, Asia
Scientific name: *Asio otus*

Owls

There are 170 or so kinds of owls found over most of the world. Most look similar, with their large, disklike faces and huge eyes. Typically, an owl sits on a branch watching and listening for the slightest movement of prey. When it hears something, it pinpoints the direction of the prey with its extraordinarily acute hearing before flying down to grab it. The edges of an owl's feathers are soft and fluffy, not hard like those of most birds. This cuts down the noise of flight so the hunter can fly almost silently in the darkness.

Size: 20½–25½ in (52–65 cm)
Range: Arctic to northern U.S.A.
Scientific name:
    Nyctea scandiaca

Snowy owl

Snowy owl

The snowy owl hunts during the day as well as at night for birds and for mammals such as mice, hares, and lemmings. The female owl is up to 20 percent bigger than the male and has dark markings on her mainly white feathers. She lays 4 to 15 eggs.

Barn owl

Barn owl

The barn owl is easily recognized by its pale, heart-shaped face. During the day it roosts in a sheltered spot. At dusk it comes out to hunt for food, usually small creatures such as rats and mice.

Size: 16 in (41 cm)
Range: worldwide, except temperate Asia, the Arctic, and many Pacific islands
Scientific name: *Tyto alba*

Birds of prey

Birds of prey hunt in a variety of ways. Some, such as goshawks and sparrow hawks, live mainly in forests and woodlands and hunt in the cover of trees. They move from one leafy perch to the next, ready to dash out to catch their prey in a sudden attack. Others, such as hawks and eagles, soar over open country, watching for live animals. Not all birds of prey are hunters. Vultures, for example, are scavengers—they eat carrion, the bodies of creatures that are already dead.

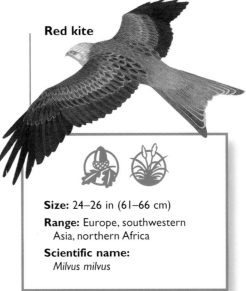

Red kite

Size: 24–26 in (61–66 cm)
Range: Europe, southwestern Asia, northern Africa
Scientific name: *Milvus milvus*

Lappet-faced vulture

Like all vultures, this bird feeds mostly on carrion. It has huge wings, on which it soars long distances searching for food, and a powerful hooked beak, which cuts easily into the flesh of dead animals. This vulture lays one egg in a nest at the top of a tree.

Size: 3¼–3¾ ft (1–1.15 m)
Range: Africa, Israel
Scientific name: *Torgos tracheliotus*

Lappet-faced vulture

Red kite

This large bird of prey has long wings and a forked tail. It hunts in woodlands and open country and often hovers briefly as it searches for rats, birds, reptiles, and other prey. Like vultures, it also eats carrion. The red kite nests in trees, and females lay up to five eggs.

Northern goshawk

A powerful, fast-moving bird, the northern goshawk hunts creatures such as rabbits and grouse. It flies through the forest, weaving in and out of trees as it chases prey. It kills its food with its strong, sharp talons and eats it on the ground.

Northern goshawk

Size: 18–24 in (46–61 cm)
Range: North America, including the West Indies
Scientific name: *Buteo jamaicensis*

Red-tailed hawk

Red-tailed hawk

A powerful, aggressive bird, this hawk can live anywhere from forests to deserts. It hunts other birds in the air or swoops down on rabbits, snakes, and lizards from a high perch. It makes a nest of twigs high in a tree or cactus plant. The female lays one to four eggs. Both parents take turns incubating the eggs.

Size: 21–26 in (53–66 cm)
Range: North America, Europe, northern Asia
Scientific name: *Accipiter gentilis*

91

Golden eagle

The magnificent golden eagle has a hooked beak, extremely sharp eyesight, and strong feet with long curved claws. When hunting, the eagle soars over land, searching for food. It eats small mammals, birds, reptiles, and carrion.

Size: 30–40 in (76–102 cm)
Range: North America, Europe, northern Asia and Africa
Scientific name: *Aquila chrysaetos*

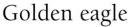

Golden eagle

Secretary bird

This long-legged bird spends much of its life on the ground, where it may walk 20 miles (30 km) or so every day. It runs to catch prey such as small mammals, birds, insects, and reptiles. It kills larger animals by stomping on them. Pairs make a nest of sticks and turf at the top of a tree. The nest is lined with grass and leaves. The female lays two or three eggs.

Size: 5 ft (1.5 m) tall
Range: Africa south of the Sahara
Scientific name: *Sagittarius serpentarius*

Secretary bird

Osprey

This bird of prey flies over water looking for fish to catch. When the bird catches sight of a fish, it plunges down, holding its feet out to seize the prey. The soles of the osprey's feet are studded with small spines to help it grip its slippery catch.

Size: 20¾–24½ in (53–62 cm)
Range: almost worldwide
Scientific name: *Pandion haliaetus*

Osprey

Eurasian kestrel

The kestrel belongs to the falcon family. It hunts by hovering above the ground on fast-beating wings, watching for prey. If it spots something, such as a small mammal or bird, the kestrel drops down and snatches the prey with its sharp-clawed feet.

Eurasian kestrel

Size: 12¼–13¾ in (31–35 cm)
Range: Europe, Asia, Africa, western Canada, Aleutian Islands
Scientific name: *Falco tinnunculus*

Peregrine falcon

One of the fastest fliers, the peregrine is an expert hunter that preys on other birds. It makes a spectacular high-speed dive toward its prey, often a pigeon or a dove, and seizes it in midair. It kills the prey with its powerful talons and takes it to the ground to eat.

Size: 16–20 in (41–51 cm)
Range: almost worldwide
Scientific name: *Falco peregrinus*

Peregrine falcon

Madagascar fish eagle

With a total population of less than 100 pairs, this fish eagle is one of the rarest birds. It usually hunts around shallow estuaries and coastal swamps, where it plunges down to catch fish with its strong feet.

Size: 26¾–31 in (68–79 cm)
Range: northwest Madagascar
Scientific name:
  Haliaeetus vociferoides

● **Madagascar fish eagle**

Size: 31 in (79 cm)
Range: Mexico, Central and South America
Scientific name:
  Sarcorhamphus papa

King vulture

With its brightly patterned, bare-skinned head, the king vulture is one of the most colorful of all birds of prey. Although it may occasionally kill some prey for itself, it feeds mostly on carrion—animals that are already dead. The king vulture is one of the few birds that is believed to use its sense of smell to find food.

King vulture

Rough-legged hawk

Rough-legged hawk

The rough-legged hawk hovers over the tundra as it hunts for prey, such as lemmings and voles. It nests in the far north, laying up to four eggs in a nest of twigs made on rock outcrops or along eroded riverbanks. After the breeding season, this hawk flies south for the winter.

Size: 19¾–23½ in (50–60 cm)
Range: North America, northern Europe and Asia
Scientific name:
  Buteo lagopus

Bald eagle

The national bird of the United States, the bald eagle was almost extinct in the 1960s but has been increasing in numbers since then. Bald eagles gather around Alaskan rivers to catch exhausted salmon as they migrate upriver. The eagle's nest is made of sticks and is one of the largest bird nests.

Size: 31–37 in (79–94 cm)
Range: Canada and U.S.A.
Scientific name:
  Haliaeetus leucocephalus

Bald eagle

Eagles

Eagles are large birds of prey with strong hooked beaks, sharp talons, and big golden eyes. There are about 60 kinds of eagles living all over the world.

Typically, a hunting eagle soars over the land for long periods, searching for food. With its keen eyesight, an eagle spots prey from a great distance and then makes a rapid dive to the ground to seize and kill the animal with its talons. But some eagles hunt in different ways. Harpy eagles chase their prey through the trees, and sea eagles seize fish from the water.

Eagles usually build their nests in trees or on cliffs. The nests are made of sticks and branches and may be used year after year.

A snake hunter

Like other snake eagles, the crested serpent eagle feeds mostly on snakes and other reptiles. This eagle generally hunts by perching in a tree to watch for prey on the ground then dropping down onto it. The eagle's short, strong toes have a rough surface that helps it grip its wriggling catch.

Rain forest eagle

The harpy is the world's biggest and most powerful eagle. It lives in the rain forests of Mexico and Central and South America. Instead of soaring high in the air, this eagle makes short flights from tree to tree, looking for prey. The harpy hunts mostly monkeys, sloths, and tree porcupines. As soon as it spots its prey, the harpy usually chases it through the trees at high speed then catches the animal in its strong talons.

94

Fish-eating eagle

Fish is the main food of sea eagles, such as the white-tailed eagle pictured. The bird soars over the ocean looking for prey then swoops down to the surface to seize a fish in its talons. Sea eagles also catch other creatures and rob smaller birds of their prey. These eagles may also dive repeatedly at water birds such as ducks until they are exhausted and easy to catch. There are several different types of sea eagles. The largest is the Steller's sea eagle, which lives on North Pacific Ocean coasts.

This **bald eagle** is feeding its hungry chicks. The young stay in the nest for about ten weeks. They often fight each other, and sometimes the weakest of the brood is killed.

Birds of the trees and masters of the air

One of the many advantages of flight is that it allows birds to fly up into trees. There, among the branches, they find havens from ground-living hunters as well as safe places to roost and make nests. Many birds also gather much of their food in trees. Pigeons and parrots feed mostly on seeds, nuts, and fruits. Others, such as woodpeckers and cuckoos, eat insects that they find on leaves and tree trunks. Some birds are more skillful fliers than others. Hummingbirds, for example, are true masters of the air and perform extraordinary aerial acrobatics. Swifts are so used to life in the air that they rarely, if ever, walk on land.

Crested treeswift

Size: 8 in (20.5 cm)
Range: Southeast Asia
Scientific name:
Hemiprocne longipennis

Crested treeswift

This swift catches insects in the air to eat. It makes a tiny cup-shaped nest from thin flakes of bark glued together with spit. There is room for just one egg, which both parents take turns incubating.

European nightjar

The nightjar becomes active at sunset, when it takes to the air to dart after moths and other night-flying insects. The nightjar's tiny beak opens very wide and is fringed with bristles that help trap its prey.

Size: 10¼ in (26 cm)
Range: Europe, Asia, Africa
Scientific name:
Caprimulgus europaeus

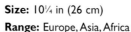

European nightjar

Common potoo

The potoo feeds at night, flying out from a perch to capture insects in its large beak. By day, it sits upright and very still on a broken branch or stump. With its head and beak pointing upward, the potoo looks like part of the tree and is hidden from its enemies. It lays its single egg on top of a tree stump.

Common potoo

Size: 16¼ in (41 cm)
Range: Central America, tropical South America
Scientific name:
Nyctibius griseus

Ruby-throated hummingbird

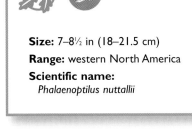
Common poorwill

Size: 3½ in (9 cm)
Range: Canada, U.S.A.; winters in Central America
Scientific name: *Archilochus colubris*

Size: 7–8½ in (18–21.5 cm)
Range: western North America
Scientific name: *Phalaenoptilus nuttallii*

Ruby-throated hummingbird

Like all hummingbirds, the ruby-throated variety plunges its beak deep inside flowers to feed on nectar. After breeding in Canada and the eastern United States, this amazing small bird travels some 2,000 miles (3,200 km) to winter in Central America.

Barn swallow

The barn swallow eats insects, which it catches in the air or snatches from the surface of water. Both male and female help to make a nest of mud and grass on the wall of a building. The female lays four or five eggs.

Common poorwill

Named after its call, which sounds like "poor will," this bird is rarely seen during the day but comes out to hunt insects at dusk and before dawn. It darts out from a perch or from the ground to capture prey such as moths and beetles in its wide mouth. It does not make a nest. Females lay their two eggs on the ground.

Bank swallow

The bank swallow is also known as the sand martin. A lively bird, it darts in the air as it chases and snaps up insects. It lives in a burrow that it digs into sandbanks near water, using its beak and feet. Martins lay up to eight eggs in a nest at the end of the burrow.

Barn swallow

Size: 6½–7¾ in (17–19 cm)
Range: almost worldwide
Scientific name: *Hirundo rustica*

White-throated swift

Swifts are fast and expert fliers. They catch insects, eat, drink, and even mate while flying. Their legs and feet are tiny and rarely used for walking. The white-throated swift makes a cup-shaped nest from feathers and grass glued together with spit. The nest is built in a crack or crevice in a cliff or mountainside. The female lays four or five eggs.

Bank swallow

Size: 4¾–5½ in (12–14 cm)
Range: parts of Europe, Asia, and North America; winters in South America, Africa, and Southeast Asia
Scientific name: *Riparia riparia*

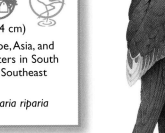

White-throated swift

Size: 6–7 in (15–18 cm)
Range: western U.S.A., Mexico, Central America
Scientific name: *Aeronautes saxatalis*

Rufous-tailed jacamar

Size: 9–11 in (23–28 cm)
Range: southern Mexico, Central America, South America
Scientific name: *Galbula ruficauda*

Rufous-tailed jacamar

This brightly plumaged, long-billed bird sits on a branch, watching for insects. When it spots something, it darts after the prey and snatches it in midair. The jacamar then flies to a perch and may bang a large insect against a branch to kill it before eating it. The female jacamar digs a breeding tunnel in the ground and lays two to four eggs. Both parents incubate the eggs for 19 to 23 days, then feed and care for their young until they can fly: about three weeks.

Hoopoe

This bird catches insects and other small creatures in trees and on the ground. It makes a nest in a hole in a tree, a wall, or in the ground. The female lays two to nine eggs and is fed by her mate while she incubates them for 16 to 19 days.

Hoopoe

Size: 11 in (28 cm)
Range: Europe, Asia, Africa
Scientific name: *Upupa epops*

Resplendent quetzal

Resplendent quetzal

The male has a train of long tail feathers that wave and flutter as he flies and performs courtship displays. These feathers are shed after each breeding season and then regrown. The ancient Maya and Aztec peoples of Central America and Mexico believed the quetzal was a sacred bird, and its feathers were highly prized. The female does not have a red breast or long train.

Size: 15–16 in (38–40.5 cm); tail feathers 24 in (61 cm)
Range: Mexico, Central America
Scientific name: *Pharomachrus mocinno*

Victoria crowned pigeon

The world's largest pigeon, the Victoria crowned pigeon has been hunted heavily and is now rare. This beautiful bird usually feeds on the ground, eating fallen fruit, seeds, and berries. If disturbed, it flies off to perch in a tree.

Size: 23–29 in (58.5–73.5 cm)
Range: New Guinea
Scientific name: *Goura victoria*

○ **Victoria crowned pigeon**

Blue-crowned motmot

This bird has an unusual tail made up of two long central feathers with racket-shaped tips. With its tail swinging from side to side like a pendulum, the motmot sits on a branch, watching for prey. It darts out from its perch to catch insects, spiders, and lizards then returns to eat them.

Blue-crowned motmot

Size: 15–16¼ in (38–41 cm)
Range: Mexico, Central and South America
Scientific name: *Momotus momota*

Size: 9 in (23 cm)
Range: central Africa
Scientific name:
Lybius bidentatus

Double-toothed barbet

Belted kingfisher

This kingfisher is an agile flier. It watches for prey from a tree overhanging a river or stream, then dives down to seize a fish or frog from the water. A breeding pair digs a long nesting tunnel in a riverbank. The female lays five to eight eggs in a nest made at the end of the tunnel.

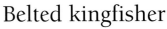

Pileated woodpecker

Ants, beetles, and termites are the main food of this woodpecker. Clinging tightly to a tree trunk with its sharp claws, the bird hammers into the bark with its strong beak to find prey. It also feeds on fruit. The female bird lays four eggs in a tree-hole nest.

Double-toothed barbet

This barbet has two sharp, toothlike edges on its upper beak. It perches in trees and bushes, feeding on figs, bananas, and other fruit and also darts out to catch flying termites.

Belted kingfisher

Size: 15–19 in (38–48 cm)
Range: U.S.A.
Scientific name:
Dryocopus pileatus

Eurasian collared dove

This common dove lives close to people in towns and the countryside. It feeds mainly on seeds, but it also eats berries, other plant foods, and scraps put out by people.

Size: 11–14 in (28–35.5 cm)
Range: North America
Scientific name:
Ceryle alcyon

Size:
12½ in
(31.5 cm)
Range: parts of Europe and Asia; introduced into the Bahamas and mainland North America
Scientific name:
Streptopelia decaocto

Eurasian collared dove

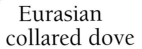

Bee-eater

True to its name, this bird eats bees as well as wasps. It rubs its prey on a branch to remove the venom from the stinger before eating the insect. Bee-eaters nest in tunnels that they dig in riverbanks.

Size: 11 in (28 cm)
Range: Europe, Asia, Africa
Scientific name:
Merops apiaster

Pileated woodpecker

99

Bee-eater

BIRDS OF THE TREES AND MASTERS OF THE AIR

Red-crested touraco

The red-crested touraco lives in trees and does not often come down to the ground. It is a poor flier but runs, hops, and climbs well among the branches. It eats fruit and insects.

Red-crested touraco

Size: 24 in (61 cm)
Range: Amazon and Orinoco River basins
Scientific name: *Opisthocomus hoazin*

Size: 16 in (40.5 cm)
Range: central Africa
Scientific name: *Tauraco erythrolophus*

Hoatzin

Although it lives in trees, the hoatzin is a poor flier. It clambers along branches, feeding on fruit, buds, and leaves.

Hoatzin

Common cuckoo

The cuckoo does not make a nest but lays her eggs in the nests of other birds. She usually lays 8 to 12 eggs, all in different nests. Each egg hatches in about 12 days and the young cuckoo ejects the host's young from the nest so it gets all the food. Cuckoos eat insects, especially caterpillars.

Common cuckoo

Size: 13 in (33 cm)
Range: Europe, Africa, Asia
Scientific name: *Cuculus canorus*

Size: 33½ in (85 cm)
Range: southern Mexico, Central America, northern South America
Scientific name: *Ara macao*

Scarlet macaw

Scarlet macaw

These spectacular birds are usually seen in pairs or in flocks of up to 20 birds. At sunrise the birds fly, screeching noisily, from their roost sites to feeding areas high in the trees. There they feast on seeds, fruit, and leaves. At dusk they return to their roosts.

Great pied hornbill

This hornbill lives high in the rain forest, eating fruit and catching small animals. The female hornbill is smaller and does not have such a large beak as the male. In the breeding season, she lays one to three eggs in a tree hole. Once she has laid her eggs, she seals up the nest hole, leaving only a slitlike opening. The male brings her food and passes it through this slit. The female stays walled up until the young are hatched.

Great pied hornbill

Size: 5 ft (1.5 m) tall
Range: India, Southeast Asia, Sumatra
Scientific name: *Buceros bicornis*

Toco toucan

Although the toucan's colorful beak is up to 7 inches (18 cm) long, it is not solid, so it is not as heavy as it looks. Inside the largely hollow beak are crisscrossed rods of bone that give it strength. The toucan feeds on fruit. It picks up food in the tip of its beak, then tosses the morsel into its mouth.

Size: 24 in (61 cm)
Range: eastern South America
Scientific name:
 Ramphastos toco

Toco toucan

Rainbow lorikeet

Rainbow lorikeet

The pattern of the colorful feathers of the rainbow lorikeet varies slightly from bird to bird. Screeching, chattering flocks of up to 100 lorikeets fly among the branches, eating fruit, insects, pollen, and nectar.

Size: 10¼ in (26 cm)
Range: Indonesia, New Guinea, Australia
Scientific name:
 Trichoglossus haematodus

Size: 7 in (18 cm)
Range: Australia; introduced into Florida
Scientific name:
 Melopsittacus undulatus

Budgerigar

Budgerigar

As cage birds commonly called parakeets or "budgies," these small, fast-moving parrots have many color variations. In the wild they are mainly green. Flocks search the ground for seeds.

Eclectus parrot

The male eclectus parrot has mostly green feathers, whereas the female is bright red with a blue belly. Both feed mainly on fruit, nuts, flowers, and nectar. They usually make a nest in a hole high in a tree. The female lays two eggs and incubates them for about 26 days.

Female

Male

Eclectus parrots

Greater sulphur-crested cockatoo

These noisy parrots gather in huge flocks to feed on seeds, fruit, palm hearts, and insects. In the breeding season cockatoos separate into pairs or family groups. A pair makes a nest in a tree, and both parents incubate the two or three eggs.

Greater sulphur-crested cockatoo

Size: 13¾ in (35 cm)
Range: New Guinea, northeastern Australia, Solomon Islands, Indonesia
Scientific name: *Eclectus roratus*

Size: 19¾ in (50 cm)
Range: Melanesia, New Guinea, Australia, Indonesia
Scientific name:
 Cacatua galerita

Hummingbirds

Beautiful hummingbirds are more agile in the air than any other group of birds. They are named after the humming sound made by the rapid beating of their wings as they hover in front of flowers while they feed. Their wings beat so fast that they are almost invisible. The birds can fly up, down, sideways, and even backward. Hummingbirds live only in North, Central, and South America, mostly in the warmest parts. They measure from just over 2 inches (5 cm) to about 7¾ inches (20 cm) long, but the tail feathers make up as much as half of this length. Many have colorful, iridescent plumage and decorative head crests and tail feathers. Females usually have duller plumage than males. The sweet nectar contained in flowers is the main food of hummingbirds. Most have long beaks, which they plunge deep into flowers to reach the nectar.

White-tipped sicklebill

The long, strongly curved beak of the white-tipped sicklebill is perfect for taking nectar from deep flowers.

The smallest bird

The bee hummingbird is the world's tiniest bird. The male is only about 2 inches (5 cm) long, including its beak and tail. Females are about ¼ inch (0.5 cm) longer.

The longest beak

The swordbilled hummingbird has a longer beak than any other hummingbird. The beak allows the bird to reach nectar inside the deepest tube-shaped flowers. This bird also eats insects, which it catches in the air.

A colorful hummingbird

The male crimson topaz is one of the most beautiful hummingbirds, with colorful plumage and long, curving tail feathers. It takes nectar from a wide range of flowers and also eats insects. The female bird has mostly green feathers.

102

○ **Marvelous spatuletail**

Courtship display

This hummingbird, known as the marvelous spatuletail, has only four full-grown tail feathers, two of which have a long, bare shaft ending in a broad wedge shape, or spatule. During courtship displays the male shows off these decorative feathers as he flies to and fro in front of the female.

Male crimson topaz

A male **violet sabrewing** hummingbird hovers on rapidly beating wings as he feeds on nectar from a ginger flower. Like many hummingbirds, this bird has iridescent feathers.

Purple honeycreeper

Groups of purple honeycreepers feed in trees on fruit (especially bananas), and insects. They also perch on flowering plants and suck nectar from them with their long, curved beaks. The female honeycreeper builds a cup-shaped nest in the fork of a tree or bush. She lays two eggs, which she incubates for 12 to 14 days.

Purple honeycreeper

Size: 4 in (10 cm)
Range: Trinidad, South America
Scientific name:
Cyanerpes caeruleus

Northern parula

This little warbler feeds mainly on caterpillars and other insects that it finds in trees. It creeps over the branches and hops from perch to perch as it looks for prey. It makes its nest in Spanish moss, which hangs from trees. The female usually lays four or five eggs that she incubates for 12 to 14 days. Both parents feed and care for the young when they hatch.

Northern parula

Size: 4¼ in (11 cm)
Range: eastern North America
Scientific name:
Parula americana

Pine grosbeak

A type of finch, the pine grosbeak uses its bill to crush the stones of fruit such as cherries and plums. It also eats seeds, buds, and insects. A breeding pair makes a nest in a tree, and the female lays two to five eggs.

Pine grosbeak

Size: 7¾–9 in (20–23 cm)
Range: northern Europe, northern Asia, North America
Scientific name:
Pinicola enucleator

Snow bunting

Size: 6¼ in (16 cm)
Range: Arctic region, northern Europe, North America
Scientific name:
Plectrophenax nivalis

House sparrow

The house sparrow has been introduced almost worldwide and is an extremely common and adaptable bird. A few birds were taken to New York in 1850, and they have now spread over much of North and South America. Seeds are the sparrow's main food, but it also eats insects and scraps put out by people.

Northern cardinal

Only the male cardinal has brilliant red plumage. The female is mainly brown, with a red beak. Cardinals eat primarily insects, fruit, seeds, and buds.

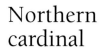

Size: 7¾–9 in (20–23 cm)
Range: mostly eastern U.S.A.
Scientific name:
Cardinalis cardinalis

Northern cardinal

Snow bunting

The snow bunting breeds farther north than almost any other land bird. To escape the cold, it sometimes burrows in the snow. After breeding, it flies south for the winter. Seeds and insects are its main food.

House sparrow

Size: 5¾–6¼ in (14.5–16 cm)
Range: Europe, Asia; introduced worldwide, except in very hot or very cold regions
Scientific name: Passer domesticus

Zebra finch

Size: 3½ in (9 cm)
Range: Australia
Scientific name:
Poephila guttata

Large flocks of zebra finches feed on seeds and insects. They usually live near water, but in dry areas these birds wait for rain before breeding. They make a domed nest low in a tree or bush, where the female lays four to six eggs.

Scarlet tanager

Size: 7½ in (19 cm)
Range: eastern U.S.A.; winters in South America
Scientific name:
Piranga olivacea

The scarlet tanager nests in woodlands, eating fruit and bees, wasps, and other insects and their larvae. After breeding, male tanagers molt their scarlet feathers and become olive green like the female birds, but keep black wings.

Red-billed quelea

Size: 5 in (12.5 cm)
Range: Africa, south of the Sahara
Scientific name:
Quelea quelea

In huge flocks of thousands of birds, red-billed queleas move like clouds across the sky. They feed on grain crops and can destroy whole fields. Queleas breed in colonies. They lay two or three eggs at a time in a kidney-shaped nest that hangs from a branch and has a side entrance.

Golden oriole

Most of the golden oriole's life is spent high in the trees, feeding on insects and fruit with the help of its sharp beak. Its nest is like a tiny hammock made of grass and hung from a forked branch. Golden orioles lay three or four eggs.

Golden oriole

Size: 9½ in (24 cm)
Range: Europe, Asia, Africa
Scientific name:
Oriolus oriolus

American dipper

This little bird lives around streams. It can swim underwater and even walk on the bottom of a stream as it searches for insects and other small creatures. The female dipper makes a domed nest of moss and grass in a crevice in a stream bank. She lays three to six eggs.

Size: 5½–8¾ in (14–22 cm)
Range: western North America
Scientific name:
Cinclus mexicanus

American dipper

○ **Ribbon-tailed astrapia**

Birds of paradise

Birds of paradise are named for their beautiful plumage and are among the most spectacular of all birds. Although some are mainly black, with bright patches of shimmering iridescent feathers, others are colored brilliant blue, red, and yellow. Many have long, strangely shaped feathers on their heads or tails.

There are more than 40 species, ranging in body size from about 5 to 42 inches (13 to 107 cm) long. Most live in the rain forests of New Guinea, but a few birds of paradise are found in the nearby Molucca Islands and the forests of northeastern Australia. Fruit is their main food, but they also catch insects, spiders, and, occasionally, frogs and lizards. Only the males have the colorful and decorative head and tail feathers for which birds of paradise are famed. The females look quite different, with dull, usually brownish plumage.

Ribbon-tailed astrapia

The male of this kind of bird of paradise has patches of shiny green feathers around his head and ribbonlike tail feathers nearly 3¼ feet (1 m) long. He twitches these tail feathers from side to side as he displays to females.

King of Saxony bird of paradise

King of Saxony bird of paradise

Two wirelike plumes, up to 19¾ inches (50 cm) long, extend from the male bird's head. During courtship, he holds them high and bounds up and down, hissing loudly. As the female approaches, the male sweeps his long head feathers down in front of her. He follows her, and they mate.

An upside-down display

The male blue bird of paradise hangs upside down in an effort to attract females. His long tail streamers form a graceful arc over the cascade of magnificent blue plumage. He swings to and fro while making a grating call.

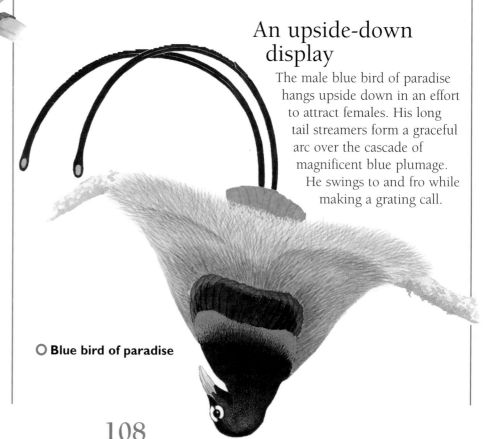

○ **Blue bird of paradise**

108

A group display

Most male birds of paradise display alone, but the raggianas gather in groups. When females appear, the males hop around, flapping their wings and calling excitedly. Each then tries to outdo the others in showing off his glorious plumage. At the peak of the display, the male birds make a series of high-pitched calls.

Raggianas bird of paradise

Tail plumes

The male Wilson's bird of paradise has two coiled tail feathers. They are held at right angles to the body when the bird displays.

Wilson's bird of paradise

The striking colors and magnificent tail plumes of the **greater bird of paradise** are a spectacular sight as it perches on a branch in the rain forest.

Royal flycatcher

This flycatcher has an amazing crest that normally lies flat but is opened and closed like a fan during courtship displays. Like all flycatchers, it feeds on insects that it snaps up while flying.

Rufous hornero

Size: 7½–8 in (19–20.5 cm)
Range: eastern South America
Scientific name: *Furnarius rufus*

Size: 6½ in (16.5 cm)
Range: southern Mexico, West Indies, Central and South America
Scientific name: *Onychorhynchus coronatus*

Royal flycatcher

Rufous hornero

The rufous hornero searches for food on the ground, digging out earthworms and insects with its sharp beak. It makes a dome-shaped nest of mud and straw, and the female lays up to five eggs.

Eastern kingbird

Superb lyrebird

Superb lyrebird

Only the male lyrebird has a long lyre-shaped tail. In the breeding season, he displays to the female by spreading his tail feathers over himself and dancing. The lyrebird rarely flies but hops up into trees to roost at night. The lyrebird scratches on the ground to find insects to eat.

Size: 8–9 in (20.5–23 cm)
Range: North America; winters in South America
Scientific name: *Tyrannus tyrannus*

Size: male 31½–37½ in (80–95 cm); female 29¼–33 in (74–84 cm)
Range: Australia
Scientific name: *Menura novaehollandiae*

Eastern kingbird

This noisy bird attacks anything that enters its territory, particularly larger birds. It eats many different types of insects, which it catches in the air or on the ground or scoops out of water. It also hovers in the air to pick berries from trees. The female lays three to five eggs.

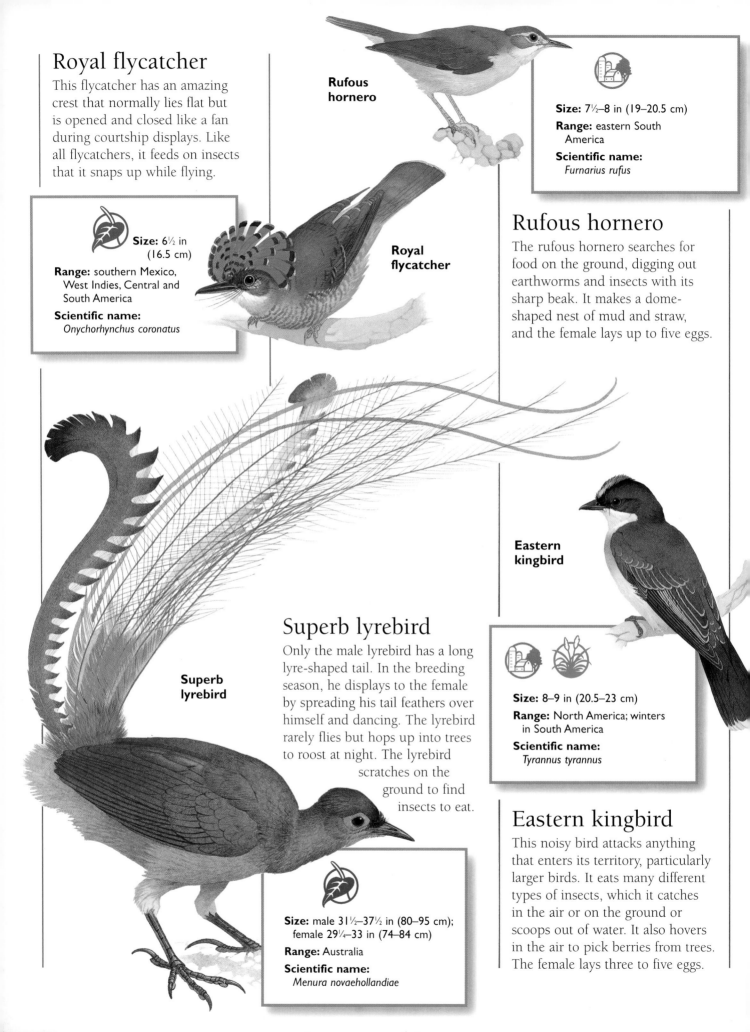

Size: 6 in (15 cm)
Range: Malaysia, Sumatra, Borneo
Scientific name:
Pitta granatina

Garnet pitta

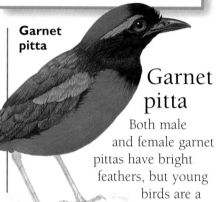

Wire-tailed manakin

Size: 4½ in (11.5 cm)
Range: South America
Scientific name:
Pipra filicauda

Garnet pitta

Both male and female garnet pittas have bright feathers, but young birds are a dull brown. This bird spends much of its time on the ground, catching ants, beetles, and other insects. It also eats seeds and fruit and can fly short distances.

Wire-tailed manakin

Only the male manakin has dramatic black, red, and yellow plumage, but both male and female have long, wiry tail feathers. The male shows off his bright colors in courtship displays. These birds usually feed alone, searching for insects and fruit in forests and cocoa plantations.

Torrent tyrannulet

This bird usually lives by fast-flowing streams. It often plucks insects from rocks surrounded by foaming water, drenching itself in the process. A breeding pair makes a cup-shaped nest that usually hangs over water. The female lays two eggs, which she incubates while the male stays nearby. Both parents feed the young insects.

Torrent tyrannulet

Size: 4 in (10 cm)
Range: Central and South America
Scientific name:
Serpophaga cinerea

Andean cock-of-the-rock

In the breeding season, the brilliantly colored male cocks-of-the-rock perform group displays, competing for the attention of the plainer females. They leap, call, and flick their wings. These birds feed mainly on fruit.

Size: 15 in (38 cm)
Range: northwestern South America
Scientific name:
Rupicola peruviana

Long-billed woodcreeper

Using its long beak, this woodcreeper searches rain forest plants for insects and spiders to eat. It also finds prey under the bark of trees. An expert climber, it uses its stiff tail for support as it clambers around in trees. The female lays two eggs in a tree-hole nest and incubates them for about 14 days.

Long-billed woodcreeper

Size: 14 in (35.5 cm) including bill
Range: northern South America
Scientific name:
Nasica longirostris

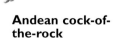

Andean cock-of-the-rock

111

American crow

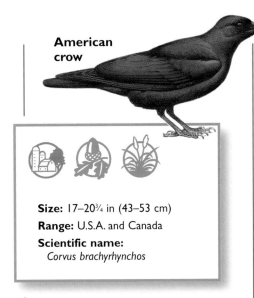

American crow

Size: 17–20¾ in (43–53 cm)
Range: U.S.A. and Canada
Scientific name:
Corvus brachyrhynchos

American crow

This large black bird eats almost anything it can find, including insects, spiders, frogs, and birds and their eggs. It also scavenges on garbage. A nest of sticks and twigs is made in a tree or bush. The female lays three to six eggs in it.

Size: 6¼ in (16 cm)
Range: Europe, Asia, North America, northern Africa
Scientific name:
Eremophila alpestris

Horned lark

Horned lark

Only the male bird has black tufts of feathers on his head. He raises them during courtship displays or when defending his territory. Shore larks eat seeds, buds, insects, and other small creatures. A simple nest of plant stems, surrounded with pebbles, is made on the ground. The female lays four eggs.

Black-billed magpie

The magpie eats insects, spiders, and snails but also flies up into trees to snatch young birds from their nests. A breeding pair makes a large nest in a tree or bush. The female lays five to eight eggs and incubates them while the male keeps her supplied with food.

Black-billed magpie

Size: 17¼–22½ in (44–57 cm)
Range: Europe, northern Africa, Asia, western North America
Scientific name: *Pica pica*

Northern shrike

The northern shrike keeps watch for prey from a perch and makes short flights to catch insects. It also hovers in the air, waiting to pounce on small birds and mammals. Usually the shrike carries its catch back to a perch to eat, but when food is plentiful it stores the extra insects, spiked on a thorn or sharp twig.

Northern shrike

Size: 9½ in (24 cm)
Range: North America, Asia, Europe, northern Africa
Scientific name:
Lanius excubitor

Water pipit

The water pipit makes its nest in high mountain areas, usually close to rushing streams. In winter, harsh weather drives it down to damp lowland meadows. Water pipits eat water worms and insects, which they catch by wading into shallow pools and onto mud flats.

Water pipit

Size: 6–7 in (15–18 cm)
Range: Europe, Asia, southern U.S.A., and Central America
Scientific name: *Anthus spinoletta*

Male

Crimson sunbird

Size: 4½ in (11.5 cm)
Range: India, Sumatra, Borneo, Malaysia
Scientific name:
Aethopyga siparaja

Crimson sunbird

This sunbird eats flower nectar as well as insects. It hovers in front of tube-shaped flowers and reaches into them with its long bill. When feeding from big blooms such as hibiscus, it pierces the petals to get the nectar at the base.

Scarlet-tufted malachite sunbird

Cardinal honeyeater

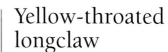

Yellow-throated longclaw

This bird gets its name from the back claw on each foot which is nearly 2 inches (5 cm) long. The bird is often seen on farmlands and feeds on insects, which it usually finds in grass. In the breeding season the male makes a special courtship flight and fans his tail and sings. The female lays three or four eggs in a nest hidden in long grass.

Yellow-throated longclaw

Size: 8 in (20.5 cm)

Range: Africa south of the Sahara

Scientific name:
Macronyx croceus

Size: 5 in (13 cm)

Range: Pacific islands: Vanuatu, Samoa, Santa Cruz, Solomon

Scientific name:
Myzomela cardinalis

Cardinal honeyeater

The cardinal honeyeater feeds by sipping nectar from flowers and picking insects from leaves. The female is duller than the colorful male. She has olive gray feathers with red patches. This bird's cup-shaped nest hangs from a forked branch, and the female lays two or three eggs.

Scarlet-tufted malachite sunbird

This sunbird lives only on high mountain slopes, where it feeds on the nectar of plants such as giant lobelias and protea flowers. Its main food is insects, particularly flies, which it catches while flying. It has scarlet tufts at the sides of the breast, but only the male has long central tail feathers. A nest of plant down (soft hairs) and dry stems is built in a low bush. The female lays one or two eggs.

Size: male 10–12 in (25.5–30.5 cm); female 5½–6 in (14–15 cm)

Range: East Africa

Scientific name:
Nectarinia johnstoni

Blue jay

Size: 11¾ in (30 cm)
Range: eastern Canada and U.S.A.
Scientific name:
Cyanocitta cristata

Blue jay

Noisy groups of blue jays are a familiar sight in backyards. Seeds and nuts are their main food, and they bury extra supplies to save for the winter. Blue jays also eat insects and even steal eggs and chicks from the nests of other birds. A breeding pair makes its nest in a tree or bush, and the female lays two to six eggs.

How do animals communicate?

Almost all animals have ways of keeping in touch with others of their own kind. Many, such as birds, whales, dogs, and monkeys, make a wide range of sounds, each with its own meaning. Other animals communicate by smell. They use scents to announce to others that they are ready to mate or that a particular area is their territory. Sight is also important. Courting lizards nod their heads in a special way, and the positions of the ears of animals such as dogs and cats show when they are pleased, angry, or frightened.

Like all wild dogs, the **coyote** communicates with barks and yaps as well as by using its tail and ears to show its mood. The coyote's howl is a way of signaling its ownership of territory, warning rival animals, and finding other members of its pack.

A male moth's antennae allow him to detect the scent given off by a female of his own kind from more than ½ mile (1 km) away. The large feathery antennae of the male **silk moth** are especially sensitive.

Female fireflies, called **glowworms**, signal to males by making a series of flashes. Each species has a different sequence. The flashes are made by a combination of substances in the firefly's abdomen.

Male

Warblers are well known for their songs. The **fan-tailed warbler** sings during its special song-flight to attract mates. It may go up to 100 feet (30 m) or more above the ground, circling over a wide area.

Female

One of the front claws of the male **fiddler crab** is much larger than the other and boldly colored. The male crab stands outside his burrow on the seashore and waves this claw to attract the attention of females. Each species of fiddler crab has a slightly different pattern of waves.

115

Reptiles

The first reptiles evolved from amphibians about 300 million years ago. Dinosaurs, which first appeared 225 million years ago, were reptiles and were the most common land animals on Earth for 160 million years.

Today there are more than 6,500 known species of reptiles, including animals such as sea turtles, predatory crocodiles, poisonous snakes, and fast-moving lizards. Reptiles live on all continents except Antarctica. Most hunt other animals for food, but there are some plant-eating turtles, tortoises, and lizards.

One of the great advantages reptiles have over amphibians is the structure of their eggs. The eggs have a tough shell to protect the baby reptile and a yolky foodstore to feed it as it grows. This means the eggs do not have to be laid in water, where there are many predators. Most baby reptiles hatch from eggs laid and incubated in the soil. Some develop inside the female's body and either hatch from eggs soon after they are laid or are born live. In all cases, baby reptiles are born as fully formed, miniature adults.

The **emerald tree boa** is a bright green snake that spends much of its life in trees, where it wraps its gleaming coils around a branch. It watches for prey, such as lizards and small mammals, which it catches and kills with its sharp fangs. The fastest-moving of all the boas, it is also a good swimmer.

Loggerhead sea turtle

Green iguana

What is a reptile?

Reptiles are vertebrate animals—like mammals and birds, they have a backbone made up of small bones called vertebrae. Their bodies are covered in tough waterproof scales. Most reptiles live on land, but turtles and some snakes live in water, and crocodiles spend time in water and on land.

Reptiles are cold-blooded and need the sun's warmth to be active. As a result, most live in warm climates. Reptiles usually switch between basking in the sun to gain heat and moving to shade or burrows to cool down.

Kinds of reptiles

Four groups of reptiles survive today. Turtles and tortoises have short, broad bodies, enclosed by a bony shell. Crocodiles and alligators are hunters and the largest living reptiles. The third group includes lizards and snakes. All snakes and most lizards are predators. The last group, the tuataras of New Zealand, has only two living species.

TURTLES AND TORTOISES
EASTERN BOX TURTLE

- Hard shell
- Flexible neck
- Head
- Hard beak
- Clawed feet
- Four legs

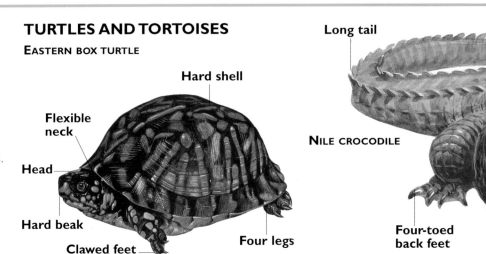

- Long tail
- **NILE CROCODILE**
- Four-toed back feet

TUATARAS

- Crest on back
- Large head
- **TUATARA**
- Four legs

LIZARDS

- **RACE RUNNER**
- Ear openings
- Slender body
- Four legs
- Long tail

A long spine and a strong tail help the **crocodile** move efficiently in the water. Its legs are short but strong, and it has long jaws studded with many sharp teeth.

SNAKES

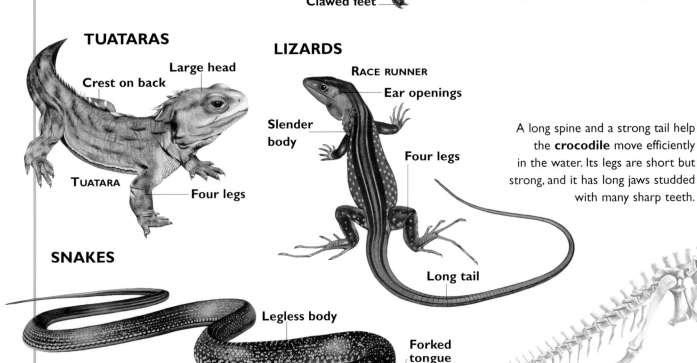

- **DARK GREEN WHIPSNAKE**
- Legless body
- Forked tongue
- Tailbones

Python incubating eggs

Egg-laying reptiles

Most reptiles lay eggs from which their young hatch, although some give birth to live young. The egg is protected by a tough shell. Inside is a yolk sac that provides food for the developing young, or embryo. The embryo grows inside the egg until it is ready to hatch out as a small version of the adult, able to live independently.

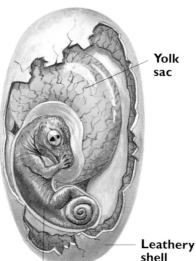

Yolk sac

Leathery shell

Embryo reptile

Turtle laying eggs

Most reptiles, such as **turtles,** simply lay their eggs in a safe place and leave them to hatch by themselves. Some snakes, such as **pythons,** curl around their eggs to keep them warm.

CROCODILES AND ALLIGATORS

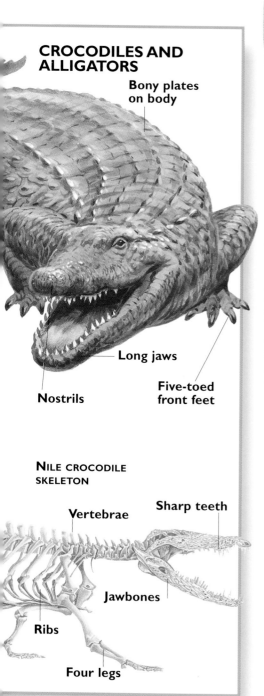

Bony plates on body

Long jaws

Nostrils

Five-toed front feet

NILE CROCODILE SKELETON

Vertebrae

Sharp teeth

Jawbones

Ribs

Four legs

Prehistoric reptiles

Although not the first reptiles, dinosaurs were the most successful, dominating the Earth for 160 million years. Like reptiles today, they had scale-covered skin and laid eggs. Many, such as *Lambeosaurus,* were plant eaters. Others, such as *Tyrannosaurus rex,* were fierce hunters.

Lambeosaurus with young

Crocodiles, alligators, turtles, and tortoises

All of these kinds of reptiles are armored, but in different ways. A typical turtle or tortoise has a hard shell that protects its soft body. Crocodiles and alligators are covered with hard scales and have thickened bony plates on the back for extra protection. The turtle group includes freshwater turtles and terrapins, sea turtles, and land tortoises. The crocodile group includes three families: crocodiles, alligators and caimans, and the gavial, which consists of only two species.

Size: up to 18 ft (5.5 m)
Range: southeastern U.S.A.
Scientific name:
Alligator mississipiensis

American alligator

Crocodiles and alligators

There are 13 species of crocodiles, 7 species of alligators and caimans, and 2 species of gavials. All are powerful creatures that live on land and in water and hunt a range of other animals. They live in tropical and subtropical areas. Males and females generally look alike, but males tend to grow larger. Both crocodiles and alligators have a pair of large teeth near the front of the lower jaw for grasping prey. In crocodiles, these teeth fit into notches in the upper jaw and can be seen when the jaw is closed. In alligators and caimans, the large teeth fit into bony pits in the upper jaw and cannot be seen when the mouth is closed.

American alligator

At one time American alligators came close to extinction because hunters killed so many for their skins. Efforts to protect the species have been very successful, and it is no longer endangered. These alligators usually mate in spring. The female lays about 50 eggs in a mound of leaves and other plant material and guards the nest while the eggs incubate. The young stay with their mother for up to two years.

Gavial

The gavial has long jaws studded with about 100 small teeth—ideal equipment for seizing fish and frogs under the water. The most aquatic of all the crocodiles, it moves awkwardly on land and rarely leaves the water except to nest. The female hauls out onto the shore where she lays 35 to 60 eggs at night in a pit that she digs with her back feet. She stays nearby while the eggs incubate for as long as 94 days. The gavial has been hunted for its skin and is now endangered.

Size: 23 ft (7 m)
Range: southern Asia from Myanmar to Nepal and northern India
Scientific name:
Gavialis gangeticus

🄌 **Gavial**

120

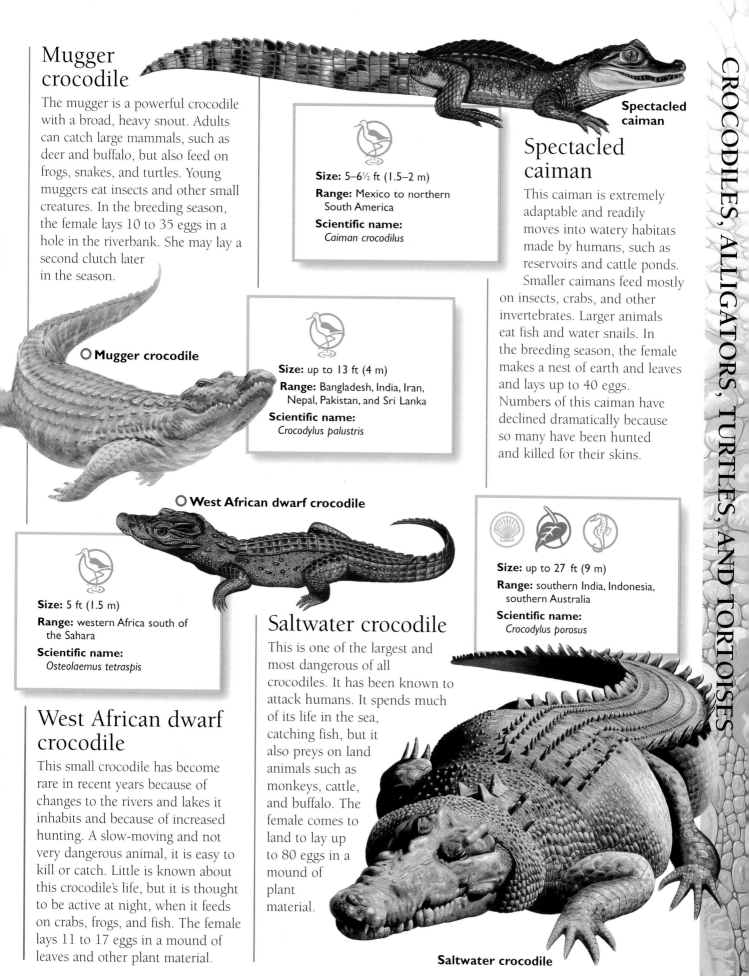

Mugger crocodile

The mugger is a powerful crocodile with a broad, heavy snout. Adults can catch large mammals, such as deer and buffalo, but also feed on frogs, snakes, and turtles. Young muggers eat insects and other small creatures. In the breeding season, the female lays 10 to 35 eggs in a hole in the riverbank. She may lay a second clutch later in the season.

Size: 5–6½ ft (1.5–2 m)
Range: Mexico to northern South America
Scientific name: *Caiman crocodilus*

Size: up to 13 ft (4 m)
Range: Bangladesh, India, Iran, Nepal, Pakistan, and Sri Lanka
Scientific name: *Crocodylus palustris*

O **Mugger crocodile**

O **West African dwarf crocodile**

Size: 5 ft (1.5 m)
Range: western Africa south of the Sahara
Scientific name: *Osteolaemus tetraspis*

West African dwarf crocodile

This small crocodile has become rare in recent years because of changes to the rivers and lakes it inhabits and because of increased hunting. A slow-moving and not very dangerous animal, it is easy to kill or catch. Little is known about this crocodile's life, but it is thought to be active at night, when it feeds on crabs, frogs, and fish. The female lays 11 to 17 eggs in a mound of leaves and other plant material.

Spectacled caiman

Spectacled caiman

This caiman is extremely adaptable and readily moves into watery habitats made by humans, such as reservoirs and cattle ponds. Smaller caimans feed mostly on insects, crabs, and other invertebrates. Larger animals eat fish and water snails. In the breeding season, the female makes a nest of earth and leaves and lays up to 40 eggs. Numbers of this caiman have declined dramatically because so many have been hunted and killed for their skins.

Size: up to 27 ft (9 m)
Range: southern India, Indonesia, southern Australia
Scientific name: *Crocodylus porosus*

Saltwater crocodile

This is one of the largest and most dangerous of all crocodiles. It has been known to attack humans. It spends much of its life in the sea, catching fish, but it also preys on land animals such as monkeys, cattle, and buffalo. The female comes to land to lay up to 80 eggs in a mound of plant material.

Saltwater crocodile

Nile crocodiles

Unlike most reptiles, the female Nile crocodile is a devoted parent. After mating, the female digs a pit near the river with her back legs and lays 16 to 80 eggs. She covers the nest with soil, then both parents stay close by to guard it while the eggs incubate for six to eight weeks. The female does not leave the nest area even to find food during this time. When they are about to hatch, the baby crocodiles call out to their mother from inside their shells. She uncovers the nest so that the young can get out. The mother may continue to care for her young until they are six months old. By then they are about 17¾ inches (45 cm) long and can find food for themselves.

The crocodile's nest

The nest is usually made near water on a sandy beach or riverbank and is 7¾–17¾ inches (20–45 cm) deep. Once she has dug the nest burrow, the female lies over it and deposits her eggs inside.

Beginning life

When ready to hatch, the young crocodiles are very sensitive to any movements on the earth above them. When they hear their mother's footsteps they call out. Once she has uncovered the nest, each young uses the sharp egg tooth on its jaw to chip its way out of its shell. The mother may help to pull the babies free. Once the hatchlings are out of the eggs they must find shelter from the many predators waiting to catch them. The mother picks the babies up, a few at a time, and carries them to a safe nursery site. She does not close her mouth, and the tiny crocodiles look like prisoners behind the bars of her big, sharp teeth. She releases her babies in a quiet pool and defends them fiercely.

122

The **Nile crocodile** does not live only in the Nile River. It is found in rivers and lakes all over tropical and southern Africa. Adults can measure more than 16½ feet (5 m) long.

Fierce hunter

The Nile crocodile is a wiley hunter. It lurks in the water, often with only its eyes and nostrils above the surface, waiting for prey to come to the riverbank to drink. The crocodile then seizes its prey, drags it into the water, and drowns it.

Turtles and tortoises

There are about 270 species of turtles and tortoises. Typically, they have a hard shell to protect the soft body. The shell is in two parts—the carapace on the back and the plastron underneath. The ribs and most of the vertebrae are attached to the shell, and most turtles and tortoises can pull their head inside the shell for protection. Turtles and tortoises have hard beaks instead of teeth for tearing off pieces of food. All turtles and tortoises lay eggs. Most bury them in sand or earth and leave the hatchlings to make their own way out.

Arrau river turtle

Size: 34¼ in (87 cm)
Range: northern South America
Scientific name:
Podocnemis expansa

Arrau river turtle

This is the largest of the turtles known as sidenecks—a sideneck retracts its head by moving it sideways into the shell. Females gather in huge numbers on sandbanks to lay their eggs. When the young hatch, they must make their own way to the water.

Wood turtle

This rough-shelled turtle stays near water but spends most of its life on land. It is a good climber and feeds on fruit, worms, and insects. In May or June females lay six to eight eggs. These may hatch before autumn, but the eggs of turtles in northern areas usually do not hatch until the next spring.

Size: 5–9 in (12.5–23 cm)
Range: eastern Canada, northeastern to midwestern U.S.A.
Scientific name: Clemmys insculpta

◐ **River terrapin**

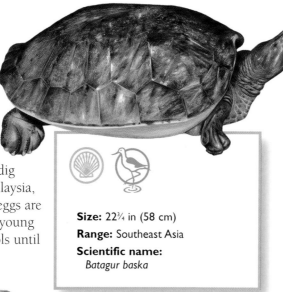

River terrapin

A large plant-eating turtle, the river terrapin, or batagur, lives in salt water as well as in rivers. It nests on sandbanks, so it is easy for people to catch it and dig up its eggs for food. In Malaysia, to save the river terrapin, eggs are taken to hatcheries where young turtles are kept safe in pools until they are two years old.

Size: 22¾ in (58 cm)
Range: Southeast Asia
Scientific name:
Batagur baska

Pond slider

Size: 5–11¾ in (13–30 cm)
Range: U.S.A., Central America to Brazil
Scientific name:
Trachemys scripta

Pond slider

The pond slider rarely moves far from water and often basks on floating logs. Young pond sliders feed mainly on insects, tadpoles, and other small invertebrate animals, but as they grow they also eat plants. In summer the female pond slider lays up to three clutches of 4 to 23 eggs each.

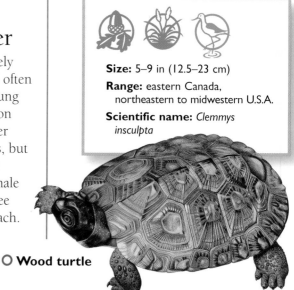

○ **Wood turtle**

Galápagos giant tortoise

This huge tortoise may weigh more than 475 pounds (215 kg)—males are usually larger than females. It lives on land and feeds on almost any plants it can find. Some have a shell that curves up behind the head, allowing the tortoise to reach higher plants. The female digs a pit with her back feet and lays 4 to 10 eggs. She covers the eggs with soil and leaves them to incubate. The young dig themselves out of the pit when they hatch.

O **Galápagos giant tortoise**

Size: up to 4 ft (1.2 m)
Range: Galápagos Islands
Scientific name:
   Geochelone elephantopus

Pancake tortoise

Pancake tortoise

This remarkable tortoise has a soft, flexible shell. If in danger, it crawls into a rocky crevice and breathes in lots of air. Its body expands so much that it becomes stuck tight in the hole and very difficult to pull out. But this does not protect the animal from people, who catch large numbers for the pet trade.

Size: 6 in (15 cm)
Range: Africa
Scientific name:
   Malocochersus tornieri

Spur-thighed tortoise

This rare tortoise is native to dry, scrubby regions around the Mediterranean Sea that are being changed by farming and the building of vacation homes. Millions of these tortoises have been captured and sold as pets. Some trade still goes on but is now banned by most countries.

Size: 6 in (15 cm)
Range: northern Africa, southeastern and southwestern Europe, southwestern Asia
Scientific name:
   Testudo graeca

Schweigger's hingeback tortoise

Schweigger's hingeback tortoise

This tortoise eats some small animals but feeds mainly on plants and spends much of its life hiding among plant debris. Its shell is unique. A hinge allows the rear of the shell to be lowered to protect the animal's hindquarters if it is attacked. Young tortoises do not have a hinge—it develops as they grow.

Size: 13 in (33 cm)
Range: western and central Africa
Scientific name:
   Kinixys erosa

O **Spur-thighed tortoise**

125

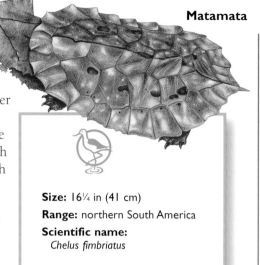

Matamata

Matamata

The irregular shape of this turtle keeps it well hidden as it lies among dead leaves and other debris on the riverbed. Fleshy flaps at the sides of the head wave in water and may attract small fish and sense movement. When a fish comes close, the turtle opens its mouth, taking in the fish and water with it. The turtle closes its mouth, leaving only a slit for the water to flow out.

Size: 16¼ in (41 cm)
Range: northern South America
Scientific name:
  Chelus fimbriatus

Murray River turtle

Murray River turtle

The shape of the Murray River turtle's shell changes as it develops. Newly hatched young have almost circular shells. As they grow, the shell becomes wider at the back. Adult shells are oval. This active turtle feeds on frogs, tadpoles, and plants. In summer the female lays between 10 and 15 eggs in a hole dug in the riverbank. The eggs hatch in about 10 or 11 weeks.

Size: 11¾ in (30 cm)
Range: southeastern Australia
Scientific name:
  Emydura macquarri

Hawksbill

Hawksbills have long been hunted for their beautiful shells as well as for their eggs. There are now strict controls on hunting, but numbers are still extremely low. This sea turtle has an unusual diet. In addition to eating mollusks and crustaceans, it feeds on sponges. Many of these contain poisons, but the toxins do not seem to affect the turtles.

Size: 30–36 in (76–91 cm)
Range: tropical Atlantic, Pacific, and Indian Oceans, Caribbean
Scientific name:
  Eretmochelys imbricata

● **Hawksbill**

◑ **Leatherback**

Leatherback

The world's largest sea turtle, the leatherback weighs about 800 pounds (360 kg). Its shell is not covered with hard plates but is made of a thick, leathery material. It feeds mostly on jellyfish. Leatherbacks travel long distances between the areas where they feed and their nesting sites. Most breed only every other year, laying up to nine clutches in the breeding year. Newly hatched young have small scales on their shells and skin, but these soon disappear.

Size: 5 ft (1.5 m)
Range: tropical Atlantic, Pacific, and Indian Oceans, but migrates to temperate waters
Scientific name:
  Dermochelys coriacea

◗ Loggerhead turtle

Size: 30–80 in (76–200 cm)

Range: temperate and tropical areas of Pacific, Indian, and Atlantic Oceans, Mediterranean Sea

Scientific name: *Caretta caretta*

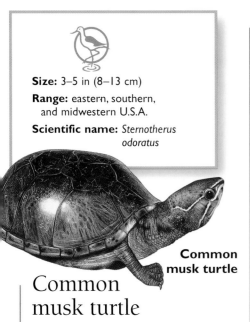

Size: 3–5 in (8–13 cm)

Range: eastern, southern, and midwestern U.S.A.

Scientific name: *Sternotherus odoratus*

Common musk turtle

Common musk turtle

Also known as the stinkpot, this turtle oozes a strong-smelling fluid from special glands if attacked. It eats insects and mollusks but also feeds on carrion (creatures that are already dead) and small quantities of fish and plants. It rarely strays far from the water.

Spiny softshell

Softshell turtles have rounded, flexible shells. They can move fast on land and in water but spend most of their lives in water. The spiny softshell feeds on insects, crayfish, and some fish and plants. It breeds in summer, when the female lays about 20 eggs.

Loggerhead turtle

Like most sea turtles, breeding loggerheads return to the same beaches where they hatched. In the United States, they nest on summer nights at special beaches from New Jersey to Texas. Females dig holes in the sand and lay about 100 eggs. Two months later, hatchlings dig out and run to the water, but most are eaten by birds. Others wander away from the sea, attracted by house and streetlights, and die.

Atlantic green turtle

This turtle spends most of its life in the sea, feeding on seaweed and sea grasses. It may travel great distances to lay its eggs on the beach where it was born. The female drags herself onto the sand, where she digs a pit and lays 100 or more eggs. She covers them with sand and returns to the sea. When the young hatch, they must struggle out of the pit and down to the sea.

Size: 3¼–4 ft (1–1.25 m)

Range: tropical Atlantic, Pacific, and Indian Oceans

Scientific name: *Chelonia mydas*

◗ Atlantic green turtle

Alligator snapping turtle

This turtle can weigh up to 200 pounds (91 kg). It has a lumpy shell that makes it hard to see as it lies on the riverbed, watching for prey. It waits with its large mouth open to show a pink fleshy flap on its lower jaw. Passing creatures come to try this "bait" and are quickly swallowed or sliced in half by the turtle's strong jaws.

Size: 14–26 in (36–66 cm)

Range: central U.S.A.

Scientific name: *Macroclemys temmincki*

○ Alligator snapping turtle

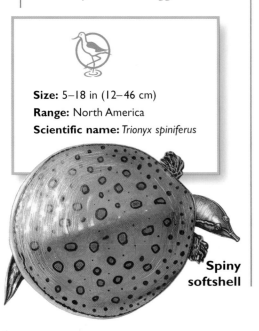

Size: 5–18 in (12–46 cm)

Range: North America

Scientific name: *Trionyx spiniferus*

Spiny softshell

127

Lizards and snakes

Lizards and snakes belong to a large group of reptiles, all of which have a body covered with scales. There are at least 3,500 species of lizards living over most of the world except the far north and Antarctica. Most live on land or in trees, but the marine iguana spends much of its time in the sea. There are more than 2,400 species of snakes. Like lizards, they live mainly in warmer parts of the world, and there are none in the polar regions. Most snakes live on land, but there are some freshwater and marine species.

Lizards

Lizards are the largest group of reptiles. They range from tiny geckos only 3 inches (7.5 cm) long to huge Komodo dragons that measure up to 10 feet (3 m). A typical lizard has four legs, but there are some legless species and others, such as the skinks and snake lizards, that have extremely small limbs. Most have ear openings and movable eyelids. In general, lizards lay eggs in a hole or a safe place under a rock and give them no further attention. But a few types keep their eggs inside their bodies until the young are quite well developed. They either hatch almost as soon as the eggs are laid or are born live.

Chuckwalla

Size: 11–16½ in (28–42 cm)
Range: southwestern U.S.A., Mexico
Scientific name:
Sauromalus obesus

Chuckwalla

This plump lizard lies among rocks at night and comes out in the morning to warm its body by basking in the sun. A plant eater, it spends the day feeding on leaves, buds, and flowers. If in danger, it hides in a rock crevice and puffs its body up with air so it is almost impossible to remove.

Size: 5 in (12.5 cm)
Range: southwestern Africa
Scientific name:
Palmatogecko rangei

Web-footed gecko

Leaf-tailed gecko

Leaf-tailed gecko

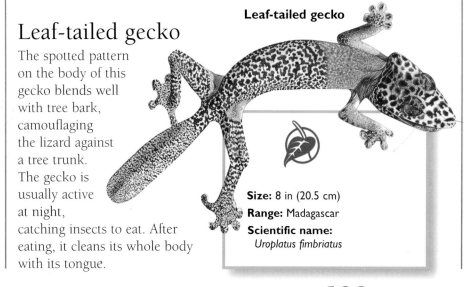

The spotted pattern on the body of this gecko blends well with tree bark, camouflaging the lizard against a tree trunk. The gecko is usually active at night, catching insects to eat. After eating, it cleans its whole body with its tongue.

Size: 8 in (20.5 cm)
Range: Madagascar
Scientific name:
Uroplatus fimbriatus

Web-footed gecko

This desert-living gecko has webbed feet that act like snowshoes to help it run over soft sand. It also uses its feet for burrowing into the sand to hide from enemies or the burning sun. It sits in the burrow with its head facing the entrance, waiting to pounce on insects such as termites.

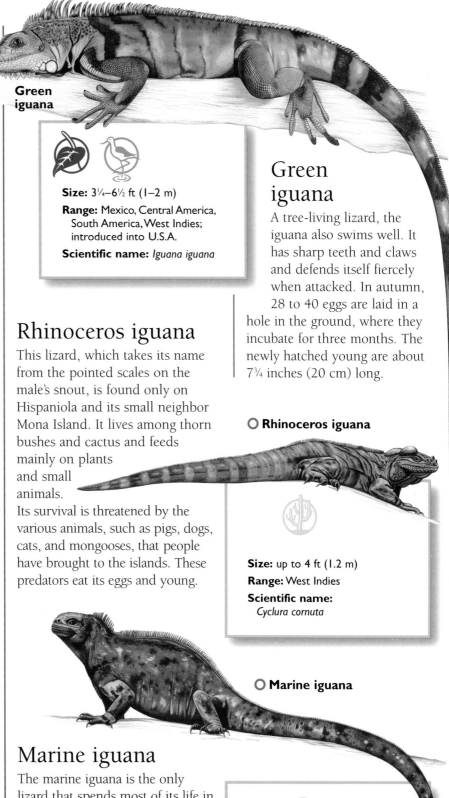

Arabian toad-headed agamid

A burrowing lizard, this agamid digs tunnels for shelter or buries itself in the sand. If alarmed, it takes up a defensive position to warn off the enemy—it lifts its tail high, rolls it up, and then unrolls it again.

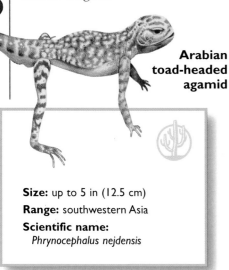

Green iguana

Arabian toad-headed agamid

Size: up to 5 in (12.5 cm)
Range: southwestern Asia
Scientific name:
   Phrynocephalus nejdensis

Size: 3¼–6½ ft (1–2 m)
Range: Mexico, Central America, South America, West Indies; introduced into U.S.A.
Scientific name: *Iguana iguana*

Rhinoceros iguana

This lizard, which takes its name from the pointed scales on the male's snout, is found only on Hispaniola and its small neighbor Mona Island. It lives among thorn bushes and cactus and feeds mainly on plants and small animals.
Its survival is threatened by the various animals, such as pigs, dogs, cats, and mongooses, that people have brought to the islands. These predators eat its eggs and young.

Green iguana

A tree-living lizard, the iguana also swims well. It has sharp teeth and claws and defends itself fiercely when attacked. In autumn, 28 to 40 eggs are laid in a hole in the ground, where they incubate for three months. The newly hatched young are about 7¾ inches (20 cm) long.

○ Rhinoceros iguana

Size: up to 4 ft (1.2 m)
Range: West Indies
Scientific name:
   Cyclura cornuta

Tuatara

There are only two species of tuataras, which are very similar to relatives that lived 130 million years ago and that are known only from fossils. Tuataras live on the ground and take shelter in burrows. They eat insects and other small invertebrates as well as small birds and lizards.

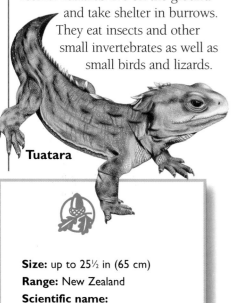

Tuatara

Size: up to 25½ in (65 cm)
Range: New Zealand
Scientific name:
   Sphenodon punctatus

○ Marine iguana

Marine iguana

The marine iguana is the only lizard that spends most of its life in the sea, swimming and diving as it searches for algae, which it scrapes off rocks and eats. When in the water, the iguana uses its powerful tail to push itself along. It has to come to the surface to breathe, but when it dives, its heart rate slows so its body uses less oxygen.

Size: 4–5 ft (1.2–1.5 m)
Range: Galápagos Islands
Scientific name:
   Amblyrhynchus cristatus

Green anole

Size: 3¾–5 in (9.5–12.5 cm)
Range: southwestern U.S.A.
Scientific name:
Xantusia vigilis

Size: 4¾–7¾ in (12–20 cm)
Range: southern U.S.A., except the far West
Scientific name:
Anolis carolinensis

Green anole

The anole's long-toed feet help it climb in trees, where it searches for insects and spiders to eat. The male anole has a flap of pink skin on his throat that he fans in a display to mark his territory. During the breeding season, the female lays one egg on the ground among leaves or rocks about once a week. The eggs hatch in five to seven weeks.

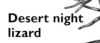

Desert night lizard

Desert night lizard

This lizard lives among desert plants such as yucca and agave and feeds on termites, ants, flies, and beetles. It does not lay eggs but gives birth to one to three live young, which develop inside the female's body and receive all the nourishment they need from her.

○ **Gila monster**

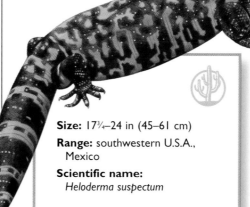

Size: 17¾–24 in (45–61 cm)
Range: southwestern U.S.A., Mexico
Scientific name:
Heloderma suspectum

Gila monster

This is one of only two poisonous lizards. Its poison is made in glands in the lower jaw, and as the Gila bites its prey, poison flows into the wound. Eggs, baby birds, and mammals are its main food. If food is scarce, the Gila can live off fat reserves stored in its tail.

Jungle runner

This very active lizard hunts on the ground. It has a long, forked tongue, which it flicks out to "smell" for insects and other invertebrates. The female is smaller than the male, and her body is marked with stripes instead of spots.

Western blue-tongued skink

This plump-bodied lizard has a large head and tiny legs. It scurries around in the daytime, searching for insects, snails, and berries. It sometimes takes shelter from the scorching sun in a rabbit burrow. The young grow inside the female's body and are born fully developed, 5 to 25 at a time.

Size: 17¾ in (45 cm)
Range: southern Australia
Scientific name:
Tiliqua occipitalis

Size: 2½–9½ in (6–24 cm)
Range: Central America, South America east of the Andes; introduced into Florida
Scientific name: *Ameiva ameiva*

Jungle runner

Western blue-tongued skink

Size: 10 ft (3 m)
Range: Komodo and some neighboring islands in the Lesser Sunda Islands
Scientific name: *Varanus komodoensis*

Slow worm

The slow worm gives birth to live young, which the female can keep in her body for up to a year if the weather is unfavorable. It sleeps under rocks or logs. In the morning it hunts for slugs, worms, insects, and other prey.

Slow worm

Komodo dragon

This creature dwarfs most other lizards and is large and strong enough to kill deer, wild boar, and pigs. It has a heavy body; a long, thick tail; and strong legs with talonlike claws. Despite its size it is a good climber and moves surprisingly fast. It swims well and is often found near water.

○ **Komodo dragon**

Size: 13¾–21¼ in (35–54 cm)
Range: parts of Europe and western Asia, northwestern Africa
Scientific name: *Anguis fragilis*

Frilled lizard

This lizard has a collar of skin that normally lies in folds around its neck. But if the lizard is disturbed, its collar stands up like a frill, making the lizard look larger and more frightening than it really is. It eats insects and other creatures that it finds in trees and on the ground.

Great Plains skink

This lizard is unusual because the female guards her eggs carefully while they incubate and protects them from predators. She even helps the young wriggle free of their shells, then cares for them for about 10 days.

Size: 26–36 in (66–92 cm)
Range: Australia and New Guinea
Scientific name: *Chlamydosaurus kingii*

Frilled lizard

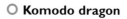

Transvaal snake lizard

With snakelike movements of its long body and tail, this lizard streaks through the grass in search of insects and spiders to eat. Its tiny legs are often held off the ground as it moves like a snake. The female's two to four eggs develop inside her body. The fully formed young break from their shells as the eggs are laid.

Size: 15¾ in (40 cm)
Range: South Africa
Scientific name: *Chamaesaura aena*

Transvaal snake lizard

Size: 6½–13¾ in (16.5–35 cm)
Range: central U.S.A., Mexico
Scientific name: *Eumeces obsoletus*

Great Plains skink

131

LIZARDS AND SNAKES

Chameleons

There are about 130 species of these tree-living lizards. Most live in Africa, including Madagascar, but some occur in southwestern Asia, India, and Sri Lanka. A typical chameleon has a body that is flattened side to side, large eyes that move independently of each other and magnify distant objects, and a strong tail that can be used to grip branches tightly. Most chameleons are between 6 and 11¾ inches (15 and 30 cm) long, but one Madagascan species grows up to 31½ inches (80 cm). Chameleons can change their skin color to help them hide from prey and predators and can mimic the movement of swaying leaves.

Changing color

A chameleon can lighten or darken its skin almost instantly, which helps it hide in its leafy surroundings. But in the breeding season, color changes may have other meanings. When two males compete for territory or females, the winning chameleon displays bright coloration, whereas the loser becomes a darker green and less visible.

Catching prey

Once the chameleon is close enough to its prey, it judges its position with its superb eyesight and takes aim. Shooting out its tongue, which may be as long as its body, the chameleon traps the insect on the sticky pad at the tongue's tip then retracts its tongue. This all happens very fast: in less than one-twentieth of a second.

132

Flap-necked chameleon

This reptile has flaps of skin at the back of its head, which it can extend to threaten a rival of its own species. It spends nearly all its life in trees and only comes down to move to another tree or to lay eggs.

Jackson's chameleon

The male of this species has three large horns on his head. Females have one small horn on the nose and tiny horns by each eye. The green of its skin keeps it camouflaged on lichen-covered tree bark.

Meller's chameleon

The bold markings on this chameleon make it extremely hard to see against the leaves of a tree as it sits motionless on a branch, watching for prey. Meller's chameleon grows up to 22¾ inches (58 cm) long.

This little chameleon looks like the dead leaves it hides among on the forest floor. It even has lines on its body that resemble the veins of a leaf. Unlike most chameleons, the **dwarf chameleon** spends its life on the ground and cannot grip with its tail.

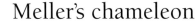

Snakes

Snakes are slender, legless creatures that range in size from 4 inches (10 cm) to 30 feet (9 m). Although limbless, snakes can move fast and hunt successfully. By using special belly scales (called scutes) and their flexible bodies, snakes can move across the ground or even up tree trunks. A snake's eyes are always open and alert to movement. Snakes have no ear openings but "hear" by sensing vibrations. Their long, forked tongues collect scents and help them find food and avoid enemies. To kill their food, some snakes, such as boas, use their strong body coils to squeeze prey, causing it to suffocate. Others, such as vipers, have a poisonous bite.

Western blind snake

Size: 7–15 in (18–38 cm)
Range: southwestern U.S.A.
Scientific name:
Leptotyphlops humilis

Western blind snake

The western blind snake has a blunt head and tail. It lives where there is sandy or gravelly soil and spends much of its time underground. It eats ants, termites, and insect larvae, which it finds by smell. Its body is slender enough to slide into their nests.

Anaconda

One of the longest of all snakes, the anaconda spends much of its life in slow-moving water. When an animal comes to drink, the anaconda seizes the victim with its mouth, then coils around it and squeezes. Female anacondas produce up to 40 live young, each 26 inches (66 cm) long.

Indian python

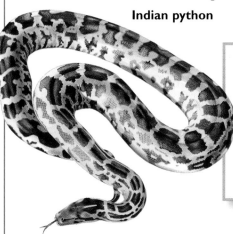

Size: 16½–20 ft (5–6.1 m)
Range: India, Southeast Asia, Indonesia
Scientific name:
Python molurus

Indian python

One of the largest snakes in the world, the Indian python basks in the sun by day or rests in a cave or other shelter. At night it prowls around, searching for prey such as birds, small deer, and boar or waits near a water hole where animals are sure to come. The female lays up to 100 eggs and coils her body around them to keep them warm while they incubate.

Boa constrictor

The boa constrictor kills prey, such as birds and mammals, by wrapping the victim in the strong coils of its body and squeezing until the animal suffocates. The boa spends most of its life on the ground, but it does climb trees and can grip branches with its tail.

Size: 30 ft (9 m)
Range: South America east of the Andes
Scientific name: *Eunectes murinus*

Anaconda

Boa constrictor

Size: up to 18½ ft (5.6 m)
Range: Mexico, Central and South America
Scientific name:
Boa constrictor

Eastern hognose snake

If in danger, the hognose snake gives an impressive warning display, inflating its body and hissing loudly. If this does not scare off its enemy, the snake plays dead, lying still with its tongue hanging from its open mouth. Usually active in the daytime, it hunts frogs, toads, and lizards.

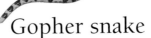

Gopher snake

Gopher snake

This large snake is a good climber and burrower. Usually active in the daytime, it hunts rats and mice as well as rabbits and birds. If alarmed, it flattens its head, hisses loudly, and shakes its tail before attacking the enemy. Gopher snakes mate in spring, and the female lays up to 24 eggs in a burrow or under a log.

Size: 4–8¼ ft (1.2–2.5 m)
Range: southwestern Canada, U.S.A., Mexico
Scientific name: *Pituophis melanoleucus*

Size: up to 6½ ft (2 m)
Range: Europe (including western Russia), northwestern Africa, western Asia
Scientific name: *Natrix natrix*

Size: 20–45 in (50–115 cm)
Range: eastern U.S.A.
Scientific name: *Heterodon platyrhinos*

Eastern hognose snake

Grass snake

Size: 11¾–39 in (30–100 cm)
Range: Australia
Scientific name: *Enhydris punctata*

Spotted water snake

Able to move swiftly both in water and on land, this snake preys on creatures such as fish and frogs. Its eyes and nostrils are on the upper surface of the head. Pads of skin close off the nostrils completely when the snake swims underwater. It is mildly poisonous.

Grass snake

The grass snake is a good swimmer and hunts fish and frogs in woodland rivers as well as mice on land. It is one of the most common snakes in Europe. In the breeding season the male courts the female by rubbing his chin over her body before mating. She lays 30 to 40 eggs in a warm spot.

Spotted water snake

Grass snake

135

Scarlet kingsnake

Scarlet kingsnake

This kind of kingsnake spends much of its life hidden under rotting logs or tree stumps. It is often mistaken for the highly venomous coral snake (see below).

A simple rhyme teaches the difference between the two: Red touch yellow—kill a fellow. Red touch black—friend of Jack.

Size: 14–27 in (35.5–69 cm)
Range: southeastern Canada, contiguous U.S.A., Mexico
Scientific name:
Lampropeltis triangulum

Sidewinder

This poisonous snake hides under a bush or in a burrow during the day and comes out at night to hunt for mice, rats, and lizards. A desert dweller, the sidewinder has a special way of moving over sand. It presses its tail down, throws the rest of its body to one side, then moves its tail up and repeats the action, moving sideways across the sand.

Size: 17–32¼ in (43–82 cm)
Range: southwestern U.S.A. and Mexico
Scientific name:
Crotalus cerastes

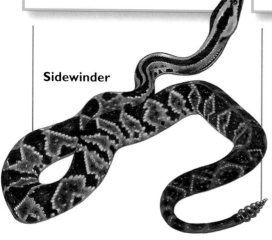
Sidewinder

Paradise tree snake

Size: up to 4 ft (1.2 m)
Range: Philippines to Indonesia
Scientific name:
Chrysopelea paradisi

Paradise tree snake

This snake is an excellent climber and spends much of its life in trees. Also known as the flying snake, it spreads its ribs to flatten its body so it can glide 65 feet (20 m) or more from tree to tree in the rain forest. It does not have much control over its "flight" and cannot glide upward or steer.

Banded sea snake

Size: 6½ ft (2 m)
Range: coastal areas of Indian and Pacific Oceans
Scientific name:
Hydrophis cyanocinctus

Banded sea snake

This snake spends all its life in the sea, never going on land. Its body is slightly flattened, and its paddle-shaped tail helps it move through the water. It breathes air but can stay underwater for up to two hours. Like all sea snakes, it eats fish and has a poisonous bite.

Eastern coral snake

The colorful markings of the coral snake are a warning to enemies that it is highly poisonous. This snake spends much of its time buried in sand or dead leaves. In the morning and late afternoon it moves around searching for small snakes and lizards, which it kills with its poisonous bite.

Size: 22–48 in (56–120 cm)
Range: southeastern U.S.A., northeastern Mexico
Scientific name:
Micrurus fulvius

Eastern coral snake

Eastern diamondback rattlesnake

Eastern diamondback rattlesnake

This is the most dangerous snake in the United States, with poison that attacks its victims' blood cells. Like all rattlesnakes, it makes a rattling sound with a series of hard, hollow rings of skin at the end of its tail. Each ring was once the tip of the tail, and a new one is left behind each time the snake sheds its skin.

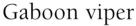

Size: 3¼–7¾ ft (1–2.4 m)

Range: eastern to midwestern U.S.A.

Scientific name:
Crotalus adamanteus

Indian cobra

This large, very poisonous cobra feeds on mice, lizards, and frogs. It can attack or defend itself from a distance by "spitting" out jets of poison. This can cause severe pain if it reaches the eyes of mammals. To threaten enemies, the cobra raises the front of its body and spreads the ribs and loose skin at its neck to form a hood shape. Eyelike markings on the hood confuse the enemy further.

Indian cobra

Gaboon viper

The patterns on the Gaboon viper's body help keep it hidden as it lies among dead leaves on the forest floor. It hunts at night, preying on mice, frogs, and birds. Its fangs are up to 2 inches (5 cm) long, the longest of any viper, and it has powerful poison. The female viper gives birth to litters of as many as 30 live young.

Gaboon viper

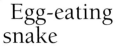
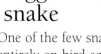

Size: 4–6½ ft (1.2–2 m)

Range: western Africa south of the Sahara

Scientific name:
Bitis gabonica

Egg-eating snake

One of the few snakes to feed entirely on bird eggs, this snake has special equipment for dealing with the hard shells. The mouth can stretch to engulf an egg much larger than the snake's head. The whole egg passes down into the throat, where special back bones crush the shell open. The contents then pass into the stomach and the pieces of shell are regurgitated.

Egg-eating snake

Size: 29½ in (75 cm)

Range: Africa south and east of the Sahara

Scientific name:
Dasypeltis scabra

Size: 6–7¼ ft (1.8–2.2 m)

Range: India, central and southeastern Asia, Philippines

Scientific name:
Naja naja

Amphibians

Amphibians were the first vertebrate animals to live on land. They evolved from fish about 370 million years ago, and modern amphibians still spend part of their lives in water. Many also mate and lay their eggs in water. The eggs hatch into water-living larvae that have tail fins and gills. As they grow, they lose their gills and develop lungs, so that they are able to live on land. Some amphibians such as mudpuppies, however, spend their whole lives in water and keep their feathery gills.

There are about 4,550 known species of amphibians, but new species are being discovered all the time, particularly in tropical areas, so there are likely to be more than 5,000. These consist of two main groups: salamanders and newts; frogs and toads. There is also a third, smaller group of legless, long-bodied amphibians called caecilians, which look similar to earthworms.

True to its name, the boldly colored **spotted salamander** has a line of irregular spots running down its back from head to tail. Normally a peaceful creature, the male can be aggressive when defending his territory against intruders. The male may bite the nose of a rival.

Oriental fire-bellied toad

What is an amphibian?

A mphibians are cold-blooded vertebrates. They cannot control their own body temperature. Some bask in the sun to warm up or enter water to cool down. Although most have lungs, amphibians gain much of the oxygen they need through their skin, which is not scaly and must be kept moist.

Taking off

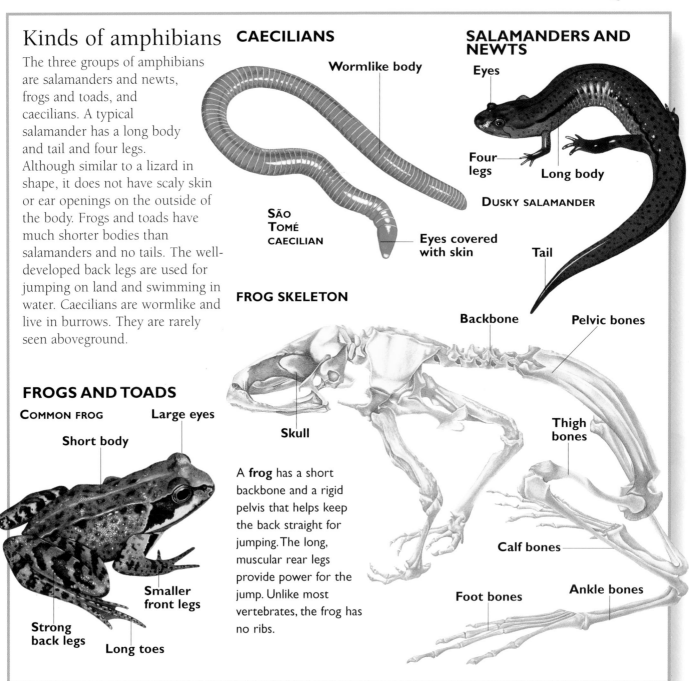

Kinds of amphibians

The three groups of amphibians are salamanders and newts, frogs and toads, and caecilians. A typical salamander has a long body and tail and four legs. Although similar to a lizard in shape, it does not have scaly skin or ear openings on the outside of the body. Frogs and toads have much shorter bodies than salamanders and no tails. The well-developed back legs are used for jumping on land and swimming in water. Caecilians are wormlike and live in burrows. They are rarely seen aboveground.

CAECILIANS

Wormlike body

SÃO TOMÉ CAECILIAN

Eyes covered with skin

SALAMANDERS AND NEWTS

Eyes

Four legs

Long body

DUSKY SALAMANDER

Tail

FROG SKELETON

Backbone

Pelvic bones

Skull

Thigh bones

Calf bones

Foot bones

Ankle bones

FROGS AND TOADS

COMMON FROG

Large eyes

Short body

Smaller front legs

Strong back legs

Long toes

A **frog** has a short backbone and a rigid pelvis that helps keep the back straight for jumping. The long, muscular rear legs provide power for the jump. Unlike most vertebrates, the frog has no ribs.

Back legs fully stretched

Getting ready to land

Leaping frog

On land, the frog crouches with its long back legs folded. The foot, calf, and thigh are all about the same length. As the frog leaps, the legs unfold to push it into the air. When stretched out, the frog's back legs are usually longer than its body.

From egg to adult

A typical frog develops in stages known as a life cycle. The amount of time each stage takes varies from species to species, ranging from 24 hours to several weeks. The eggs, which have a protective jellylike coating, are usually laid in water. They hatch into tadpoles, which have a tail and, in most species, feathery gills. As each tadpole grows, it develops legs and lungs, and the gills disappear. When it has grown into a miniature version of the adult, the tadpole loses its tail. Not all frogs follow this cycle. Some keep their developing eggs inside their body.

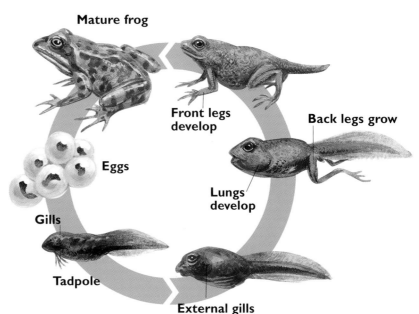

Mature frog

Front legs develop

Back legs grow

Eggs

Lungs develop

Gills

Tadpole

External gills disappear

Poison-arrow frog

South American false-eyed frog

Spotted salamander

Beware of bright colors

Many amphibians have extremely brightly colored and patterned skins. This is usually a warning to potential predators that the amphibian's skin contains nasty-tasting secretions. These can cause severe irritation in mammals, and some even contain poisons that can kill. The South American false-eyed frog has large eyelike markings on its rear. If attacked, it displays these most likely to fool its enemy into thinking it is larger than it really is.

Prehistoric amphibians

Amphibians such as *Ichthyostega* were the first known land animals. *Ichthyostega* was a strongly built creature with four legs. Like its fish ancestors, it had a tail fin and bony scales on its belly and tail.

Ichthyostega

Salamanders and newts

There are about 350 species of salamanders and newts, divided into 10 groups, or families. Sirens, amphiumas, olms, and mudpuppies are all long-bodied amphibians with small, almost useless legs. These creatures all live in water and have feathery gills for breathing, which many of them keep throughout their lives.

The lungless salamanders are the largest group of salamanders. With no lungs, they obtain almost all their oxygen through their moist skin. There are several other groups of salamanders, most of which have sturdy bodies and well-developed legs. There are about 53 species of newts. There are water- and land-living newts, but most stay near water.

Two-toed amphiuma

Size: 17¾–45½ in (45–116 cm)
Range: southeastern U.S.A.
Scientific name:
Amphiuma means

Two-toed amphiuma

The amphiuma lives only in water. It has a long body and tiny legs that are useless for walking. It usually hunts at night for creatures such as crayfish and frogs. During the day it may hide in a burrow that it digs in the mud or takes over from another creature. Amphiumas mate in water, and the female lays about 200 eggs in a long string. She curls around the eggs and protects them until they hatch.

California slender salamander

True to its name, this salamander has a long, slim body and tail. Its legs and feet are tiny, with four toes on each foot. It generally lives on land and moves by wriggling its body rather than by using its legs. During the day it hides among damp plants, coming out at night to hunt for creatures such as worms and spiders.

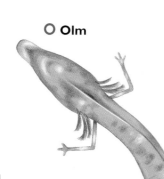

○ **Olm**

Olm

This strange-looking salamander has a long body and red feathery gills. Its tail is flattened and it has small, weak legs. It is almost blind and lives in total darkness in the streams and lakes of caves. There it rummages in the mud to find food such as worms and small crustaceans. Animal collectors have taken so many of these fascinating creatures from the wild that new areas where they have been found are kept secret.

Size: 3–5½ in (7.5–14 cm)
Range: western U.S.A.: Oregon, California
Scientific name:
Batrachoseps attenuatus

California slender salamander

Size: 7¾–11¾ in (20–30 cm)
Range: Balkan Peninsula and Italy
Scientific name: *Proteus anguinus*

142

Mudpuppy

The mudpuppy spends all its life in water. It hunts worms, crayfish, and insects at night. The female lays up to 190 eggs, each of which is stuck separately to a log or rock. Mud puppy larvae take four to six *years* to mature.

Red salamander

Mudpuppy

Size: 7¾–17 in (20–43 cm)
Range: southern Canada, U.S.A.
Scientific name:
 Necturus maculosus

Red salamander

The brilliantly colored red salamander has a stout body and a short tail and legs. It spends much of its time on land but usually stays near water. Earthworms, insects, and smaller salamanders are its main food. After courting and mating, the female salamander lays between 50 and 100 eggs. The larvae hatch about two months later but do not become adults until they are about two years old.

Size: 3¾–7 in (9.5–18 cm)
Range: eastern U.S.A.
Scientific name:
 Pseudotriton ruber

◯ **Texas blind salamander**

Size: 3½–5¼ in (9–13.5 cm)
Range: U.S.A.: southern Texas
Scientific name:
 Typhlomolge rathbuni

Texas blind salamander

This salamander lives in water in underground caves in total darkness. It cannot see, and although its blood makes it look pink, the skin is colorless. The Texas blind salamander eats cave-dwelling invertebrates that feed on the droppings left by bats that roost in the caves.

Greater siren

The siren has a long eel-like body and tiny front legs with four toes on each foot. It has no back legs and swims by fishlike movements of its body. During the day, it hides under rocks or burrows into the muddy riverbed. At night, it comes out to feed on snails, insect larvae, and fish.

Spotted salamander

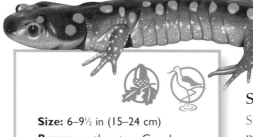

Size: 19¾–38½ in (50–97.5 cm)
Range: southeastern U.S.A.
Scientific name:
 Siren lacertina

Size: 6–9½ in (15–24 cm)
Range: southeastern Canada, eastern U.S.A.
Scientific name:
 Ambystoma maculatum

Spotted salamander

Spotted salamanders spend most of their time alone and out of sight, burrowing through damp soil. But every spring they gather in crowds around pools to mate and lay eggs in the water. Where acid rain has polluted breeding pools, this spectacle no longer occurs.

Greater siren

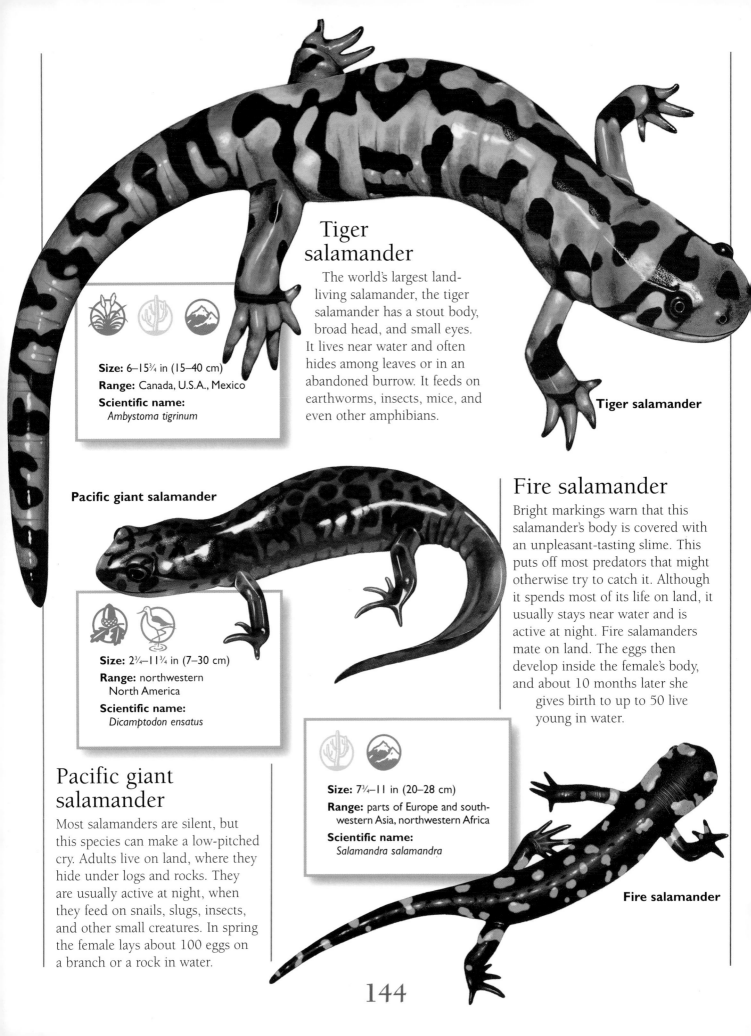

Tiger salamander

The world's largest land-living salamander, the tiger salamander has a stout body, broad head, and small eyes. It lives near water and often hides among leaves or in an abandoned burrow. It feeds on earthworms, insects, mice, and even other amphibians.

Size: 6–15¾ in (15–40 cm)
Range: Canada, U.S.A., Mexico
Scientific name:
   Ambystoma tigrinum

Tiger salamander

Pacific giant salamander

Size: 2¾–11¾ in (7–30 cm)
Range: northwestern North America
Scientific name:
   Dicamptodon ensatus

Pacific giant salamander

Most salamanders are silent, but this species can make a low-pitched cry. Adults live on land, where they hide under logs and rocks. They are usually active at night, when they feed on snails, slugs, insects, and other small creatures. In spring the female lays about 100 eggs on a branch or a rock in water.

Fire salamander

Bright markings warn that this salamander's body is covered with an unpleasant-tasting slime. This puts off most predators that might otherwise try to catch it. Although it spends most of its life on land, it usually stays near water and is active at night. Fire salamanders mate on land. The eggs then develop inside the female's body, and about 10 months later she gives birth to up to 50 live young in water.

Size: 7¾–11 in (20–28 cm)
Range: parts of Europe and south-western Asia, northwestern Africa
Scientific name:
   Salamandra salamandra

Fire salamander

144

Axolotl

This unusual salamander is now rare because so many have been collected for the pet trade, and predatory fish have been introduced into the lake where it lives. Many axolotls remain as larvae with feathery gills all their lives, but some do become land-living adults without gills.

○ **Axolotl**

Size: up to 11½ in (29 cm)
Range: Lake Xochimilco in Mexico
Scientific name:
Ambystoma mexicanum

Warty newt

The male of this large rough-skinned newt develops a jagged crest on his back in the breeding season. Females are often larger than males. Warty newts feed on small invertebrates; they also eat small fish and other amphibians and their eggs.

Warty newt

Size: 5½–7 in (14–18 cm)
Range: parts of Europe, central Asia
Scientific name: *Triturus cristatus*

South American caecilian

Caecilians are not salamanders but belong to a separate group of blind, burrowing amphibians. This caecilian has a short, thick body, but unlike most caecilians, it has no scales on its skin. It spends most of its life underground, where it feeds on earthworms.

South American caecilian

Size: 13¾ in (35 cm)
Range: South America east of the Andes
Scientific name:
Siphonops annulatus

Size: 2½–5½ in (6.5–14 cm)
Range: eastern North America
Scientific name:
Notophthalmus viridescens

Hellbender

Despite its fierce name, this large salamander is a harmless creature that hides under rocks in the water during the day. At night it hunts crayfish, snails, and worms, which it finds by smell and touch rather than by sight. In autumn the female lays up to 500 eggs in a hollow made by the male on the streambed.

Eastern newt

Size: 12–29¼ in (30.5–74 cm)
Range: U.S.A.
Scientific name:
Cryptobranchus alleganiensis

Hellbender

Eastern newt

This newt breeds in early spring. The female lays up to 400 eggs on water plants, and larvae hatch two months later. After a few months, the larvae turn into sub-adults called efts. They leave the water and spend up to three years on land. Then they return to the water and grow into adults.

Frogs and toads

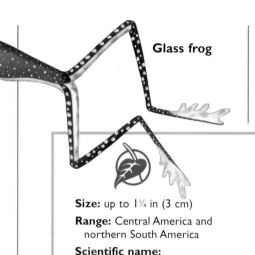

Glass frog

There are more than 3,500 species of frogs and toads. All have a similar body shape whatever their lifestyle. Typically, an adult frog or toad has long back legs, webbed toes, and no tail. The skin is either smooth or warty. Like all amphibians, frogs and toads are sometimes at home on land and sometimes in fresh water. They can swim and hop. Some even climb trees. Most feed on small creatures such as slugs, snails, and insects, which they catch with their long, sticky tongue.

Frogs and toads usually breed in water, laying eggs that hatch into tailed, swimming young known as tadpoles. The tadpoles live in water, breathing through feathery gills at the sides of the head and eating plants. As the tadpoles grow, they develop legs, lungs replace the gills, and they finally lose their tails and become frogs or toads (see page 141).

Size: up to 1¼ in (3 cm)
Range: Central America and northern South America
Scientific name:
Centrolenella albomaculata

Glass frog

This delicate little frog lives in small trees and bushes, usually near running water. It has sticky disks on its toes, which help it grip when climbing. The female lays her eggs in clusters on the undersides of leaves overhanging water. When the tadpoles hatch, they tumble into the water below, where they complete their development.

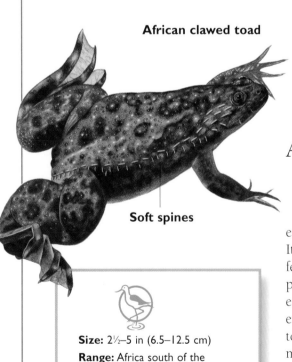

African clawed toad

Soft spines

Size: 2½–5 in (6.5–12.5 cm)
Range: Africa south of the Sahara
Scientific name:
Xenopus laevis

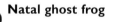

Natal ghost frog

African clawed toad

This toad moves as fast in the water as any fish and is even able to swim backward. It uses the claws on its front feet to dig in the mud around pools and streams for food. It eats any creatures it can find, even its own tadpoles. The toads mate in water, and the male makes a soft buzzing sound underwater to attract the female. The eggs are attached to water plants and hatch after 36 hours.

Size: up to 2 in (5 cm)
Range: northeastern South Africa
Scientific name:
Heleophryne natalensis

Natal ghost frog

This frog lives in fast-flowing mountain streams. The female lays her eggs in a pool or on wet gravel. Once hatched, the tadpoles move into the streams, where they hold on to stones with their suckerlike mouths to stop themselves from being swept away.

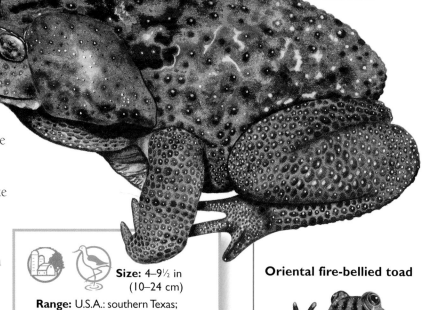

Cane toad

Cane toad

One of the largest toads in the world, the cane toad has been introduced into many areas outside its natural range so it will feed on insects that destroy crops. Glands at the sides of the toad's body make a poisonous liquid that may cause irritation and even death in mammals that try to eat it. Eggs are laid in water, where they hatch into tadpoles three days later.

Size: 4–9½ in (10–24 cm)
Range: U.S.A.: southern Texas; Mexico, Central and South America, Africa, southern Asia, Australia
Scientific name: *Bufo marinus*

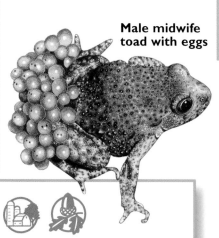

Male midwife toad with eggs

Size: up to 2 in (5 cm)
Range: western Europe, Morocco
Scientific name: *Alytes obstetricans*

Midwife toad

The midwife toad hides by day under logs or in cracks in walls. At night it feeds on insects and other small creatures. After the female has laid her eggs, the male winds the strings of eggs around his back legs and carries them while they develop. When they are ready to hatch, he places them in shallow water, and the tadpoles swim away.

Western spadefoot

An expert burrower, the western spadefoot toad has a hard spike on each back foot that helps it dig. It spends the day in its burrow and comes out at night to feed. The spadefoot waits for rain to fall before mating. Its eggs are laid in a rainpool and hatch when two days old.

Western spadefoot

Size: 1¼–2½ in (3.5–6.5 cm)
Range: western U.S.A., Mexico
Scientific name: *Scaphiopus hammondi*

Oriental fire-bellied toad

Size: 2 in (5 cm)
Range: Siberia, northeastern China, Korean Peninsula
Scientific name: *Bombina orientalis*

Oriental fire-bellied toad

The brilliantly colored rough skin of this toad gives off a milky substance that irritates the mouth and eyes of any attacker. The female fire-bellied toad lays her eggs on the undersides of stones in water. The eggs are laid in small clumps of two to eight and left alone to hatch by themselves.

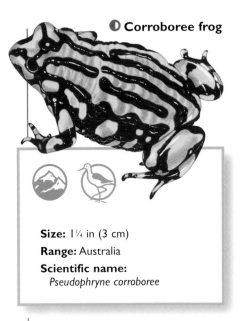

Corroboree frog

Size: 1¼ in (3 cm)
Range: Australia
Scientific name:
  Pseudophryne corroboree

Corroboree frog

This frog lives on land near water and takes shelter under logs or in a burrow that it digs. In summer pairs make a nesting burrow in a bog. The female lays up to 12 large eggs, and one parent usually guards the eggs while they develop. Most often the tadpoles stay in the eggs until there is enough rain to wash the eggs into a creek, where they hatch at once.

Gold frog

This tiny frog often lives among dead leaves on the forest floor but may also hide in cracks in trees or rocks in dry weather. It has a bony shield on its back and may use this to block off the entrance of its hiding place to keep the atmosphere inside moist.

Gold frog

Size: up to ¾ in (2 cm)
Range: southeastern Brazil
Scientific name:
  Brachycephalus ephippium

Marsupial frog

The marsupial frog has an unusual way of caring for its eggs. As the female lays her eggs, the male helps her pack them into a skin pouch on her back. A few weeks later, she finds some shallow water and releases her brood, which have hatched into tadpoles. She uses the long toe on her back foot to open the pouch.

Marsupial frog

Size: up to 1½ in (4 cm)
Range: northwestern South America
Scientific name:
  Gastrotheca marsupiata

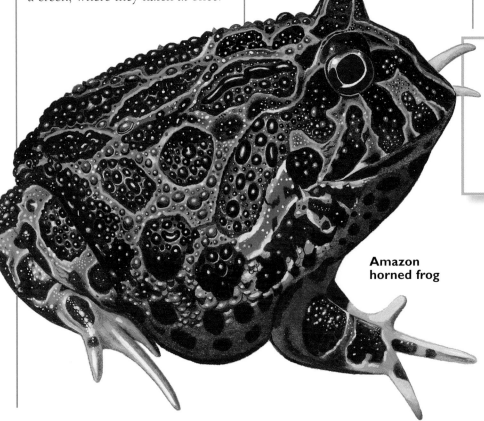

Amazon horned frog

Size: up to 7¾ in (20 cm)
Range: northern and central South America
Scientific name:
  Ceratophrys ornata

Amazon horned frog

This horned frog is almost as broad as it is long and has a wide head and large mouth. It has a lump on each upper eyelid. Even though it spends much of its life half-buried in the ground, its back toes are partly webbed. It feeds on snails, small frogs, and mice and probably also eats tadpoles of its own species.

Darwin's frog

Darwin's frog

This frog has unusual breeding habits. The female lays 20 to 45 eggs on land. Several males stand guard for up to 20 days until the young begin to move around inside the eggs. Each male then gathers up to 15 eggs in his mouth and lets them slide into the large sac under his chin. The tadpoles continue to develop inside the sac. When they have grown into tiny frogs, the males let them go in water.

Size: 1¼ in (3 cm)

Range: southern Chile and southern Argentina

Scientific name: *Rhinoderma darwinii*

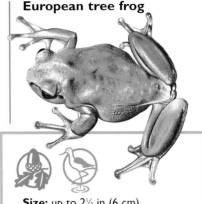

European tree frog

Size: up to 2½ in (6 cm)

Range: central and southern Europe; western Asia, northwestern Africa

Scientific name: *Hyla arborea*

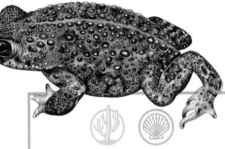

Natterjack toad

Natterjack toad

The male natterjack has the loudest call of any European toad. His croak carries 1¼ miles (2 km) or more. The natterjack usually lives on land but is often found near the sea and may even breed in salty pools. These toads mate at night, and the female lays strings of up to 4,000 eggs in shallow water. The eggs hatch into tadpoles in about ten days.

Size: 2¾–4 in (7–10 cm)

Range: western and central Europe

Scientific name: *Bufo calamita*

European tree frog

This smooth-skinned frog spends most of its life in trees. It can change color with amazing speed, turning from bright green in sunlight to dark gray in shade. The frogs breed in early summer, and the female lays up to 1,000 eggs in water.

Spring peeper

Size: ¾–1¼ in (2–3 cm)

Range: southeastern Canada, eastern U.S.A.

Scientific name: *Hyla crucifer*

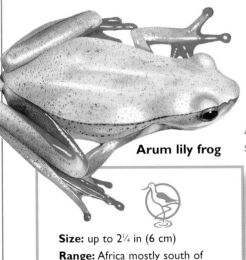

Arum lily frog

Arum lily frog

A good climber, this frog has large sticky disks on each toe that help it grip. The undersides of its legs are orange, but the rest of the body changes color according to available light. In bright sun it is light cream, and in shade it turns dark brown. Courting males often climb onto arum lilies to call to females. They mate in water and lay eggs on submerged water plants.

Size: up to 2¼ in (6 cm)

Range: Africa mostly south of the Sahara

Scientific name: *Hyperolius horstockii*

Spring peeper

This agile frog can climb trees and jump heights of more than 17 times its own body length. It feeds mainly on small spiders and insects, including flying insects, which it leaps into the air to catch. In the breeding season, males sit in trees courting females with their high-pitched whistle calls.

FROGS AND TOADS

149

Size: 4 in (10 cm)
Range: Sumatra and Borneo
Scientific name:
Rhacophorus nigropalmatus

Wallace's flying frog

Wallace's flying frog

This frog does not really fly but glides from tree to tree in the rain forest. Its large webbed feet and the flaps of skin on its front legs act like a parachute to help it float as far as 24½ feet (7.5 m) through the air. It can even steer by changing the position of its feet. Little is known about this frog's breeding habits, but it is thought to lay its eggs in a mass of foam, which protects them while they incubate.

**Red-banded
crevice
creeper**

Size: 2 in (5 cm)
Range: Africa south of the Equator
Scientific name:
Phrynomerus bifasciatus

South African rain frog

This plump frog spends much of its life in underground burrows, which it digs with its strong back feet. It comes aboveground only during wet weather to hunt insects and other small creatures. Its young develop completely inside eggs, so frogs hatch out, not tadpoles.

**South African
rain frog**

Size: 1¼ in (3 cm)
Range: South Africa, Namibia, Botswana, Zimbabwe
Scientific name:
Breviceps adspersus

Eastern narrow-mouthed frog

An excellent burrower, this small frog can disappear into the earth in a moment. It rests in a burrow during the day and comes out at night to hunt for ants and other insects. It breeds in summer when there is heavy rain.

**Eastern narrow-
mouthed frog**

Red-banded crevice creeper

Termites and ants are the main food of this frog. It digs in burrows or climbs trees to find insects. Its bright markings warn that its skin contains a substance that irritates the mouth or skin of predators. It breeds in shallow pools. The jelly-coated eggs attach to plants or lie at the bottom of the pool until they hatch.

Size: ¾–1½ in (2–4 cm)
Range: southeastern U.S.A.
Scientific name:
Gastrophryne carolinensis

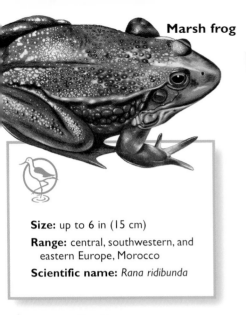

Marsh frog

Mottled burrowing frog

Mottled burrowing frog

This frog has a small pointed head, with a hard snout used for burrowing. It digs headfirst, pushing into the soil with its snout and clawing its way forward with its strong legs. The female lays her large eggs in a burrow. When the young hatch, she digs a tunnel for the tadpoles to swim to the nearest water.

Size: up to 6 in (15 cm)
Range: central, southwestern, and eastern Europe, Morocco
Scientific name: *Rana ridibunda*

Size: up to 1¼ in (3 cm)
Range: Africa south of the Sahara
Scientific name: *Hemisus marmoratum*

Marsh frog

This noisy frog spends most of its life in water but comes out onto banks or to float on lily pads. It catches small invertebrates and also eats small birds and mammals. Males call night and day, particularly in the breeding season. The female lays thousands of eggs in several large clusters.

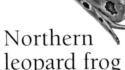
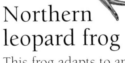

European common frog

Much of this frog's life is spent on land, feeding on insects, spiders, and other small creatures. It breeds in spring, when males attract females with their deep croaking calls. They mate in water, and the females lay clusters of thousands of eggs.

European common frog

Northern leopard frog

This frog adapts to any watery home and eats almost any creatures it can find. If disturbed when hunting on land, it leaps away to water in a series of zigzagging jumps. In the breeding season males attract females with low grunting calls. Each female lays about 5,000 eggs, which lie at the bottom of the water until they hatch about ten days later.

Northern leopard frog

Size: 2–5 in (5–12.5 cm)
Range: most of northern North America except Pacific coast
Scientific name: *Rana pipiens*

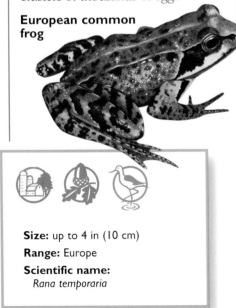

Size: up to 4 in (10 cm)
Range: Europe
Scientific name: *Rana temporaria*

Bullfrog

The largest North American frog, the bullfrog lives in water but also spends time on land at the water's edge. It hunts at night, catching insects, fish, smaller frogs, and even birds and snakes. It is a good jumper and can leap nine times its own length. In the breeding season the female lays up to 20,000 eggs in water.

Size: 3½–8 in (9–20.5 cm)
Range: southeastern Canada, eastern and central U.S.A., northern Mexico
Scientific name: *Rana catesbeiana*

Bullfrog

151

Golden poison-arrow frog

The poison in the skin of the neon-bright, golden poison-arrow frog may come partly from its food, such as small beetles and millipedes. Although deadly to its enemies, the frog's poison may have value. Doctors are investigating its use in a medicine for heart-attack patients.

Poison-arrow frogs

Poison-arrow frogs (also called poison-dart frogs) are among the most colorful of all amphibians. But the jewel-like appearance of some is a warning to predators to keep their distance because the skin contains extremely strong poison. The frogs do not inject their poison into predators. It is produced in special glands and simply released into the skin, making the frog a dangerous meal for a predator. Poison-arrow frogs live in the tropical rain forests of Central and South America. There are about 155 species of poison-arrow frogs, but only 55 of these are actually poisonous.

Small but lethal

One of the most deadly of all poison-arrow frogs is *Phyllobates terribilis*. This frog is only 2 inches (5 cm) long, but its poison is at least 20 times as strong as that of any other frog and can be lethal for humans even to touch. It is one of only three species traditionally used by local tribesmen for tipping hunting arrows. The arrow is simply rubbed over the frog's body, and it is ready to use. The poison remains strong for more than a year.

1. The eggs are laid on a leaf.

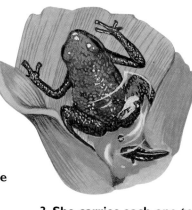

2. Once hatched, the tadpoles wriggle one at a time onto the mother's back.

3. She carries each one to a leaf pool high in a tree.

Caring for young

The female flaming poison-arrow frog lays her eggs on a leaf. She then looks after her tadpoles while they develop into frogs, carrying them on her back up into a tree and placing them in groups of about four in tiny pools of water contained in plants. She checks on them every few days and even gives them some unfertilized eggs to eat. The young are not poisonous at this stage, so they are safe for other creatures to catch and eat.

Among the most beautiful of all poison-arrow frogs is **Dendrobates tinctorius,** with its shiny blue markings. It is one of the 55 poisonous species.

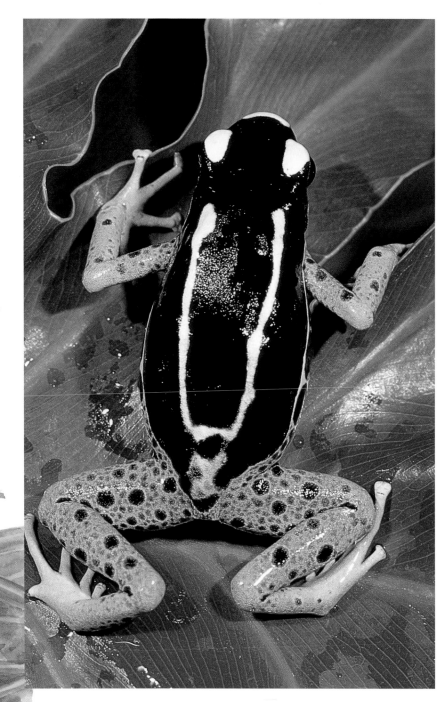

153

Why are some animals poisonous?

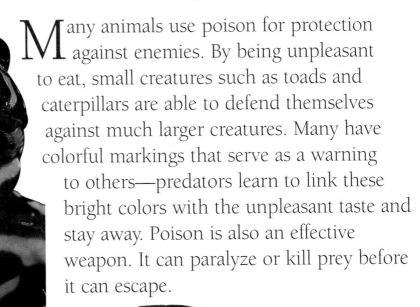

Many animals use poison for protection against enemies. By being unpleasant to eat, small creatures such as toads and caterpillars are able to defend themselves against much larger creatures. Many have colorful markings that serve as a warning to others—predators learn to link these bright colors with the unpleasant taste and stay away. Poison is also an effective weapon. It can paralyze or kill prey before it can escape.

The **Oriental fire-bellied toad** has small poison glands all over its body that produce an unpleasant-tasting substance. If threatened, the toad reveals the bright scarlet markings on the underside of its body to warn off its attacker.

The **cobra** uses poison to kill its prey. As it bites the animal, poison passes from glands in the head, through special canals in the hinged fangs at the front of the jaw into its prey. Some species also spray venom to blind their enemies.

The **scorpion** paralyzes and kills prey with a poisonous sting. Near the sharp stinger at the end of its body are poison glands. When the scorpion attacks, it swings its tail forward over its body and into the prey. Muscles force poison down into the hollow stinger. Some scorpions have poison strong enough to kill a human.

The **monarch butterfly caterpillar** feeds on the poisonous milkweed plant. The poison in the plant does not affect the caterpillar but is stored in its body and makes the caterpillar taste extremely unpleasant. Its bold stripes warn predators to leave it alone. Even as a butterfly, this insect is poisonous.

Fish

There are more than 24,000 species of fish in the world today, more than any other type of vertebrate. They range from tiny species such as the pygmy goby, which is only about ⅓ of an inch (1 cm) long, to giants such as the whale shark, which can measure as much as 39½ feet (12 m).

All fish live in water. There are at least 14,000 species in the sea, and the rest live in freshwater lakes and rivers all over the world. Special structures called gills allow fish to get oxygen they need from the water. Instead of legs, they have fins and a tail to help them push their bodies through water.

Fish feed in a wide variety of ways. Some eat aquatic plants. Others catch tiny animals or strain them from the water through comblike structures attached to their gills. Many are active, fast-moving hunters with sharp teeth, but some, such as the anglerfish, lie hidden on the seafloor and wait for prey to come close enough to catch.

Like many other kinds of fish, these **bluestripe snappers** swim in a large group called a school, or shoal. The exact reasons for schooling are not known, but there is certainly safety in numbers. Many predators are confused by the school, which can turn and change direction with breathtaking speed.

Lionfish

157

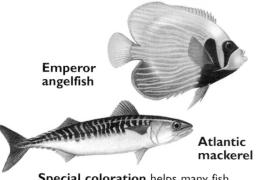

Emperor angelfish

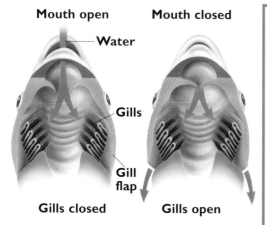

Atlantic mackerel

Special coloration helps many fish hide from their enemies. The angelfish's markings and the mackerel's light belly and darker back break up their body outlines and make them harder to see.

What is a fish?

Fish were the first vertebrates—animals with backbones—to live on Earth. The earliest fish lived about 500 million years ago. All except the group that includes lampreys and hagfish have a backbone made of bones called vertebrae, although in the sharks and rays this is made of cartilage.

GILLS OF BONY FISH

Mouth open

— Water

Mouth closed

Gills

Gill flap

Gills closed

Gills open

How fish breathe

Fish breathe through special structures called gills at the sides of the head. These are made up of large numbers of delicate plates, packed with blood vessels. As water flows through the gills, molecules of oxygen pass into the blood and are carried around the body. Each set of gills in a bony fish has one combined opening to the outside, which is covered by a protective flap. In sharks and rays, each gill has its own exit to the water.

GILLS OF SHARKS

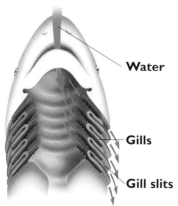

Water

Gills

Gill slits

Structure of a fish

There are three main groups of fish and their relatives. The most primitive group includes the lampreys and hagfish. These fishlike animals have no jaws, only a suckerlike mouth. The second group includes all the sharks and rays. These are known as cartilaginous fish because their skeletons are made of a gristly substance called cartilage, not bone. The third, and largest, group contains the bony fish. As their name suggests, these fish have skeletons made of bone.

JAWLESS FISHLIKE ANIMAL

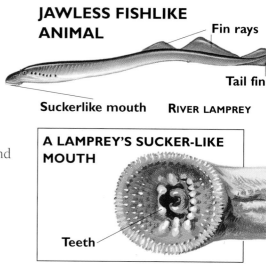

Fin rays

Tail fin

Suckerlike mouth   RIVER LAMPREY

A LAMPREY'S SUCKER-LIKE MOUTH

Teeth

BONY FISH SKELETON

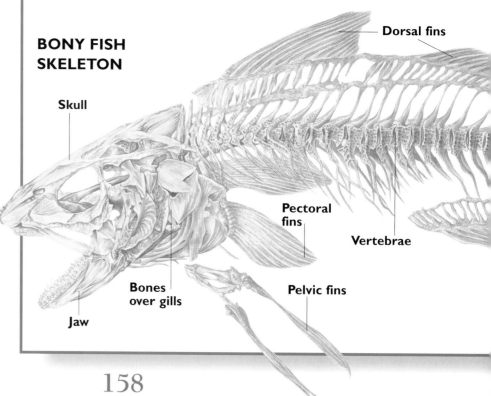

Dorsal fins

Skull

Pectoral fins

Vertebrae

Bones over gills

Jaw

Pelvic fins

Eggs and young

Most female fish lay large numbers of small eggs into the water. Males then release sperm to fertilize the eggs, which float in surface waters or sink to the bottom. The eggs hatch into tiny larvae, many of which are eaten by other creatures. Some survive to develop into juveniles, with a more adultlike body. The juveniles feed and grow into adult fish.

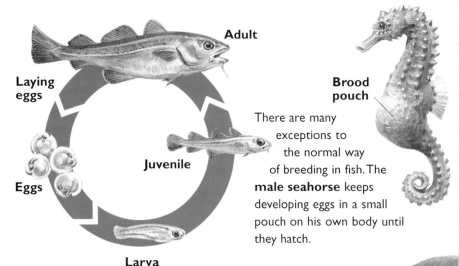

Adult

Laying eggs

Juvenile

Eggs

Larva

Brood pouch

There are many exceptions to the normal way of breeding in fish. The **male seahorse** keeps developing eggs in a small pouch on his own body until they hatch.

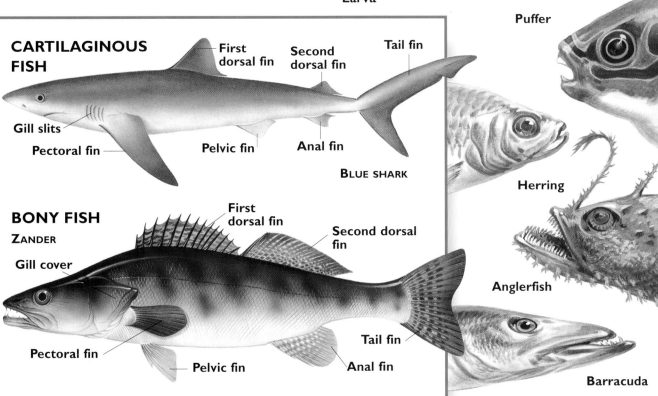

CARTILAGINOUS FISH

First dorsal fin

Second dorsal fin

Tail fin

Gill slits

Pectoral fin

Pelvic fin

Anal fin

BLUE SHARK

BONY FISH

ZANDER

Gill cover

First dorsal fin

Second dorsal fin

Pectoral fin

Pelvic fin

Tail fin

Anal fin

Dorsal fin

Tail fin

Anal fin

Special bones cover the gills on each side of a fish's head. In the fins there are small bones called spines. These bones keep the fins stiff and spread out.

Puffer

Herring

Anglerfish

Barracuda

Fish mouths

The mouth of a fish is adapted to suit the food that it eats. Fierce hunting fish, such as the barracuda, have a long snout and lots of sharp teeth for seizing prey. The anglerfish uses its very wide mouth for engulfing prey that it lures near with its "fishing rod." Many, such as the puffer, have a hard beaklike mouth for crushing hard-shelled creatures. The herring filters tiny animal plankton from the water through special structures called gill rakers that are linked to its gills.

159

Hagfish, lampreys, sharks, and rays

Hagfish and lampreys are primitive fishlike animals that have no true jaws. Hagfish have a slitlike mouth surrounded by small tentacles. Lampreys have a sucking disk for feeding on the blood of other creatures. All hagfish live in the sea, but there are some freshwater lampreys.

Sharks, sawfish, rays, and their relatives are all cartilaginous fish—they have skeletons made of cartilage, not bone. There are about 850 known species of cartilaginous fish, and all live in the sea. Most are active hunters, equipped with sharp-edged teeth in both jaws. A few of the largest, such as the whale shark, are not hunters. They use rakers on their gills to filter small creatures from the water.

Short fin mako shark

A powerful fish with a slender body and a pointed head, the mako is a fast-swimming, aggressive hunter. It usually feeds on surface-living fish, such as tuna and mackerel. The female mako gives birth to live young, which develop inside her body.

Short fin mako shark

Size: 6½–13 ft (2–4 m)

Range: Atlantic, Pacific, and Indian Oceans

Scientific name: *Isurus oxyrinchus*

Greater sawfish

Size: 25½ ft (7.7 m)

Range: temperate and tropical oceans

Scientific name: *Pristis pectinata*

Smooth hammerhead shark

This shark has one eye and one nostril on either side of its elongated head. This spacing of its features may improve its sight and sense of smell. It is known to attack people.

Size: 14 ft (4.3 m)

Range: all oceans

Scientific name: *Sphyrna zygaena*

Smooth hammer-head shark

Sandy dogfish

A small shark, the sandy dogfish lives on sandy and muddy seafloors, where it feeds on fish and bottom-living invertebrates. The female's eggs are laid in hard cases, which lodge among seaweed or other objects. The young dogfish hatch 5 to 11 months later and are about 4 inches (10 cm) long.

Sandy dogfish

Size: 23½–39½ in (60–100 cm)

Range: North Atlantic Ocean

Scientific name: *Scyliorhinus canicula*

Greater sawfish

Also known as the smalltooth, the greater sawfish has a long bladelike snout. Each side is studded with 24 or more large teeth. The sawfish lives on the seafloor in shallow water and uses its saw to dig in the sand and mud for small invertebrates to eat. It may also swim into a school of smaller fish and lash its toothed saw from side to side to stun prey.

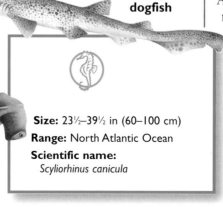

160

White shark

A large, aggressive hunter equipped with jagged triangular teeth, the white shark (also called the great white) kills seals, dolphins, and even other sharks. It also feeds on dead animals and waste. White sharks have been involved in a number of attacks on people.

Size: 19½ ft (6 m)
Range: Atlantic, Pacific, and Indian Oceans
Scientific name:
Carcharodon carcharias

White shark

Atlantic manta

With its huge pointed pectoral fins, the manta is the biggest of the rays. Like the whale shark, this giant feeds mostly on tiny animal plankton, which it filters from the water. It also eats fish. The manta often basks near the surface with the tips of its pectoral fins out of the water.

Size: 17 ft (5.2 m) long; 22 ft (6.7 m) wide
Range: Atlantic Ocean
Scientific name:
Manta birostris

Size: 24 in (61 cm)
Range: Arctic and North Atlantic Oceans
Scientific name:
Myxine glutinosa

Atlantic hagfish

Atlantic hagfish

The hagfish has no jaws, just a slitlike mouth surrounded by small tentacles. It feeds on crustaceans, but it also eats dead and dying fish. Using its toothed tongue, the hagfish bores into the prey's body and eats its flesh.

Atlantic manta

Sea lamprey

The adult sea lamprey is a blood-feeding parasite. It has no true jaws and uses its sucking, disklike mouth to attach itself to its prey so firmly that it is almost impossible to remove. A special substance in its mouth keeps the host's blood flowing so the lamprey can feed. The host often dies from blood loss.

Size: 35½ in (90 cm)
Range: Mediterranean Sea and Atlantic Ocean; larvae live in fresh water
Scientific name:
Petromyzon marinus

Sea lamprey

Size: up to 60 ft (18 m)
Range: all oceans
Scientific name:
Rhincodon typus

Whale shark

Whale shark

The whale shark is the biggest of all fish. Despite its size, it is not a fierce hunter and eats tiny animal plankton that it filters from the water. The shark opens its mouth and takes in a rush of water, which contains lots of small creatures. The water flows out through the gill slits, leaving the plankton in the mouth.

Skates, rays, and seafloor sharks

There are more than 300 different species of skates and rays found worldwide. Most have an extremely broad, flattened body and huge winglike fins, giving them a diamond shape. As they swim, the fish flap their fins up and down and appear almost to be flying through the water. Skates and rays spend much of their lives on or near the seafloor. Their flattened bodies make them hard to see as they lie half-covered with sand. Small openings, called spiracles, on the upper surface of the head allow them to breathe as they lie on the seafloor. They feed mostly on mollusks, crustaceans, and fish, and they also scavenge any dead creatures and other waste that falls to the seafloor.

Sharks are usually thought of as fast-swimming fish that live in the surface waters of the sea, but some are seafloor dwellers. Horn sharks, nurse sharks, and carpet sharks lurk on the bottom, moving only to catch passing prey.

Nurse shark

A slow-moving bottom dweller, the nurse shark has lots of short sharp teeth, ideal for crushing shellfish. The sensitive fleshy whiskers on its flattened head are thought to help it find hidden prey on the seafloor. This shark spends much of its time on the sea bottom and tends to crawl away if disturbed, rather than swim.

Skate

The skate's flattened body is covered with tiny spines, and a line of larger spines runs down the middle of the tail. The spines help the skate defend itself against attackers. The female lays her eggs in a leathery case with long tips at each corner, which is left on the seafloor. When the young fish hatch, they are about 8 inches (20 cm) long.

Horn shark

This shark has a long, tapering body and a large, blunt head. It gets its name from the sharp spines in front of the fins on its back. Active at night, it feeds on prey such as sea urchins, crabs, and worms on the seafloor. It crushes hard-shelled food with the large, flat teeth at the back of its jaws.

Horn shark

Camouflaged by its coloring and the many flaps of skin at the sides of its body, the **carpet shark** lies on the seafloor waiting for prey to come near.

Stingray

Stingray and spotted eagle ray

Both of these fish have long whiplike tails that they use to lash out at prey and enemies. Spines on the tail are linked to venom glands and can cause serious injury to humans. Rays have flattened teeth with which they crush the hard shells of prey such as crabs and mollusks.

Spotted eagle ray

163

Sturgeons, gars, and their relatives

A ll of these fish live in fresh water, but most sturgeons spend most of their adult life in the sea. They travel into rivers to lay their eggs, and the young remain there for several years, feeding and growing before making their first journey to the sea, where they spend their adult lives. Sturgeons are increasingly rare, partly because people kill the female fish to eat their eggs as a food called caviar. Gars, bichirs, and bowfins are separate groups of fish. They generally occur in areas where there is a dense growth of water plants.

Goldeyes, pirarucus, and elephant-snout fish belong to a group of about 220 species of freshwater fish. Most live in the southern half of the world, but there are two species of goldeyes in North America. They all eat fish and insects.

Bowfin

This fish lives in slow-moving waters with dense plant life. In spring the male clears a hollow in the riverbed and makes a nest of plant roots and gravel. The female then lays her eggs and the male guards them for 8 to 10 days until they hatch.

Bowfin

Size: 36 in (91 cm)
Range: northeastern U.S.A.
Scientific name: *Amia calva*

Longnose gar

As its name suggests, this gar has extremely long jaws, studded with sharp teeth. It hides among water plants, waiting for fish and shellfish to come near. It then dashes forward and seizes its prey. It lays eggs in spring in shallow water. The eggs are sticky and attach themselves to stones or waterweeds so they are not carried away by the current.

Size: 5 ft (1.5 m)
Range: North America
Scientific name:
Lepisosteus osseus

Bichir

A long-bodied fish covered with hard diamond-shaped scales, the bichir lives among water plants at the edges of rivers and lakes. It has an unusual dorsal fin made up of small flaglike sections, each supported by a bony spine. The bichir feeds mainly on fish, frogs, and newts.

Size: 15¾ in (40 cm)
Range: central Africa
Scientific name:
Polypterus weeksi

Bichir

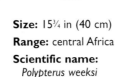

Longnose gar

Elephant-snout fish

This fish gets its name from its long trunklike snout. The muscles along its body are adapted to produce weak electric charges that set up an electric field in the water around the body. The fish can sense any disturbances in this field. This helps it find prey at night or in murky water.

Elephant-snout fish

Size: 31½ in (80 cm)
Range: Nile River
Scientific name:
Mormyrus kannume

Goldeye

The goldeye belongs to a small family of fish known as mooneyes. They have big golden eyes that provide good vision at night, when they are generally active. The goldeye has a large number of small, fine teeth, and it feeds mainly on insects and their larvae as well as on fish.

Goldeye

Size: 11¾–15¾ in (30–40 cm)
Range: North America
Scientific name:
Hiodon alosoides

Pirarucu

One of the largest freshwater fish in the world, the pirarucu may weigh up to 440 pounds (200 kg). It has large scales on its body but none on its head. Other fish and insect larvae are its main food. Pirarucus breed in sandy-bottomed water. The eggs are laid in a hollow in the riverbed, and the parents guard them until they hatch.

Pirarucu

Size: up to 13 ft (4 m)
Range: South America
Scientific name:
Arapaima gigas

 Paddlefish

Size: 6½ ft (2 m)
Range: Mississippi River and some of its tributaries
Scientific name:
Polyodon spathula

Atlantic sturgeon

Sturgeons spend most of their lives in the sea, feeding on worms and other invertebrates, but they lay their eggs in rivers. In spring, sturgeons migrate to rivers, where each female lays thousands of sticky black eggs. The eggs hatch in about a week. The young fish remain in the river for about three years before traveling to the sea.

Size: 10 ft (3 m)
Range: Europe
Scientific name:
Acipenser sturio

Paddlefish

The paddlefish is a relative of the sturgeon. It swims with its large mouth open and its lower jaw dropped. Small creatures in the water are caught on comblike structures in the fish's mouth. Eggs are laid in spring. Newly hatched fish do not have long snouts, which develop in two or three weeks.

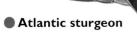

Atlantic sturgeon

Eels, tarpon, and herring

Most of these fish live in the sea, but some eels and tarpon spend at least part of their lives in fresh water. There are more than 730 species of eels. They live in all oceans, except in polar areas, and there are a few freshwater species. All have slender bodies and long fins on the back and belly.

Tarpon belong to a small family of marine fish that are related to eels and herring. They are slender-bodied fish with deeply forked tails. The herring group includes more than 350 species, some of which are important commercially as food fish, such as herring, sardines, and anchovies. Most are marine and live in schools in surface waters in the open sea or near coasts.

Sardine

The sardine is similar to the herring but has a more rounded body and larger scales. Schools of sardines swim in surface waters, feeding on animal plankton. Sardines are a valued food fish, and large numbers are caught by people every year.

Sardine

Size: 9¾ in (25 cm)
Range: coasts of Europe
Scientific name:
   Sardina pilchardus

Alewife

Alewife

A member of the herring group, the alewife feeds mostly on plankton and small fish. Although alewives live in the sea, they swim into rivers to mate and lay eggs, so they are often found in fresh water. Alewives that spend all their lives in lakes are only about half the size of sea-living alewives.

Size: 15 in (38 cm)
Range: Atlantic coast of North America; northeastern Pacific
Scientific name:
   Alosa pseudoharengus

Tarpon

A strong, fast-swimming fish, the tarpon feeds on many types of fish and on crabs. The female lays millions of eggs in coastal waters, but many of the larvae drift into rivers, where they remain until they grow larger.

Tarpon

Atlantic herring

Herring have long been an important food for people, and large numbers of these fish are caught every year. In the sea they are also preyed on by birds, other fish, dolphins, and seals. Herring feed on plankton, small crustaceans, and fish.

Atlantic herring

Size: 15¾ in (40 cm)
Range: Atlantic and Pacific Oceans
Scientific name:
   Clupea harengus harengus

Size: 4–7¾ ft (1.2–2.4 m)
Range: Atlantic Ocean
Scientific name:
   Tarpon atlanticus

Snipe eel

This deep-sea eel has an extremely long, thin body, with fins that run almost its whole length. It has narrow beaklike jaws and sharp backward-facing teeth, which it uses to trap prey such as fish and crustaceans.

Size: 4 ft (1.2 m)
Range: North Atlantic Ocean
Scientific name:
Notacanthus chemnitzii

Spiny eel

Spiny eel

The spiny eel has a long, slender body, but it is not a true eel. It has short spines on its back and belly. Little is known about this deep-sea fish, but it is thought to feed head down on the seafloor, eating bottom-living animals such as sea anemones.

Snipe eel

Size: 3¼–4 ft (1–1.2 m)
Range: Atlantic, Pacific, and Indian Oceans
Scientific name:
Nemichthys scolopaceus

Mediterranean moray

Like all of the 100 or so different species of moray eels found in warm seas, this moray has a scaleless, boldly patterned body; powerful jaws; and strong, sharp teeth. A fierce hunter, the Mediterranean moray usually hides among rocks underwater with only its head showing, watching out for prey such as fish, squid, and cuttlefish.

Mediterranean moray

Size: 4¼ ft (1.3 m)
Range: Northeastern Atlantic, Mediterranean Sea
Scientific name:
Muraena helena

European eel

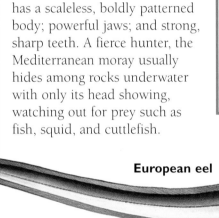

Size: 19¾–39½ in (50–100 cm)
Range: North Atlantic Ocean
Scientific name:
Anguilla anguilla

Conger eel

Conger eel

This eel is common on rocky North Atlantic shores. It usually lives in shallow water, where it hides among rocks and comes out to find fish, octopus, and other prey. Conger eels travel to deeper water to mate and lay their eggs. The eggs hatch into small transparent larvae that drift in the sea for a year or two before developing into small eels.

Size: 8¾ ft (2.7 m)
Range: coastal waters of North Atlantic Ocean
Scientific name: *Conger oceanius*

European eel

Young eels live in fresh water, where they feed on insects, crustaceans, and fish. When they are ready to breed, they swim as far as 3,000 miles (4,800 km) out to sea, where they mate, lay eggs, then die. The eggs hatch and the larvae drift for about three years. They then swim into rivers, and the cycle starts again.

Carp, bream, and piranhas

Carp, bream, roach, and their relatives, such as the bigmouth buffalo and the white sucker, belong to a group of about 2,700 freshwater fish. They dominate the streams, rivers, and lakes of Europe, northern Asia, and North America and are also found in Africa. Most have scales on the body, but not on the head, and a single fin on the back. These fish eat a wide range of prey, and some also feed on plant material.

Piranhas and pacus belong to a separate group of freshwater fish, most of which live in lakes and rivers in Central and South America. Some relatives of the piranha also live in Africa. Meat-eating piranhas have strong jaws and sharp teeth.

Goldfish

The colorful goldfish belongs to the carp family. In the wild, it lives in ponds and lakes where there are plenty of water plants, but it is best known as an ornamental fish, bred for keeping in aquariums and garden pools. Goldfish are now found all over the world.

Goldfish

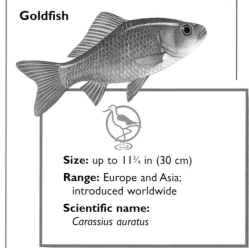

Size: up to 11¾ in (30 cm)

Range: Europe and Asia; introduced worldwide

Scientific name: *Carassius auratus*

Red piranha

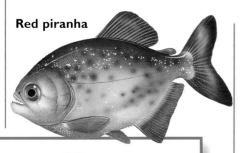

Size: up to 11¾ in (30 cm)

Range: northern South America

Scientific name: *Serrasalmus nattereri*

Red piranha

Piranhas are not large fish, but they swim in such large schools that together they can catch and kill animals much larger than themselves. Usually, however, they feed on fish, seeds, and fruit. Piranhas have strong jaws and razor-sharp teeth.

Pacu

Not all piranhas are fierce hunters. Some are peaceful plant-eating fish, such as the pacu. These fish feed on the many fruits and seeds that fall from the forest trees bordering the rivers where they live. They use their strong teeth to crush them. Plant-eating piranhas are slower swimmers than the meat-eating species.

Size: 27½ in (70 cm)

Range: South America

Scientific name: *Colossoma nigripinnis*

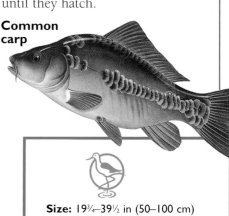

Pacu

Common carp

The carp is a sturdy, deep-bodied fish. It usually lives in slow-moving water where there is plenty of plant life. It feeds mostly on crustaceans and insect larvae as well as some plants. The eggs are laid in shallow water, where they stick to plants until they hatch.

Common carp

Size: 19¾–39½ in (50–100 cm)

Range: southern Europe; introduced into many other areas

Scientific name: *Cyprinus carpio*

Roach

Bigmouth buffalo

This powerful fish feeds on crustaceans and insect larvae as well as some plant material. In spring adults gather in shallow water, where females lay as many as 500,000 eggs. The young fish stay in the shallow breeding area for some months, feeding on plankton.

Size: 3¼ ft (1 m)
Range: North America
Scientific name:
Ictiobus cyprinellus

Size: 13¾–18 in (35–46 cm)
Range: Europe, western Asia
Scientific name:
Rutilus rutilus

Roach

This common river fish feeds on insects and their larvae as well as mollusks, crustaceans, and plants. It, in turn, is an important food for many fish-eating birds and mammals. Roach breed in shallow water, and the eggs stick to plants while they develop. The young hatch in about two weeks.

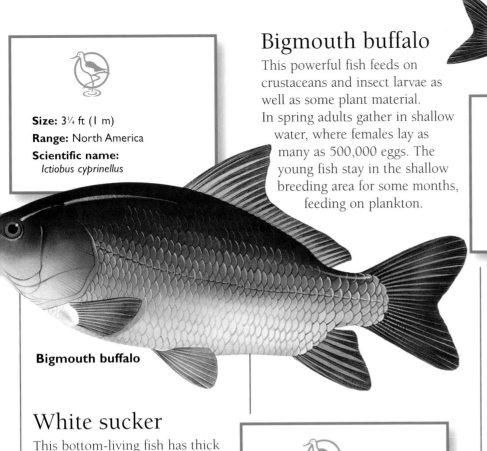

Bigmouth buffalo

White sucker

This bottom-living fish has thick suckerlike lips, which give it its common name. It feeds on insect larvae, crustaceans, and mollusks as well as some plants. White suckers breed in spring, laying their eggs at night in gravel-bottomed streams. The eggs sink to the bottom, where they stay among the gravel until they hatch.

Size: 11¾–20½ in (30–52 cm)
Range: North America
Scientific name:
Catostomus commersoni

White sucker

Tench

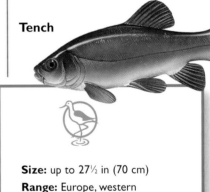

Size: up to 27½ in (70 cm)
Range: Europe, western to central Asia
Scientific name: *Tinca tinca*

Tench

A relative of the carp, the tench has a thickset body and rounded fins. The scales on the body are extremely small and covered with mucus. It usually feeds on the river- or lakebed on insect larvae, crustaceans, and mollusks. Tench breed in shallow water, shedding their eggs onto plants.

Bream

This fish uses its mouth to gather insect larvae, snails, and worms from the river bottom. It lives in schools and usually feeds at night. Bream breed in late spring or summer in shallow water. The eggs stick to water plants and hatch in about 12 days.

Size: 9–11 in (23–28 cm)
Range: Europe, northern Asia
Scientific name:
Abramis brama

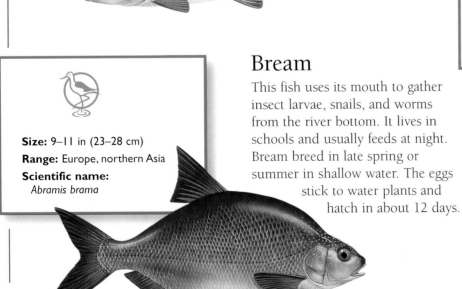

Bream

169

Catfish and relatives

There are more than 2,400 species in the catfish group, ranging from tiny fish just over ¾ of an inch (2 cm) long to giant forms measuring 5 feet (1.5 m) or more and weighing as much as 100 pounds (45 kg). Most live in rivers and freshwater lakes in the warmer parts of the world, but there are a number of sea-living species. More kinds of catfish live in South America than anywhere else. Catfish do not have small, rounded scales like most other fish. Some have bony plates that cover their bodies like jointed armor. Catfish are bottom dwellers and find their food by touch and taste, digging in the mud of a river- or lakebed until the sensitive whiskers, or barbels, around the mouth find prey. The whiskered appearance these barbels give is the reason for the catfish's common name.

Australian freshwater catfish

The second dorsal fin and the anal fin of this fish form one fin that runs right around its body. The spines on its dorsal and pectoral fins can cause painful wounds if touched. Sensory whiskers, or barbels, around the mouth help it find food, mainly mussels, prawns, and worms.

Australian freshwater catfish

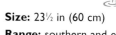

Size: 23½ in (60 cm)
Range: southern and eastern Australia
Scientific name: *Tandanus tandanus*

Surubim

This South American catfish has a long snout and a slender body, marked with dark stripes and blotches. It spends most of its life on the riverbed, where it feeds on invertebrate animals. The sensitive whiskers, or barbels, around its mouth help it find food.

Size: 19¾–35½ in (50–90 cm)
Range: South America
Scientific name: *Pseudoplatystoma fasciatum*

Surubim

Candirú

A tiny, delicate catfish, the candirú, also called the carnerd, lives on the blood of other fish. With small fish, it simply bites the skin and then feeds, but it may get inside the gill system of larger fish and stay there sucking blood. It is usually active at night and buries itself in the riverbed when not feeding.

Candirú

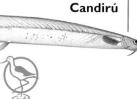

Size: up to 2 in (5 cm)
Range: South America
Scientific name: *Vandellia cirrhosa*

Cascarudo

The body of this little catfish is covered with overlapping bony plates, which help protect it from enemies. In the breeding season, the male fish makes a nest for the eggs among floating plants by blowing bubbles of air and mucus to form a foamy mass.

Size: 7 in (18 cm)
Range: tropical South America
Scientific name: *Callichthys callichthys*

Cascarudo

Glass catfish

As its name suggests, this fish is transparent, and many of the internal organs can be seen through the body. It has a long anal fin, a tiny dorsal fin, and a slightly lopsided tail fin. It sometimes balances vertically on the lower part of this tail fin. Unlike most catfish, it moves in small schools in surface waters during the day. It has become a popular species with aquarium owners.

Size: 4 in (10 cm)
Range: Malaysia, Indonesia
Scientific name:
Kryptopterus bicirrhis

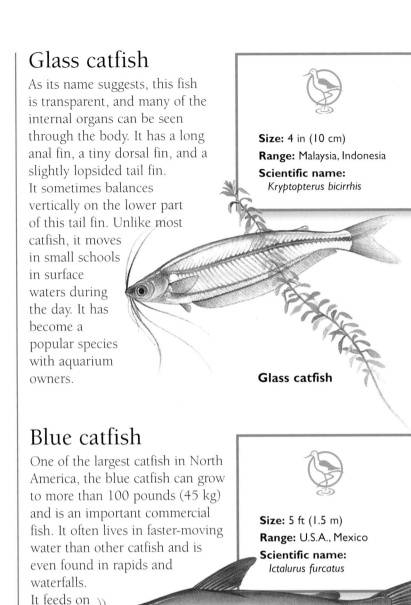

Glass catfish

Blue catfish

One of the largest catfish in North America, the blue catfish can grow to more than 100 pounds (45 kg) and is an important commercial fish. It often lives in faster-moving water than other catfish and is even found in rapids and waterfalls. It feeds on fish and crayfish. Its eggs are laid on the river- or lakebed, and both parents guard the nest and then the young.

Size: 5 ft (1.5 m)
Range: U.S.A., Mexico
Scientific name:
Ictalurus furcatus

Blue catfish

Sea catfish

This sea-living catfish is most active at night, when it feeds on crabs, shrimp, and fish. It breeds in summer, and as the eggs are laid, the male takes them in his mouth, where they incubate. He cannot eat during this time. The young fish may also swim into the male's mouth for safety after hatching.

Size: 11¾ in (30 cm)
Range: western Atlantic Ocean
Scientific name:
Aruis felis

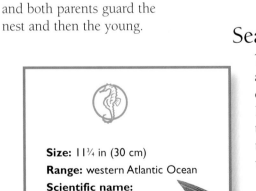

Sea catfish

Walking catfish

This catfish lives in ponds or temporary pools that may disappear in long dry periods. When this happens, the fish can move over land to another pool by making snakelike movements with its body and using its pectoral fins as "legs." It feeds on fish and invertebrate animals.

Walking catfish

Size: 11¾ in (30 cm)
Range: India, Sri Lanka, Southeast Asia; introduced into U.S.A.
Scientific name:
Clarias batrachus

Wels

A large catfish, the wels has a broad head and long anal fin. It lives in slow-moving or still waters and is usually active at night, hiding in plants near the bottom during the day. Fish are its main food, but it also eats frogs, birds, and even small mammals such as water voles.

Size: 3¼–10 ft (1–3 m)
Range: central and eastern Europe
Scientific name:
Silurus glanis

Wels

Electric eel, salmon, hatchetfish, and pike

The electric eel is the only species in its family. It is not a true eel but has a similar long body. As its name suggests, it is able to produce electric charges.

In a separate group is the hatchetfish, a deep-sea fish that has light-producing organs on its body. These help the hatchetfish recognize its own kind in the darkness of the deep sea and confuse predators.

The salmon family contains about 76 species that live in both fresh water and the sea. Some migrate from the sea into rivers to lay eggs. The smelt belong to a different group of sea fish, but they, too, travel up rivers to breed. Pike are a small group of freshwater fish.

Hatchetfish

This fish lives in water 1,300 to 2,000 feet (400 to 600 m) deep, but each night it comes up near the surface to find animal plankton to eat. On its belly are rows of light-producing organs, which give out a pale light. This confuses predators about the size and shape of the fish's body, making it harder to catch.

Hatchetfish

Size: 2¾ in (7 cm)

Range: warm and tropical areas of all oceans

Scientific name: *Argyropelecus aculeatus*

Northern pike

Northern pike

A fierce predator, the pike lurks among plants, keeping watch for prey. Young pike feed mainly on invertebrates, but adults catch other fish and even birds and small mammals. Female pike are larger than males and may weigh 50 pounds (23 kg) or more.

Size: 5 ft (1.5 m)

Range: northern Europe, Russia, Alaska, Canada, northern U.S.A.

Scientific name: *Esox lucius*

Smelt

Smelt are sea-living fish that go into fresh water to breed. In winter adult fish leave the sea to travel up rivers. In spring the females shed their eggs onto gravel on the riverbed or onto plants. When the young fish are large enough, they swim to the sea, where they grow and mature.

Size: 11¾ in (30 cm)

Range: North Atlantic Ocean

Scientific name: *Osmerus eperlanus*

Electric eel

Electric eel

Size: 7¾ ft (2.4 m)

Range: South America

Scientific name: *Electrophorus electricus*

Special muscles in the electric eel's body release high-voltage electric charges into the water. The eel uses these shocks to kill prey, usually other fish, or to defend itself from enemies. The charge can give a human a severe shock.

Smelt

Grayling

A member of the salmon family, the grayling has a high sail-like fin on its back and a forked tail. It eats insects and their larvae as well as crustaceans and mollusks. In spring the female makes a hollow in gravel in shallow water for her eggs. The eggs hatch three to four weeks later.

Grayling

Size: 18 in (46 cm)
Range: northern Europe
Scientific name:
  Thymallus thymallus

Arctic char

Arctic char spend most of their lives in polar seas, feeding on fish and mollusks. When they are ready to breed, they swim into rivers, where females lay eggs among gravel on the riverbed. The young eventually make their way back to the sea. Some arctic char live in lakes.

Size: 9¾–37¾ in (25–96 cm)
Range: Arctic and North Atlantic Oceans
Scientific name:
  Salvelinus alpinus

Arctic char

Sockeye salmon

Size: 33 in (84 cm)
Range: Pacific Ocean
Scientific name:
  Oncorhynchus nerka

Sockeye salmon

When they are about four years old, sockeye salmon move from the ocean to rivers. There they swim to the breeding grounds where they were hatched, sometimes as far as 1,000 miles (1,600 km) inland. After laying their eggs, the adult salmon die. The young spend up to three years in fresh water before migrating to the sea.

Rainbow trout

Rainbow trout

Now farmed in large quantities, rainbow trout are an important food fish. In the wild, rainbow trout live in rivers, although some spend part of their lives in the sea. In spring the female makes a shallow nest in a stream and lays her eggs, which are then fertilized and covered over by the male.

Size: up to 3¼ ft (1 m)
Range: western North America; introduced worldwide
Scientific name: *Salmo gairdneri*

Atlantic salmon

Atlantic salmon

Like the sockeye, most Atlantic salmon swim into rivers to breed. The female makes a shallow nest on the riverbed in winter and lays her eggs, which are fertilized by the male. The eggs hatch the following spring, and the young spend two to six years in the river before going to sea.

Size: up to 5 ft (1.5 m)
Range: North Atlantic Ocean
Scientific name:
  Salmo salar

173

Cod, anglerfish, and cusk eels

There are about 480 species of fish in the cod group, of which only 5 live in fresh water. The rest live in the sea, mostly in the northern half of the world, and include some of the most popular of all food fish, such as cod, haddock, hake, and ling. They hunt for their food, preying on other fish and invertebrate creatures. Many have a sensory whisker, or barbel, on the chin that helps them find food on the seabed.

The anglerfish include about 300 species. All have a large head and an extremely wide mouth filled with rows of sharp teeth. Most have a special spine on the head that they use as a lure to attract prey.

Cusk eels belong to a separate group and are small eel-like fish.

New Providence cusk eel

This little eel-like fish was discovered in 1967 and is known only from a few freshwater pools in the Bahamas. Most of its head is bare of scales, but it does have small scales covering its body. Other varieties of cusk eels live in the deep ocean, and still others live in caves.

○ **New Providence cusk eel**

Size: 4¼ in (11 cm)
Range: Bahamas
Scientific name:
  Lucifuga spelaeotes

Burbot

Size: 19¾–39½ in (50–100 cm)
Range: Canada, northern U.S.A., northern Europe, Asia
Scientific name: *Lota lota*

Rough-head grenadier

A relative of the cod, the rough-head grenadier is a deep-sea fish with a large head and a tapering tail. Its body scales are rough and toothed. Males make loud sounds by vibrating the swim bladder (a gas-filled sac inside the body) with special muscles.

Rough-head grenadier

Size: 35½–39½ in (90–100 cm)
Range: North Atlantic Ocean
Scientific name:
  Macrourus berglax

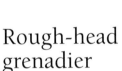

Burbot

One of the few fish in the cod group that lives in fresh water, the burbot hides among water plants by day and comes out at dawn and dusk to feed. Adults eat fish, crustaceans, and insects, whereas young burbot feed on insect larvae and small shrimp. They lay their eggs at night in winter. One female may lay as many as three million eggs.

174

Ling

The ling is most common in rocky-bottomed ocean waters, where it eats fish and large crustaceans. Although usually a deepwater fish, it may live in shallower areas where there are rocks. It breeds in spring and summer, and one female may lay as many as 60 million eggs.

Ling

Size: 5–6½ ft (1.5–2 m)
Range: northeastern Atlantic Ocean
Scientific name: *Molva molva*

Size: 35½ in (90 cm)
Range: North Pacific Ocean
Scientific name: *Theragra chalcogramma*

O **Atlantic cod**

Atlantic cod

Cod usually swim in schools in surface waters but will search for food such as other fish and worms on the seafloor. Cod is an extremely valuable food fish for humans, but because of overfishing, fewer cod are caught each year.

Size: 4 ft (1.2 m)
Range: North Atlantic Ocean
Scientific name: *Gadus morhua*

Walleye pollock

Walleye pollock

The pollock has a long, tapering body, three fins on its back, and two on its underside. Its head and mouth are large, and it has bigger eyes than most other kinds of cod. Unlike many cod, it feeds in midwaters, catching crustaceans and small fish.

Anglerfish

On its large head, the angler has a spine tipped with a flap of skin. It uses this as a fishing lure. The fish lies on the seafloor and moves its lure to attract other fish. When something comes within reach, the angler opens its huge mouth and water flows in with the prey.

Atlantic football fish

This deep-sea anglerfish has a round body studded with bony plates, each with a central spine. On its head is a lure, which carries a light-producing organ. It uses this lure to attract prey in the darkness of the deep sea.

Haddock

The haddock is a member of the cod family and feeds on bottom-living worms, mollusks, and brittle stars as well as fish. It gathers in schools to spawn, and the eggs are left to float in the surface waters until they hatch. Young haddock often find shelter among the tentacles of large jellyfish.

Atlantic football fish

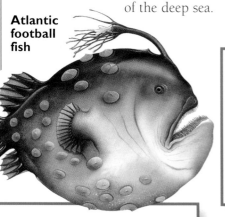

Size: 30 in (76 cm)
Range: North Atlantic Ocean
Scientific name: *Melanogrammus aeglefinus*

Anglerfish

Size: 23½ in (60 cm)
Range: all oceans
Scientific name: *Himantolophus groenlandicus*

O **Haddock**

Size: 3¼–6½ ft (1–2 m)
Range: coastal waters of Europe
Scientific name: *Lophius piscatorius*

175

Perchlike fish

This is the largest and most varied of all groups of fish, and species live in almost every watery habitat. This group is made up of at least 9,300 species such as sea bass, cichlids, gobies, and wrasses. These fish have a wide range of body forms and include fish as different as the barracuda, angelfish, swordfish, and Siamese fightingfish. Despite their differences, all perchlike fish have one or two fins on the back, and most have pelvic fins close to the head. The pelvic fins usually have a spine and five rays.

Orange-throat darter

This little member of the perch family feeds on insects and animal plankton. A breeding male has an orange throat and breast, whereas the female has a pale throat. The male chooses a nest site in a river and guards the eggs.

Orange-throat darter

Size: 3¼ in (8 cm)
Range: central U.S.A.
Scientific name:
Etheostoma spectabile

Perch

Perch

Barred markings on the perch's body help camouflage it among water plants. It lives in slow-moving water and feeds on fish. Perch breed in shallow water in spring. The eggs are shed in long strings that wind around plants or other objects. They hatch in about eight days, and the young fish feed on plankton.

Size: 13¾–19¾ in (35–50 cm)
Range: Europe
Scientific name:
Perca fluviatilis

Black grouper

Size: 4 ft (1.2 m)
Range: Atlantic coastal waters; eastern gulf of Mexico
Scientific name:
Mycteroperca bonaci

Black grouper

This common grouper may weigh up to 50 pounds (23 kg) when fully grown. It has a large head and irregular dark markings on the sides of its body. It is not a particularly fast-moving fish and tends to lurk among rocks, waiting for prey to swim by. When something comes near, the grouper opens its large mouth and sucks in the prey with a mouthful of water. Young fish usually stay in shallow coastal areas, but adults move into deeper waters.

Greater amberjack

A relative of the pompano, the greater amberjack is a large fish with a sleek body and a deeply forked tail. It feeds on many species of fish and is itself caught as a game fish.

Size: up to 6 ft (1.8 m)
Range: western Atlantic Ocean
Scientific name:
Seriola dumerili

Greater amberjack

Bluefish

An extremely fierce hunter, the bluefish kills more prey than it can eat and feeds on almost any fish, including young of its own species. Schools of bluefish travel together, often following shoals of prey fish. Young bluefish, which are known as snappers, also form their own schools.

Bluefish

Size: up to 4 ft (1.2 m)
Range: warm and tropical waters of Atlantic, Indian, and western Pacific Oceans
Scientific name: *Pomatomus saltatrix*

Florida pompano

The pompano has a rounded snout and a fairly wide body, which tapers sharply to a forked tail. It feeds mainly on mollusks and crustaceans, which it finds in the mud and sand of the seafloor. It is an excellent and valuable food fish.

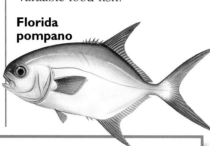

Florida pompano

Size: 17¾–25½ in (45–65 cm)
Range: western Atlantic Ocean
Scientific name: *Trachinotus carolinus*

Giant sea bass

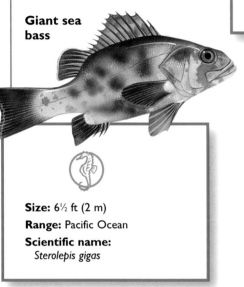

Giant sea bass

Size: 6½ ft (2 m)
Range: Pacific Ocean
Scientific name: *Sterolepis gigas*

This sea bass really is a giant. Some weigh more than 550 pounds (250 kg) and live for more than 70 years. They eat fish and crustaceans and are themselves popular as food fish. Young fish are redder in color and wider bodied than adults. They gradually develop the adult appearance by the time they are about 12 or 13 years old.

Size: up to 5 ft (1.5 m)
Range: warm and tropical waters of all oceans
Scientific name: *Coryphaena hippurus*

Dolphinfish

Dolphinfish

The brightly colored dolphinfish is easily identified by the large fin that runs along its back. The forehead of the male fish becomes steeper as he grows older; otherwise males and females look alike. Dolphinfish move in small schools and eat fish, squid, and crustaceans. They are often seen around patches of floating seaweed, where their prey may hide.

Size: 30 in (76 cm)
Range: western Atlantic Ocean, including Caribbean Sea
Scientific name: *Ocyurus chrysurus*

Yellowtail snapper

Snappers are common around coral reefs and are a popular fish for people to eat. This species is easily recognized by its bright yellow tail and the yellow stripe along each side. It feeds mostly on other fish and small crustaceans.

Yellowtail snapper

Blue parrotfish

Size: up to 4 ft (1.2 m)

Range: western Atlantic Ocean, Caribbean Sea

Scientific name:
Scarus coeruleus

Blue parrotfish

As its name suggests, this fish has beaklike jaws. Its teeth are joined together to form strong plates, which it uses to scrape algae from coral reefs. When young, these parrotfish are light blue. They turn darker blue as they get older. Old males also develop a bump on the snout.

Clown anemonefish

This boldly striped fish lives protected among the tentacles of large sea anemones. It sometimes cleans waste from its host, and it may scare away other fish that might eat the anenome. The anemone's stinging tentacles do not harm the anemonefish.

Clown anemonefish

Size: 2¼ in (6 cm)

Range: Pacific Ocean

Scientific name:
Amphiprion percula

Queen angelfish

Despite its colorful markings, this angelfish can be difficult to see among the bright corals. It has long fins on its back and belly that extend past the tail fin. It feeds on sponges and other invertebrate animals. Young queen angelfish may act as cleaners—they pick and eat parasites off other fish.

Size: up to 17¾ in (45 cm)

Range: Atlantic Ocean and Caribbean Sea

Scientific name:
Holacanthus ciliaris

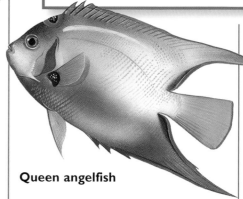

Queen angelfish

Sweetlip emperor

Copperband butterflyfish

Copperband butterflyfish

This fish uses its long beaklike snout to reach into crevices in the coral and find small creatures to eat. The large eyespot near its tail fin may confuse predators into thinking the copperband is larger than it really is.

Size: 7¾ in (20 cm)

Range: Indian and Pacific Oceans

Scientific name:
Chelmon rostratus

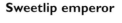

Size: 35½ in (90 cm)

Range: Australia

Scientific name:
Lethrinus chrysostomus

Scup

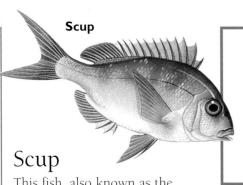

Scup

Size: 18 in (46 cm)
Range: Atlantic coast of North America
Scientific name: *Stenotomus chrysops*

This fish, also known as the northern porgy, has a strongly forked tail, and spines on both its dorsal and anal fins. It finds crustaceans, worms, and other food on the seafloor. In spring the adults breed in coastal waters, and the eggs float freely until they hatch.

Size: 13¾–19¾ in (35–50 cm)
Range: Atlantic Ocean and Mediterranean Sea
Scientific name: *Pagellus bogaraveo*

Red sea bream

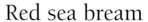

Black drum

Red sea bream

This fish has a reddish flush to its body and fins and a dark spot above its pectoral fin. Young red sea bream are paler in color and may not have a dark spot. The young fish swim in large schools in shallow waters, feeding on crustaceans. Adults live in smaller groups in deeper waters and eat fish as well as crustaceans.

Size: 4–6 ft (1.2–1.8 m)
Range: western Atlantic Ocean
Scientific name: *Pogonias cromis*

Black drum

This large fish can weigh as much as 146 pounds (66 kg). A bottom feeder, it eats mollusks and crustaceans, which it is able to crush with special flat teeth in its throat. Oysters are a favorite food, and black drums can cause a great deal of damage to commercial oyster beds. They make a booming drumlike sound during the mating season.

Size: 15¾ in (40 cm)
Range: eastern Atlantic Ocean, Mediterranean Sea
Scientific name: *Mullus surmuletus*

Sweetlip emperor

This heavy-bodied fish hunts for food around coral reefs. Its name may come from its rather large lips. It has a long snout and no scales on its cheeks. It has deep red fins, dark barring on its sides, and red patches around the eyes. It can grow to more than 20 pounds (9 kg) and is an extremely popular food fish.

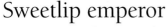

Red mullet

Red mullet

This fish searches for food on the seafloor, using the sensory whiskers, or barbels, on its chin to help it find invertebrates. Once prey is found, the red mullet digs it out of the sand or mud. It is able to change color to blend with its surroundings, varying between day and night.

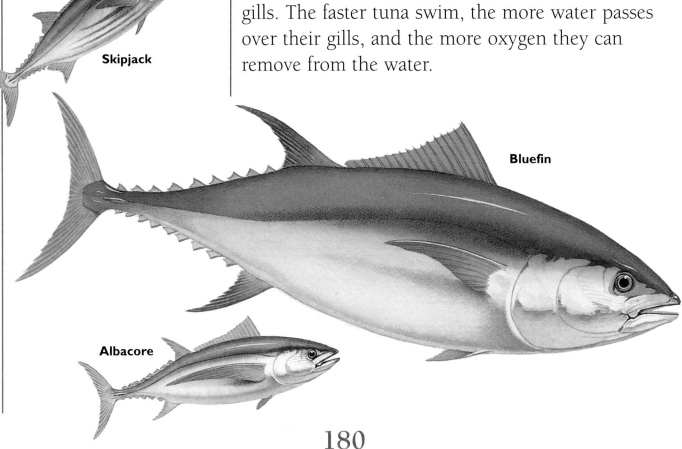

Bigeye

Tuna

Four species of tuna

The bluefin is the biggest of the tuna. It can grow to 10 feet (3 m) long and weigh more than 1,200 pounds (540 kg)—as much as seven or eight adult people. A fast swimmer, the bluefin has been known to cross the Atlantic in 199 days. The bigeye tuna grows to nearly 7¾ feet (2.4 m) long and can weigh more than 400 pounds (180 kg). The albacore and skipjack are smaller—up to 5 feet (1.5 m) and 3 feet (90 cm), respectively. The skipjack gets its name from its habit of sometimes "skipping" over the surface of the water as it chases its prey.

Among the fastest of all fish, tuna are shaped for speed and can swim at 50 miles per hour (80 km/h). They are the most streamlined of all fish, with a pointed head and a torpedo-shaped body tapering to a narrow tail stalk and a crescent tail. The 13 species of tuna live in the surface waters of warm and tropical oceans. All are hunters, feeding mainly on fish and squid. Many swim in large schools, but the biggest fish swim in smaller groups or alone.

Tuna rarely, if ever, stop swimming, because they must swim to breathe. Fish get their oxygen from water, not air; their gills take oxygen out of the water that flows past their gills. Most fish use muscles to pump water over their gills, but tuna cannot do this. They must keep swimming at all times to create a constant flow of water over their gills. The faster tuna swim, the more water passes over their gills, and the more oxygen they can remove from the water.

Skipjack

Bluefin

Albacore

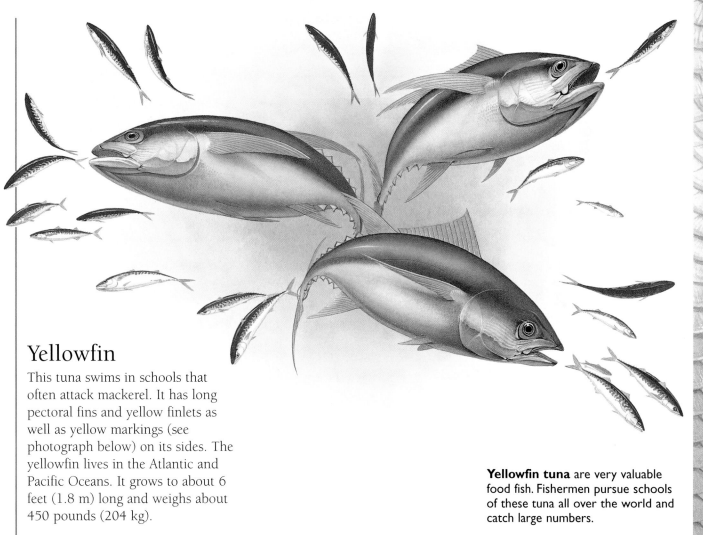

Yellowfin

This tuna swims in schools that often attack mackerel. It has long pectoral fins and yellow finlets as well as yellow markings (see photograph below) on its sides. The yellowfin lives in the Atlantic and Pacific Oceans. It grows to about 6 feet (1.8 m) long and weighs about 450 pounds (204 kg).

Yellowfin tuna are very valuable food fish. Fishermen pursue schools of these tuna all over the world and catch large numbers.

Blue tang

This fish has extremely sharp movable spines on each side of its tail that it can raise to wound an enemy. The young are bright yellow with blue markings. This color changes as the fish matures, becoming blue all over by the time it is an adult.

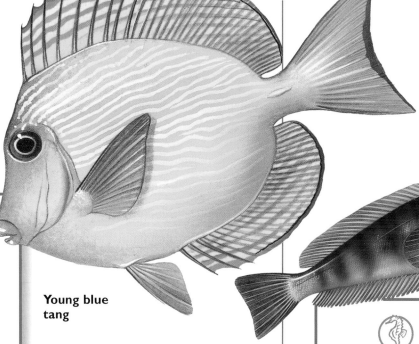

Size: 12 in (30.5 cm)
Range: western Atlantic Ocean, Caribbean Sea
Scientific name:
Acanthurus coeruleus

Young blue tang

Antarctic cod

Size: 24 in (61 cm)
Range: coastal waters of Antarctica
Scientific name:
Notothenia coriiceps

Moorish idol

This spectacular fish has bold stripes and a protruding snout. It has a wide body and long, swept-back fins. Although it is a relative of the blue tang, the moorish idol does not have tail spines. But a young fish does have a sharp spine at each corner of its mouth. These spines drop off as the fish grows bigger.

Size: 7 in (18 cm)
Range: Indian and Pacific Oceans
Scientific name:
Zanclus cornutus

Moorish idol

Antarctic cod

This fish belongs to a group known as icefish. Many of them have a special substance in their blood that lowers its freezing point. Because of this, icefish are able to survive at temperatures as low as 28.5°F (-1.9°C), at which most fish would freeze to death. This cod is a bottom dweller and eats mollusks, crustaceans, and worms as well as some algae.

Atlantic spadefish

Atlantic spadefish

The coloration of this fish changes as it grows. Young fish are black, becoming silvery gray with dark, vertical bars down the sides. These become less clear in large adults. Spadefish feed mostly on small invertebrates. They are often seen swimming around shipwrecks.

Size: 18–35½ in (46–90 cm)
Range: western Atlantic Ocean
Scientific name:
Chaetodipterus faber

Dragonet

The male dragonet is a striking fish, with his long blue-and-yellow fins. The female is smaller and does not have extended fins. Dragonets lie half-buried in the sand on the seafloor, watching for bottom-dwelling crustaceans and worms—their main food. They breed in spring or summer, and males perform displays with their decorative fins to win females.

Size: 11¾ in (30 cm)
Range: eastern Atlantic Ocean, Mediterranean Sea
Scientific name: *Callionymus lyra*

Dragonet

Northern stargazer

The northern stargazer has a large head with its mouth pointing upward; its eyes are on top of its head, also facing upward. This allows the stargazer to lie partly buried on the seafloor, with only its eyes and mouth uncovered, watching for prey such as fish and crustaceans. Behind the eyes there is a special area of electric organs. These produce electric charges that the stargazer uses to stun prey. Stargazers breed in deeper offshore waters. The young fish drift into coastal waters, where they adjust to the bottom-dwelling life of adults.

Size: up to 12 in (30.5 cm)
Range: Atlantic coast of North America
Scientific name: *Astroscopus guttatus*

Northern stargazer

Northern clingfish

Size: 6 in (15 cm)
Range: Pacific Ocean
Scientific name: *Gobiesox maeandricus*

Northern clingfish

The northern clingfish has a smooth body and a broad head. Its dorsal and anal fins are set back near its tail. Like all clingfish, its pelvic fins form part of a sucking disk on its belly. It uses this to cling to rocks or other surfaces to keep from being washed away by strong tides in the coastal waters where it lives. Mollusks and crustaceans are the clingfish's main food.

Size: 4¾ in (12 cm)
Range: western Atlantic Ocean, Gulf of Mexico, Caribbean Sea
Scientific name: *Ophioblennius atlanticus*

Redlip blenny

Redlip blenny

This fish is identified by the bristles on its rounded snout, its red lips, and red-tipped dorsal fin. It lives on rocky or coral-bottomed seafloors, where it searches for small invertebrates to eat. The female lays her eggs among coral or under rocks, and the male guards them until they hatch.

Rock goby

There are more than 1,800 kinds of gobies. Most live in the sea, but there are some freshwater species. The rock goby is one of the larger gobies but is typical of the group, with its big, blunt head and rounded tail. Its pelvic fins form a sucking disk, which it uses to cling to rocks. It feeds on small invertebrates and fish.

Size: 4¾ in (12 cm)
Range: North Atlantic Ocean and Mediterranean Sea
Scientific name: *Gobius paganellus*

Rock goby

Siamese fightingfish

Some males of these freshwater fish are bred in captivity to take part in staged fights, but in the wild males battle with rivals over territory. In the breeding season, the male blows a bubble nest made of mucus. When the female lays her eggs, the male fertilizes them and spits them into the nest to keep them safe.

Size: 2¼ in (6 cm)
Range: Thailand
Scientific name:
  Betta splendens

Siamese fightingfish

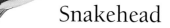

Snakehead

Snakehead

This long-bodied fish belongs to a small group of freshwater fish that live in tropical Africa and Asia. It usually lives in oxygen-poor waters and has special structures in its gills that help take some oxygen from the air. It can even survive out of water as long as it burrows into mud to keep its skin moist.

Size: 3¼ ft (1 m)
Range: India, China, Southeast Asia
Scientific name:
  Channa striatus

Man-o'-war fish

Best known for its habit of living among the trailing tentacles of the Portuguese man-of-war jellyfish, this fish does not seem to be affected by its host's stinging cells. It may even prevent them from working. The jellyfish seems not to notice the man-o'-war fish, even though the fish probably removes parasites and other debris from its host's body.

Man-o'-war fish

Size: 8¾ in (22 cm)
Range: tropical areas of Indian, Pacific, and western Atlantic Oceans
Scientific name:
  Nomeus gronovii

Blue marlin

The blue marlin is one of the fastest of all fish and has the streamlined body and crescent-shaped tail typical of high-speed swimmers. It weighs at least 400 pounds (180 kg) and has a long beaklike nose, which it may use to stun smaller schooling fish, squid, and other prey.

Size: 10–15 ft (3–4.6 m)
Range: worldwide in tropical and warm seas
Scientific name:
  Makaira nigricans

Blue marlin

184

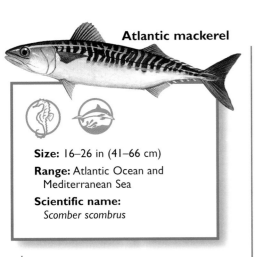
Atlantic mackerel

Size: 16–26 in (41–66 cm)
Range: Atlantic Ocean and Mediterranean Sea
Scientific name:
  Scomber scombrus

Atlantic mackerel

Mackerel move in large schools and make regular migration journeys. In spring and summer they go north, where they breed; in winter they return south again. A female may produce as many as 450,000 eggs, which float in the water until they hatch about four days later. Adult mackerel eat small fish and crustaceans; young fish feed mainly on animal plankton and fish larvae.

Wahoo

Unlike its relatives the mackerel and tuna, the wahoo is not a schooling fish. It usually swims alone or in small groups. It has a longer, thinner body than most tunas and a narrow snout that is equipped with many strong teeth. A fast swimmer, it can reach speeds of up to 41 miles per hour (66 km/h) when chasing prey.

Wahoo

Size: up to 6½ ft (2 m)
Range: worldwide in tropical seas
Scientific name:
  Acanthocybium solanderi

Swordfish

The huge, spectacular swordfish is a fast, active hunter with a streamlined body and a sickle-shaped fin on its back. It feeds on small fish as well as squid, and it may use its extremely long snout to strike at schooling fish. Young swordfish do not have a long snout; it develops as they grow.

Size: 6½–16 ft (2–4.9 m)
Range: worldwide in warm and tropical seas
Scientific name:
  Xiphias gladius

Swordfish

Size: up to 6 ft (1.8 m)
Range: worldwide
Scientific name:
  Sphyraena barracuda

Great barracuda

Sailfish

This fast-swimming fish has a tall sail-like fin on its back and long curved jaws. It is a fierce predator that eats squid and almost any kind of fish it can find. Sailfish breed in the open sea. The female sheds several million eggs, which float in surface waters until they hatch.

Great barracuda

There are about 18 different kinds of barracuda living in warm and tropical waters of all oceans. The great barracuda is typical, with its long, slender body and large jaws and teeth. A fierce predator around coral reefs, it has been known to attack people if disturbed. Young barracudas may swim in schools, but larger fish hunt alone.

Size: 12 ft (3.6 m)
Range: worldwide in warm and tropical waters
Scientific name:
  Istiophorus platypterus

Sailfish

185

Flyingfish, lanternfish, and lizardfish

The flyingfish belongs to a large group of mostly sea-living fish, which also includes halfbeaks, needlefish, sauries, and garfish. Most are active near or above the surface of the water. Flyingfish can actually lift themselves into the air with their pectoral fins and use their rapidly beating tails to help them glide short distances over the surface. Lanternfish are deep-sea fish found in all oceans from the Arctic to the Antarctic. They have light-producing organs on their bodies. The lizardfish and its relative the bummalo both live in shallow coastal waters, where they prey on small fish.

Wrestling halfbeak

This small, slender fish helps control mosquitos by feeding on their larvae. Male fish are aggressive and fight one another by sparring with their long jaws.

Wrestling halfbeak

Size: 2¾ in (7 cm)
Range: Thailand, Malaysia
Scientific name:
  Dermogenys pusillus

Tropical two-wing flyingfish

Tropical two-wing flyingfish

Size: 9 in (23 cm)
Range: all oceans
Scientific name:
  Exocetus volitans

The flyingfish escapes its enemies by leaping up and gliding over the surface of the water with the aid of its winglike fins. Unlike some other species, this flyingfish has only one pair of "wings."

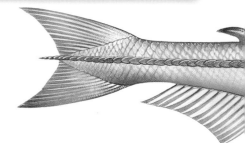

Size: 17¾ in (45 cm)
Range: Atlantic Ocean
Scientific name:
  Hemiramphus brasiliensis

Ballyhoo

Lanternfish

This fish has groups of light-producing organs on its body. The arrangement of these is different in male and female fish. The light organs may help the fish to light up the dark depths of the sea to find prey, or they may be used to confuse the fish's enemies. They feed on certain kinds of animal plankton.

Size: 4 in (10 cm)
Range: North Atlantic Ocean, Mediterranean Sea
Scientific name: Myctophum punctatum

Lanternfish

Ballyhoo

This fish cannot leap above the water like its relative the flyingfish, but it can skim over the surface. It moves in schools, feeding on sea grass and small fish, and it may use its long lower jaw to scoop up food from the water's surface.

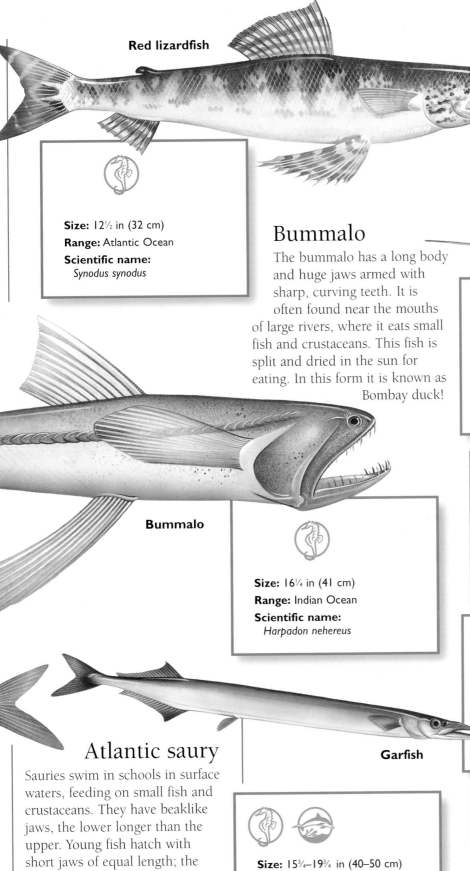

Red lizardfish

Red lizardfish

The red lizardfish has long pelvic fins and often lies on the seafloor, supporting its body on these fins. A fierce hunter, it lies in wait for prey, then suddenly darts up from the sea bottom and catches its target in its long, sharp teeth.

Size: 12½ in (32 cm)
Range: Atlantic Ocean
Scientific name:
  Synodus synodus

Bummalo

The bummalo has a long body and huge jaws armed with sharp, curving teeth. It is often found near the mouths of large rivers, where it eats small fish and crustaceans. This fish is split and dried in the sun for eating. In this form it is known as Bombay duck!

Needlefish

Size: 2 in (5 cm)
Range: South America
Scientific name:
  Belonian apodion

Needlefish

A long slender body and the position of its fins give this tiny fish a dartlike appearance. It uses its long lower jaw to scoop up animal plankton.

Bummalo

Size: 16¼ in (41 cm)
Range: Indian Ocean
Scientific name:
  Harpadon nehereus

Size: 37 in (94 cm)
Range: North Atlantic Ocean, Mediterranean and Black Seas
Scientific name:
  Belone belone

Atlantic saury

Sauries swim in schools in surface waters, feeding on small fish and crustaceans. They have beaklike jaws, the lower longer than the upper. Young fish hatch with short jaws of equal length; the long lower jaw develops as the hatchlings grow.

Garfish

Atlantic saury

Size: 15¾–19¾ in (40–50 cm)
Range: North Atlantic Ocean and Mediterranean Sea
Scientific name: *Scomberesox saurus*

Garfish

The slender garfish can live for up to 18 years. An active hunter, it eats small fish and crustaceans. Garfish breed in coastal waters, and the small, round eggs attach themselves to floating debris or seaweed.

187

Guppies, grunions, and their relatives

Guppies belong to a large group of freshwater fish that contains more than 800 species, including lyretails and four-eyed fish. Most are surface swimmers and feed on insects and plant matter that has fallen onto the water. They are extremely adaptable and able to survive in stagnant, slow-moving water that is unsuitable for most other fish.

Grunions belong to a group of more than 280 species that includes silversides, sand smelt, and rainbow fish. Most feed on animal plankton and live in large schools in lakes, estuaries, and shallow coastal waters.

Crimson-spotted rainbow fish

This colorful fish is one of about 53 kinds of rainbow fish found in Australia and New Guinea. In early summer it lays eggs, which become anchored to water plants by fine threads.

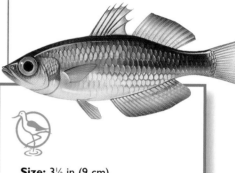

Crimson-spotted rainbow fish

Size: 3½ in (9 cm)
Range: Australia, New Guinea
Scientific name:
  Melanotaenia fluviatilis

Sand smelt

Sand smelt

This small fish swims in schools. It has a long, slender body and two widely spaced fins on its back. Animal plankton is its main food, but it also eats tiny fish. The sand smelt is in turn eaten by larger fish and by seabirds such as terns.

Size: 6–7¾ in (15–20 cm)
Range: eastern Atlantic Ocean
Scientific name:
  Atherina presbyter

Hardhead silverside

During the day, the slender body of this little fish looks almost transparent, with a narrow silvery stripe running down each side. When night falls, the color darkens. Silversides are common fish, and they swim in large schools. Their eggs have tiny threads that attach them to water plants while the embryos develop.

Hardhead silverside

Size: 5 in (12.5 cm)
Range: North Atlantic Ocean
Scientific name:
  Atherinomorus stipes

California grunion

Grunions time their breeding with the rhythms of the tides. On the night of an extremely high, or spring, tide, they swim ashore and lay their eggs in the sand. The next wave carries the fish back to the sea. Two weeks later, at the next spring tide, the eggs hatch and the young are carried out to sea.

Size: 7 in (18 cm)
Range: Pacific Ocean
Scientific name: **California**
  Leuresthes tenuis   **grunion**

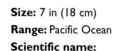

Four-eyed fish

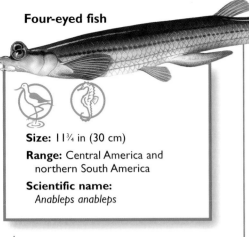

Size: 11¾ in (30 cm)
Range: Central America and northern South America
Scientific name:
Anableps anableps

Four-eyed fish

This unusual fish has, in fact, only two eyes that are divided into two parts. The top part of each eye is for seeing in the air, and the lower part is for seeing in water. The two are separated by a dark band. The fish swims at the surface, the water reaching the dividing bands on the eyes. It is able to watch for insects in the air and other prey in the water at the same time.

Cape Lopez lyretail

The male lyretail is a brightly colored fish with large, pointed fins. The female is plainer, with smaller fins. The lyretail lays its eggs in mud. If there is a long dry season, the eggs stop developing until the rains return. The embryos then start to grow again and hatch shortly afterward.

Size: 2¼ in (6 cm)
Range: Africa
Scientific name:
Aphyosemion australe

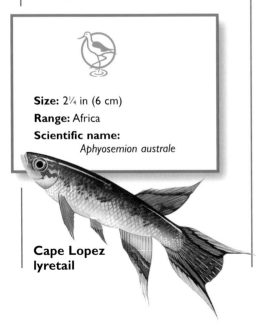

Cape Lopez lyretail

Size: 3 in (7.5 cm)
Range: Atlantic coast of U.S.A.: Cape Cod, south to Mexico
Scientific name:
Cyprinidon variegatus

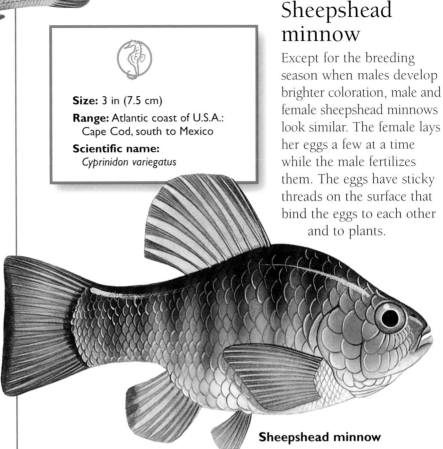

Sheepshead minnow

Mummichog

The stout-bodied mummichog is a hardy little fish that can survive in salt or fresh water and eats almost any plants and animals it can find. It breeds in spring in shallow water. The male chases his mate and then clasps her with his fins so he can fertilize the eggs as they are laid. The eggs stick together and sink to the bottom in a cluster.

Size: 4–6 in (10–15 cm)
Range: North America
Scientific name:
Fundulus heteroclitus

Mummichog

Guppy

The guppy is an extremely common fish. It is popular with people because it helps control mosquitos by feeding on their larvae. It also eats other insect larvae, small crustaceans, and the eggs and young of other fish. Many colorful forms of the guppy are bred as aquarium fish.

Sheepshead minnow

Except for the breeding season when males develop brighter coloration, male and female sheepshead minnows look similar. The female lays her eggs a few at a time while the male fertilizes them. The eggs have sticky threads on the surface that bind the eggs to each other and to plants.

Size: 2¼ in (6 cm)
Range: northern South America
Scientific name:
Poecilia reticulata

Guppy

189

Squirrelfish, oarfish, and relatives

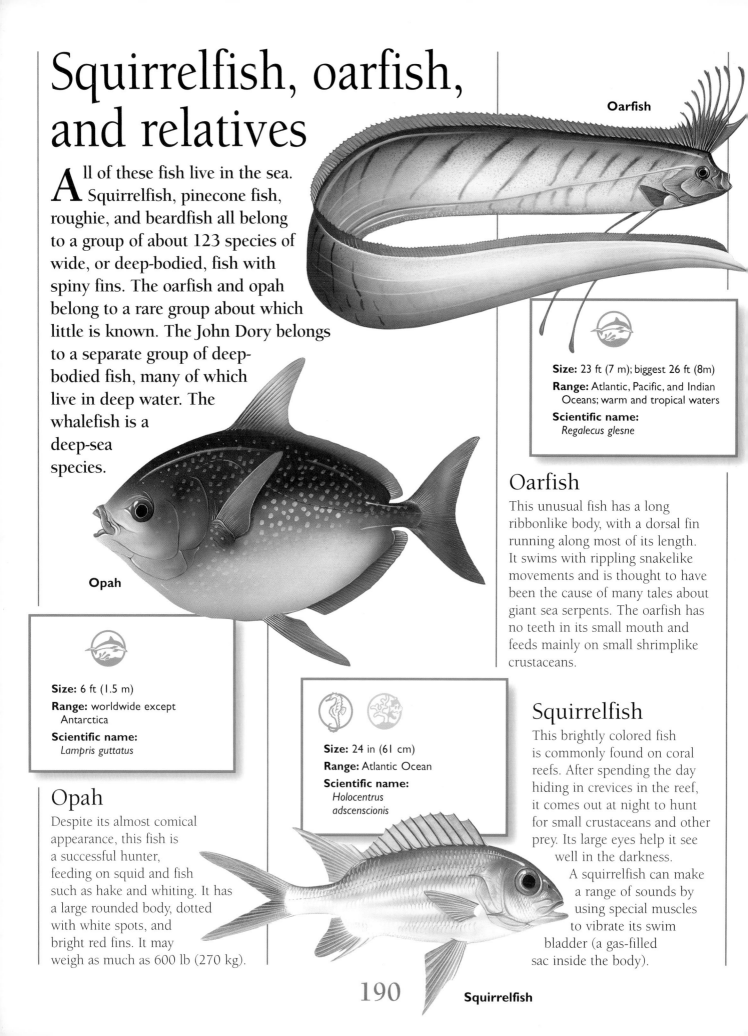

Oarfish

A ll of these fish live in the sea. Squirrelfish, pinecone fish, roughie, and beardfish all belong to a group of about 123 species of wide, or deep-bodied, fish with spiny fins. The oarfish and opah belong to a rare group about which little is known. The John Dory belongs to a separate group of deep-bodied fish, many of which live in deep water. The whalefish is a deep-sea species.

Opah

Size: 23 ft (7 m); biggest 26 ft (8m)
Range: Atlantic, Pacific, and Indian Oceans; warm and tropical waters
Scientific name:
   Regalecus glesne

Oarfish

This unusual fish has a long ribbonlike body, with a dorsal fin running along most of its length. It swims with rippling snakelike movements and is thought to have been the cause of many tales about giant sea serpents. The oarfish has no teeth in its small mouth and feeds mainly on small shrimplike crustaceans.

Size: 6 ft (1.5 m)
Range: worldwide except Antarctica
Scientific name:
   Lampris guttatus

Size: 24 in (61 cm)
Range: Atlantic Ocean
Scientific name:
   Holocentrus adscenscionis

Squirrelfish

This brightly colored fish is commonly found on coral reefs. After spending the day hiding in crevices in the reef, it comes out at night to hunt for small crustaceans and other prey. Its large eyes help it see well in the darkness.
   A squirrelfish can make a range of sounds by using special muscles to vibrate its swim bladder (a gas-filled sac inside the body).

Opah

Despite its almost comical appearance, this fish is a successful hunter, feeding on squid and fish such as hake and whiting. It has a large rounded body, dotted with white spots, and bright red fins. It may weigh as much as 600 lb (270 kg).

Squirrelfish

Size: 5 in (12.5 cm)
Range: Indian and Pacific Oceans
Scientific name:
Monocentris japonicus

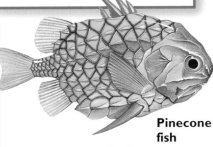

Pinecone fish

Pinecone fish

The body of the pinecone fish is protected by an armor of heavy platelike scales. Its dorsal fin is made up of thick spines, and it has more spines on its underside. Under the lower jaw it has two light-producing organs. Pinecone fish move in schools near the bottom of the sea.

Whalefish

This is a small fish with a big name. It has a big head for its size and no scales on its body. The area at the base of the dorsal and anal fins is thought to glow in the dark. It hunts for its food and seizes prey in its large jaws lined with many tiny teeth.

Size: 5½ in (14 cm)
Range: Indian Ocean
Scientific name:
Cetomimus indagator

Whalefish

Stout beardfish

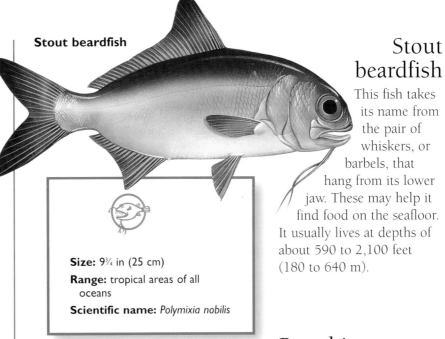

Size: 9¾ in (25 cm)
Range: tropical areas of all oceans
Scientific name: *Polymixia nobilis*

Roughie

Size: 11¾ in (30 cm)
Range: North Atlantic Ocean, south central Indian Ocean, Pacific near New Zealand
Scientific name:
Hoplostethus atlanticus

John Dory

The John Dory has 9 or 10 thick spines in the front part of its dorsal fin and 3 or 4 spines in the front part of its anal fin. This fish is not a fast swimmer and catches its food by stealth, not speed. It approaches its prey, such as small fish and crustaceans, slowly, until near enough to snap them up in its huge mouth. The John Dory is a popular food fish in Europe.

Stout beardfish

This fish takes its name from the pair of whiskers, or barbels, that hang from its lower jaw. These may help it find food on the seafloor. It usually lives at depths of about 590 to 2,100 feet (180 to 640 m).

Roughie

The brightly colored roughie has a large head and a wide body. It has sharp spines on its back in front of the dorsal fin and on its belly in front of the anal fin. Its mouth is large and upturned, and its jaws are lined with lots of tiny teeth. Little is known about the habits of this fish, but it is thought to feed on small crustaceans.

John Dory

Size: 15¾–26 in (40–66 cm)
Range: eastern Atlantic Ocean, Mediterranean Sea
Scientific name: *Zeus faber*

Seahorses, scorpionfish, and their relatives

Seahorses and sticklebacks belong to a group of more than 260 species of fish that also includes tube snouts and pipefish. Sticklebacks have between 3 and 16 spines on their back and are found in the sea and in fresh water. The extraordinary seahorses, with their horselike head, all live in the sea. The stonefish, lionfish, northern sea robin, and bullrout belong to the scorpionfish group. This includes nearly 1,300 species, most of which live in the sea. Many of these fish are chunky and spiny.

The flying gurnard belongs to a small group of only seven species of marine fish. Despite their name, these fish are bottom dwellers and have never been seen flying above the surface of the water.

Dwarf seahorse

This unusual fish moves slowly, gently pushing itself along with movements of its tiny dorsal fin. It can also attach itself to seaweed by curling its tail around it. In the breeding season the female lays 50 or more eggs, which she places in a pouch on the male's body, where they incubate.

○ **Dwarf seahorse**

Size: 1½ in (4 cm)
Range: western Atlantic Ocean, Caribbean Sea, Gulf of Mexico
Scientific name:
Hippocampus zosterae

Weedy seadragon

The leaflike flaps of skin on the body of this strange little seahorse are thought to help it hide from its enemies among fronds of seaweed. The male incubates his mate's eggs on a flap of skin beneath his tail.

Weedy seadragon

Size: 18 in (46 cm)
Range: coasts of southern Australia
Scientific name:
Phyllopteryx taeniolatus

Size: 2–4 in (5–10 cm)
Range: coasts and fresh water of North America
Scientific name:
Gasterosteus aculeatus

Three-spined stickleback

In the breeding season the male stickleback develops a bright red belly. He makes a nest from tiny bits of plants glued together with mucus. He then displays to attract females to his nest to lay their eggs. He fertilizes the eggs and guards them carefully until they hatch about three weeks later.

Three-spined stickleback

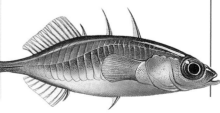

Lionfish

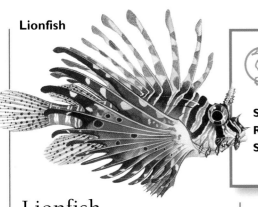

Size: 15 in (38 cm)
Range: Indian and Pacific Oceans
Scientific name:
Pterois volitans

Lionfish

With its brightly striped body and large fanlike fins, this fish is one of the most extraordinary in the sea. The spines on its back are poisonous and can be dangerous even for humans. The fish uses its spines to defend itself against enemies, not to attack prey.

Stonefish

The stonefish's mottled coloration and irregular shape keep it well hidden as it lies half-buried among stones on the seafloor. The sharp spines on its back are linked to glands containing a deadly poison that can even kill a person unlucky enough to tread on a stonefish's spines.

Stonefish

Size: 11¾ in (30 cm)
Range: Indian and Pacific Oceans
Scientific name:
Synanceia verrucosa

Bullrout

Also known as the shorthorn sculpin, this fish has spines near its gills and along each side. Females are usually larger than males. A bottom dweller, the bullrout eats seafloor crustaceans as well as worms and small fish.

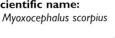

Size: 9¾–23½ in (25–60 cm)
Range: North Atlantic Ocean
Scientific name:
Myoxocephalus scorpius

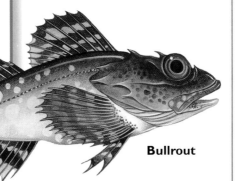

Bullrout

Northern sea robin

A relative of the lionfish, the northern sea robin spends much of its life on the seafloor, often supporting itself on its pectoral fins. It uses the first three spines of its pectoral fins to feel for prey on the seafloor. When in danger, the sea robin buries itself in sand, leaving only the top of its head and eyes showing.

Flying gurnard

A bottom-dwelling fish, the flying gurnard uses its long winglike pelvic fins to glide over the seafloor as it searches for crustaceans to eat. When alarmed, the gurnard spreads its fins wide to show off their blue spots.

Flying gurnard

Size: 11¾–16 in (30–40.5 cm)
Range: western Atlantic Ocean, Mediterranean Sea
Scientific name:
Dactylopterus volitans

Size: 16¼ in (41 cm)
Range: western Atlantic Ocean
Scientific name:
Prionotus carolinus

Northern sea robin

Flatfish

The flatfish belong to a group of about 570 species. All but three of these live in the sea. Young flatfish have rounded bodies at first, but as they grow their bodies flatten and the eye on one side moves so that both eyes are on the upper surface. A typical flatfish spends much of its life on the seafloor, lying with its eyes facing up. Some flatfish have both eyes on the right side; others have them on the left.

Adalah

The adalah is the most primitive of all flatfish. Some have eyes to the left side, others to the right, but one eye is on the edge of the head, rather than on the side with the other eye. Like other flatfish it spends much of its life on the seafloor, but it also swims in midwaters, looking for fish and other creatures to eat.

Turbot

This extremely broad-bodied flatfish varies in color, but it usually has speckled markings that help keep it hidden as it lies on the seafloor. Adult turbots feed mostly on fish, but young turbots eat small crustaceans. Turbots breed in spring or summer, and females produce as many as ten million eggs.

Turbot

Size: 3¼ ft (1 m)
Range: eastern Atlantic Ocean, Mediterranean Sea
Scientific name:
Scopthalmus maximus

Adalah

California halibut

Size: 5 ft (1.5 m)
Range: Pacific Ocean
Scientific name:
Paralichthys californicus

Size: up to 24 in (61 cm)
Range: Red Sea, Indian Ocean, western Pacific Ocean
Scientific name:
Psettodes erumei

California halibut

This halibut has a large mouth and strong, sharp teeth. It feeds on fish, particularly anchovies, and is itself eaten by creatures such as rays, sea lions, and porpoises. It is also an important food fish for people. A large halibut of this species can weigh up to 70 pounds (32 kg).

Summer flounder

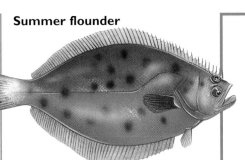

Size: up to 3¼ ft (1 m)

Range: western Atlantic Ocean

Scientific name: *Paralichthys dentatus*

Naked sole

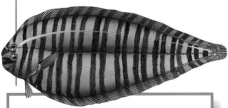

Size: up to 9 in (23 cm)

Range: northwestern Atlantic Ocean

Scientific name: *Gymnachirus melas*

Summer flounder

A slender, active fish, the summer flounder feeds on crustaceans, mollusks, and fish and will chase prey into surface waters if necessary. But although a fast swimmer, it spends much of its life lying half-buried on the seafloor. Its color varies according to the type of sea bottom it is on, but this fish is usually brownish with dark spots.

Plaice

The top side of this flatfish is a rich brown color, dotted with orange spots. Both eyes are usually on the top— on the right side of the body. Plaice with eyes on the left are rare. Plaice breed in spring, and the larvae live in surface waters for up to six weeks before starting a bottom-dwelling life. Plaice are an important food fish.

Sole

Normally a nighttime feeder, the sole usually spends the day buried in sand or mud. It breeds in shallow water, and the eggs float at the surface until they hatch. Larvae live at the surface but move to the seafloor when they are about a half inch (1.25 cm) long.

Sole

Size: 11¾–23½ in (30–60 cm)

Range: eastern Atlantic Ocean, Mediterranean Sea

Scientific name: *Solea solea*

Naked sole

The naked sole has no scales on its skin and is marked with dark stripes on its upper side. The underside is whitish in color. Most of these fish have both eyes on the right side, and the small mouth is also twisted to the right. The naked sole spends most of its life on the seafloor, but it is an active hunter and can swim well when necessary.

Blackcheek tonguefish

This flatfish has a body that is broad at the front and tapers to a pointed tail. Its dorsal and anal fins join with the tail fin. Both of its eyes are on the left of the head, and its small mouth is twisted to the left side. Like other flatfish, it lives on the seafloor and feeds on small invertebrate animals such as worms and crustaceans.

Plaice

Size: 19¾–36 in (50–91 cm)

Range: eastern Atlantic Ocean, Mediterranean Sea

Scientific name: *Pleuronectes platessa*

Size: 7¾ in (20 cm)

Range: western Atlantic Ocean

Scientific name: *Symphurus plagusia*

Blackcheek tonguefish

Coelacanth, lungfish, triggerfish, and relatives

The coelacanth is thought to resemble some of the earliest fish. Common millions of years ago, only one species now survives. Lungfish are related to early air-breathing fish and are believed to be more closely related to amphibians than any other living fish. They have lunglike breathing organs, which they use for taking breaths of air at the ocean's surface. Triggerfish and their relatives the puffer and boxfish belong to a group of about 340 species, many of which have round or boxlike bodies. Most live in the sea.

Scrawled filefish

A relative of the triggerfish, this filefish has a long spine on its back and small prickly spines on the scales of its body. It lives on bottom-living invertebrates and seaweeds and feeds nose down on the seafloor. It often lurks in clumps of eelgrass, where its coloration keeps it well hidden.

Scrawled filefish

Size: 36 in (91 cm)

Range: tropical waters of Atlantic, Pacific, and Indian Oceans

Scientific name: *Aluterus scriptus*

Porcupinefish

The body of this fish is covered with long, sharp spines that normally lie flat. But if the fish is in danger, it puffs up its body so the spines stand out, making itself almost impossible for any predator to catch. It has two teeth in each jaw. The teeth are joined together to make a sharp beak for crushing hard-shelled prey such as mollusks and crabs.

Size: 22 in (56 cm)

Range: western Atlantic Ocean, Caribbean Sea

Scientific name: *Balistes vetula*

O **Queen triggerfish**

Blue-spotted boxfish

Like all boxfish, this fish has a hard shell around its body, made up of joined plates. Its mouth, eyes, fins, and gill openings are the only breaks in the armor, which protects the fish from its enemies. It feeds mostly on bottom-living invertebrate creatures.

Size: 36 in (91 cm)

Range: tropical waters of Pacific, Indian, and Atlantic Oceans

Scientific name: *Diodon hystrix*

Queen triggerfish

On the triggerfish's back are three spines. When the first spine is upright, it is locked into place by the second. When in danger, the triggerfish can wedge itself into a crevice with this "locking" spine and become extremely hard to move. It feeds on small invertebrate creatures, particularly sea urchins.

Blue-spotted boxfish

Size: 18 in (46 cm)

Range: Indian and Pacific Oceans

Scientific name: *Ostracion tuberculatus*

Porcupinefish

Size: 6 in (15 cm)
Range: India, Myanmar, Malaysia
Scientific name:
Tetraodon cutcutia

Common puffer

Common puffer

If threatened, this fish can inflate its body until it is almost completely round and very difficult for any predator to swallow. Many kinds of puffers are popular food fish, even though parts of some puffers are very poisonous. In Japan, chefs are specially trained in preparing this fish to eat.

Coelacanth

Coelacanths were thought to have been extinct for millions of years until one was caught off the coast of South Africa in 1938. This living species is still very like its fossil relatives. It has a heavy body and fleshy sections at the base of all its fins except the first dorsal fin. It is believed to hunt other fish to eat.

Size: 6½ ft (2 m)
Range: Indian Ocean
Scientific name:
Latimeria chalumnae

Ocean sunfish

The extraordinary ocean sunfish is a relative of the triggerfish, but it is quite unlike any other fish. Its body is almost completely round and ends in a curious frill-like tail. Despite its huge size, it has a small beaklike mouth and feeds on creatures such as animal plankton and tiny jellyfish.

Ocean sunfish

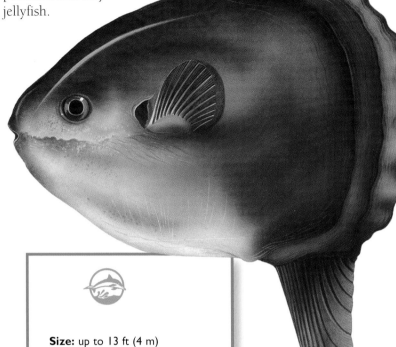

Size: up to 13 ft (4 m)
Range: Atlantic, Pacific, and Indian Oceans
Scientific name: *Mola mola*

◑ **Coelacanth**

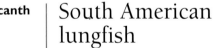

South American lungfish

This lungfish lives in swamps that dry out for part of the year. During this time, it lives in a burrow that it digs in the mud and breathes air with the help of lunglike organs in its body. When the rains return, the fish comes out of its burrow.

Size: 4¼ ft (1.25 m)
Range: central South America
Scientific name:
Lepidosiren paradoxa

South American lungfish

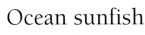

Why do some animals work together?

When animals develop close links with creatures of other species, both partners can benefit. The cleaning goby, for example, feeds on parasites and tiny scraps of food it finds on the bodies of larger fish. This goby gains a good meal, and the host has its body cleared of debris and harmful parasites. Sometimes only one partner benefits. Cattle egrets follow large mammals such as elephants to feed on the insects the animals disturb as they pass. The egrets get plenty of food, but there is no clear advantage to the mammal.

The **honey-guide** feeds on beeswax and bee larvae, but it is not able to get into bee nests by itself. Instead, the bird leads another honey-eating animal such as the **honey badger,** or ratel, to the nest and waits while it smashes open the nest. Both creatures benefit.

Black ants and several other ant species protect groups of tiny sap-sucking insects called aphids from other insects. In return, when an ant strokes an aphid's body with its antennae, the aphid produces a drop of sugary substance called honeydew—delicious food for the ant.

The **clown anemonefish** finds safety from enemies among a **sea anemone's** stinging tentacles. Its own skin is immune to the sting.

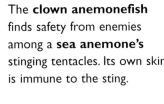

The **oxpecker** provides a very useful service for the **buffalo** while getting a good meal for itself. The bird eats the ticks and other parasites that live on the buffalo's skin.

Insects, spiders, and other invertebrates

Insects outnumber every other creature on Earth. There are more than one and a half million known animal species in the world, and about one million of those species are insects. Some experts believe that as many as 30 times this number of insects are yet to be discovered. Arachnids, like insects, are found all over the world in every kind of habitat. There are at least 75,000 species of arachnids, of which spiders are the biggest group.

Insects and spiders are not the only types of invertebrate animals. On land there are creatures such as worms, snails, centipedes, and millipedes. In the sea there is an amazing range of at least 160,000 species of invertebrates, including sponges, clams, mussels, jellyfish, and crabs.

A gleaming **mint leaf beetle** settles on a leaf of its main food plant. Leaf beetles feed on the leaves and flowers of different plants, and their larvae may attack the plant's roots. Many leaf beetles are serious pests of agricultural crops.

Garden snail

What is an invertebrate?

An invertebrate is an animal without a backbone—creatures such as crabs, worms, insects, and spiders are all invertebrates. There are invertebrates on land, in the sea, in fresh water, and in the air. These animals have an extraordinary range of lifestyles and feeding habits.

Arthropods

Arthropods are the largest group of invertebrates and some of the most successful creatures ever to live on Earth. They include creatures such as insects, spiders, and crabs. One of the reasons for the success of arthropods is that they have a hard external skeleton, called an exoskeleton, which protects the soft body within.

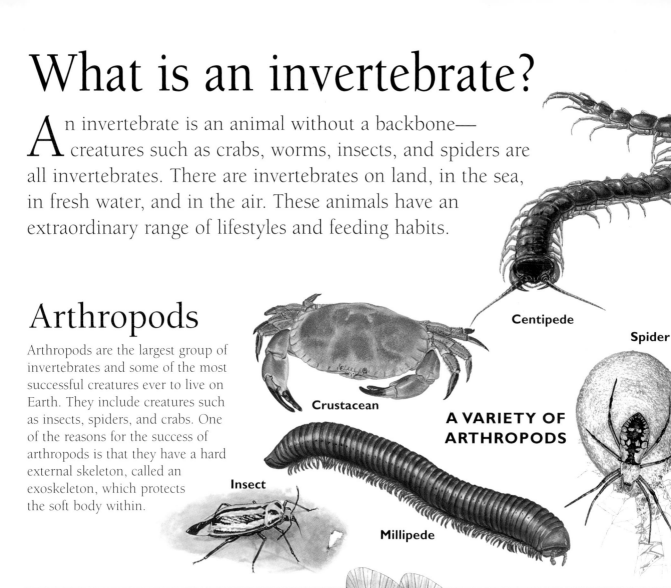

Centipede

Spider

Crustacean

A VARIETY OF ARTHROPODS

Insect

Millipede

An insect's body

An insect is divided into three parts—head, thorax, and abdomen. The head carries the eyes, a pair of sensory antennae, which the insect uses to find out about its surroundings, and the mouthparts. These vary in shape according to the insect's diet. On the thorax are three pairs of legs and usually two pairs of wings.

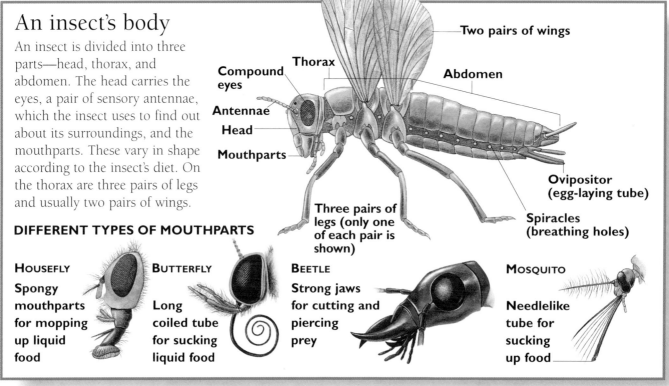

Two pairs of wings

Thorax

Compound eyes

Abdomen

Antennae

Head

Mouthparts

Ovipositor (egg-laying tube)

Three pairs of legs (only one of each pair is shown)

Spiracles (breathing holes)

DIFFERENT TYPES OF MOUTHPARTS

HOUSEFLY
Spongy mouthparts for mopping up liquid food

BUTTERFLY
Long coiled tube for sucking liquid food

BEETLE
Strong jaws for cutting and piercing prey

MOSQUITO
Needlelike tube for sucking up food

A spider's body

A typical spider's body is divided into the cephalothorax (head and thorax) and abdomen, linked by a narrow waist. At the front of the head are the jaws, called chelicerae. Behind them are the mouth and a pair of pedipalps (used in mating). At the end of the abdomen are the spinnerets, from which spiders produce silk thread. Spiders have four pairs of legs, each divided into segments and tipped with two or three claws.

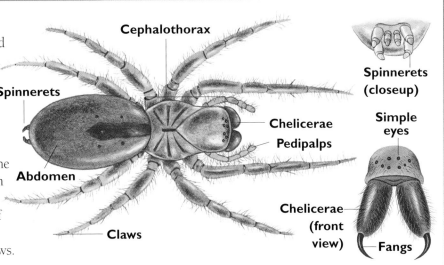

Cephalothorax

Spinnerets (closeup)

Spinnerets

Chelicerae

Pedipalps

Simple eyes

Abdomen

Chelicerae (front view)

Fangs

Claws

Other invertebrate groups

Mollusks

The three main groups of mollusks are the gastropods—creatures such as snails; the bivalves—clams, scallops, and mussels; and cephalopods—squid, cuttlefish, octopuses, and nautiluses.

Nautilus

Annelid worms

There are about 11,500 species of these worms living in water and on land. In all of them the body is divided into a number of segments.

Medical leech

Cnidarians

This group includes creatures such as sea anemones, jellyfish, and coral. Most have tubelike bodies with a central mouth surrounded by tentacles.

Purple jellyfish

Comb jellies

Comb jellies have a simple baglike body with eight lines of tiny hairs arranged down it. These hairs move and push the comb jelly through the water.

Line of hairs

Beroe comb jelly

Lamp shells

There are about 260 living species in this group, which dates back more than 550 million years. All lamp shells have an upper and a lower shell.

Lamp shell

Echinoderms

There are four main groups of echinoderms—brittle stars, starfish, sea cucumbers, and sea urchins and sand dollars. Most move around using tiny stilts called tube feet.

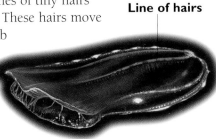

Flower urchin

Sponges

Sponges are the simplest many-celled animals. Their shapes vary from tiny cups, tubelike pipes, and tall vases to rounded masses. Special filtering cells in their bodies trap food particles from the water.

Glass sponge

WHAT IS AN INVERTEBRATE?

203

Cockroaches, earwigs, crickets, grasshoppers, and their relatives

Although these insects are not closely related, they share certain features. All of them have strong jaws for chewing, mobile heads, and most have large back wings. They also include some of the most ancient of all insect groups: Cockroaches have existed on the Earth for about 350 million years. Most of these creatures are familiar to people, and some are even unwelcome guests in our homes.

Cockroaches, earwigs, and bristletails

Most cockroaches live outdoors in every kind of habitat from mountains to rain forests, but they are best known as indoor pests. Earwigs, found in every garden, are also considered pests, since many feed on plants and flowers. Also common in houses, but less often seen, are the wingless insects known as silverfish, a type of bristletail.

Firebrat

The firebrat is a bristletail. It usually lives indoors near warm places such as ovens or furnaces. It is a fast runner and scurries around finding crumbs and other scraps of food to eat.

Firebrat

Family: Lepismatidae
Size: ⅓–¾ in (0.8–1.9 cm) long
Number of species: 200

Family: Forficulidae
Size: ⅜–1 in (0.9–2.5 cm) long
Number of species: 450

Common earwig

Young   **Eggs**

Common earwig

The female earwig lays her eggs in a burrow and stays close to look after them. Unlike most insects, she tends her young until they are able to look after themselves.

Silverfish

Fast-moving, light-shy silverfish usually live in dark corners indoors, where they eat paper, glue, and spilled foods. The long, tapering body is covered with tiny scales.

Family: Lepismatidae
Size: ⅓–¾ in (0.8–1.9 cm) long
Number of species: 200

Silverfish

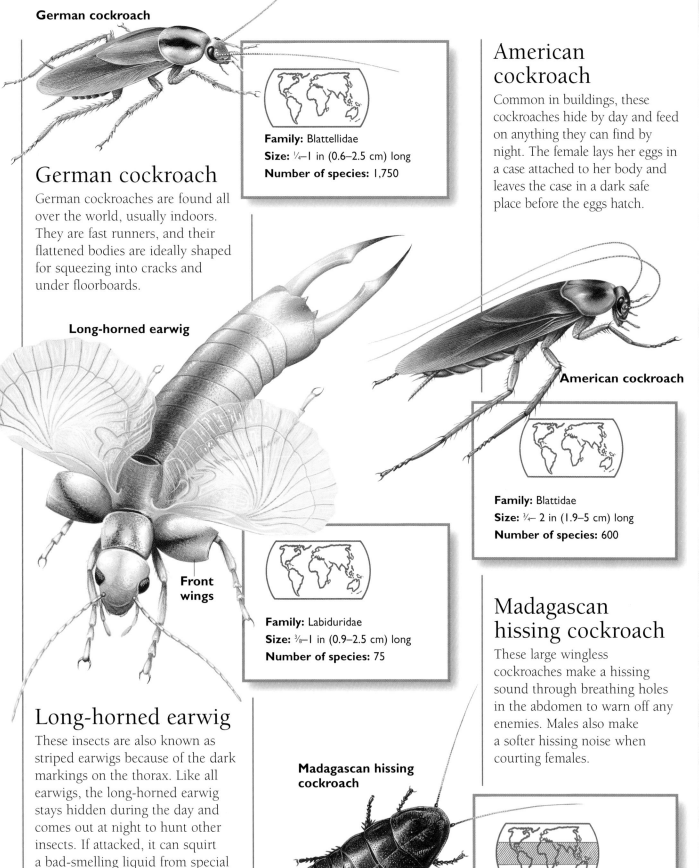

German cockroach

German cockroaches are found all over the world, usually indoors. They are fast runners, and their flattened bodies are ideally shaped for squeezing into cracks and under floorboards.

German cockroach

Family: Blattellidae
Size: ¼–1 in (0.6–2.5 cm) long
Number of species: 1,750

American cockroach

Common in buildings, these cockroaches hide by day and feed on anything they can find by night. The female lays her eggs in a case attached to her body and leaves the case in a dark safe place before the eggs hatch.

American cockroach

Family: Blattidae
Size: ¾– 2 in (1.9–5 cm) long
Number of species: 600

Long-horned earwig

Front wings

Family: Labiduridae
Size: ⅜–1 in (0.9–2.5 cm) long
Number of species: 75

Long-horned earwig

These insects are also known as striped earwigs because of the dark markings on the thorax. Like all earwigs, the long-horned earwig stays hidden during the day and comes out at night to hunt other insects. If attacked, it can squirt a bad-smelling liquid from special glands on the abdomen. It has large semicircular back wings, which have to be folded many times in order to fit under the smaller leathery front wings.

Madagascan hissing cockroach

These large wingless cockroaches make a hissing sound through breathing holes in the abdomen to warn off any enemies. Males also make a softer hissing noise when courting females.

Madagascan hissing cockroach

Family: Blaberidae
Size: 2–3 in (5–7.5 cm) long
Number of species: 1,000

Crickets, grasshoppers, and their relatives

More often heard than seen, grasshoppers are best known for their calls, usually made by males when courting females. They make these sounds by rubbing together special parts of their wings or legs. There are two main families of grasshoppers: short-horned, which include locusts, and long-horned, which include katydids. Crickets are relatives of grasshoppers that make chirping sounds. Stick and leaf insects are famous for their ability to hide themselves by looking like twigs or leaves.

Long-horned grasshopper

As their name suggests, long-horned grasshoppers have long antennae. They feed on plants, but some also eat small insects. Many are green or brown in color and can be hard to spot in the trees and bushes where they live.

Long-horned grasshopper

Family: Tettigoniidae
Size: ½–3 in (1.2–7.5 cm) long
Number of species: 5,000

Locust

Locusts are a type of grasshopper and are among the most damaging of all insects. Swarms of locusts swoop down onto crops and feed until there are scarcely any leaves left. A swarm may contain as many as 50 billion insects.

Family: Acrididae
Size: ½–3 in (1.2–7.5 cm) long
Number of species: 9,000

Locust

Short-horned grasshopper

Short-horned grasshoppers have short antennae. Like all grasshoppers, they have powerful back legs and can leap more than 200 times their own length.

Short-horned grasshopper

Family: Acrididae
Size: ½–3 in (1.2–7.5 cm) long
Number of species: 9,000

Leaf insect

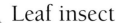

Leaf insect

These extraordinary insects are shaped just like the leaves they live on, complete with veins. Even their eggs look like plant seeds. Leaf insects live in tropical parts of Asia and Australia.

Family: Phylliidae
Size: 2–4 in (5–10 cm) long
Number of species: 50

Tree cricket

Family: Gryllidae
Size: ⅜–1 in (0.9–2.5 cm) long
Number of species: 2,000

Tree cricket

Tree crickets "sing" by rubbing together specially ridged and thickened areas of their front wings to make a high-pitched sound. They are usually colored green, black, or brown and have broad bodies and well-developed feelers at the end of the abdomen.

Mole cricket

Family: Gryllotalpidae
Size: ¾–2 in (2–5 cm) long
Number of species: 60

Mole cricket

Like tiny moles, these crickets live under the ground, where they burrow with their large spadelike front legs. A covering of fine hairs protects the body from soil. Plant roots are their main food, and they often damage crops and trees. They also eat worms and larvae.

Katydid

This insect has wings that look like leaves to help it hide among plants. The female katydid has a knifelike ovipositor (egg-laying tube). She uses this to insert eggs into slots that she cuts in the stems of plants.

Katydid

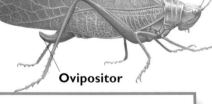

Ovipositor

Family: Tettigoniidae
Size: ½–3 in (1.2–7.5 cm) long
Number of species: 5,000

Stick insect

With its slender green or brown body, the stick insect looks so much like a leafless twig that it is hard for hungry birds to see. During the day it clings to a plant, with only its long, thin legs swaying gently, as though blown by a breeze. At night the stick insect moves around, feeding on leaves.

Family: Phasmatidae
Size: up to 11¾ in (30 cm) long
Number of species: 2,000

Stick insect

COCKROACHES, EARWIGS, CRICKETS, GRASSHOPPERS, AND THEIR RELATIVES

207

Mantids, dragonflies, and their relatives

These insects are some of the fiercest hunters in the insect world. Mantids are equipped with long front legs, which they extend at lightning speed to grasp their prey. More energetic hunters are the dragonflies, among the fastest-flying of all insects. They seize their prey in the air or pluck tiny creatures from leaves. Lacewings, antlions, snakeflies, and mantidflies are known as nerve-winged insects. They have two pairs of delicate veined wings that can be folded like a roof over the body. Their larvae feed on other small creatures, which they catch in their powerful jaws.

Angola mantis

This mantis is hard to see because it looks like lichen growing on a branch. It remains very still as it watches for food but can reach out to grab its prey in a fraction of a second. Mantid larvae hatch as tiny versions of their parents and start hunting for themselves right away.

Family: Mantidae
Size: ½–6 in (1.2–15 cm) long
Number of species: 1,500

Angola mantis

Praying mantis

The powerful front legs of the praying mantis are its hunting tools. They are lined with sharp spines, which help the insect hold on to its struggling prey as it feeds. Females are usually larger than males and sometimes attack or even eat males during mating.

Flower mantis

Some mantids are colored to match the flowers that they perch on. This helps them stay hidden from both their prey and their enemies. Mantids usually eat other insects, but they can also catch frogs and small lizards.

Flower mantis

Family: Mantidae
Size: ½–6 in (1.2–15 cm) long
Number of species: 1,500

Praying mantis

Family: Mantidae
Size: ½–6 in (1.2–15 cm) long
Number of species: 1,500

Family: Perlidae
Size: ⅜–1½ in (0.9–4 cm) long
Number of species: 350

Family: Raphidiidae
Size: ¼–1 in (0.6–2.5 cm) long
Number of species: 85

Snakefly

The snakefly gets its name from its long, snakelike neck, which it lifts as it searches for prey. Both adults and larvae hunt insects such as aphids and caterpillars.

Snakefly

Common stonefly

Stonefly nymphs (young) live in streams, where they feed mostly on plants, although some hunt insects. They can take in oxygen through their body surface but they also have gills, usually behind the first two pairs of legs, which help them breathe in the water. Adult stoneflies are poor fliers and spend much of the day resting on stones with their wings folded on their bodies. They live only two or three weeks, and most do not eat.

Common stonefly

Adult

Nymph

Family: Myrmeleontidae
Size: ⅜–2 in (0.9–5 cm) long
Number of species: 1,000

Mantidfly

This relative of the lacewing looks like a small praying mantis and catches prey in the same way. Some mantidfly larvae burrow into the nests of wasps or bees and eat their larvae. Others feed on spider eggs.

Adult

Green lacewing

Larva

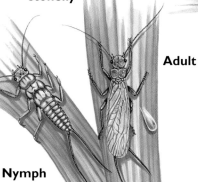

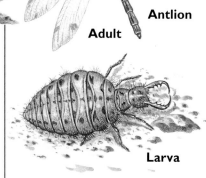

Adult

Antlion

Larva

Family: Mantispidae
Size: ⅛–1 in (0.3–2.5 cm) long
Number of species: 350

Family: Chrysopidae
Size: ⅜–¾ in (0.9–1.9 cm) long
Number of species: 1,600

Green lacewing

Adult lacewings and their larvae both feed on small insects such as aphids. The larvae suck out the body juices of their prey with special mouthparts.

Antlion

The adult antlion looks like a dragonfly but has longer antennae, with clublike tips. The name antlion comes from the larva, which is a fierce hunter with spiny jaws. The larva digs a pit in sandy soil. When an insect comes near, the antlion larva tosses soil at it until it falls into the pit.

Mantidfly

209

MANTIDS, DRAGONFLIES, AND THEIR RELATIVES

Biddy

Biddies are large dragonflies often seen around woodland streams, where they hover about 12 inches (30 cm) above the surface of the water. They are usually brownish in color and have big eyes that, depending on the species, either meet or nearly meet on the broad head. Biddy nymphs are large, and they live underwater at the bottom of streams, where they feed on insects and tadpoles.

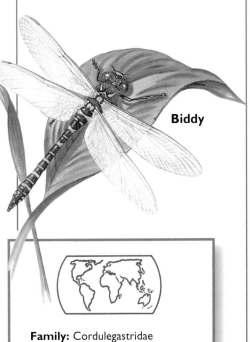

Biddy

Family: Cordulegastridae
Size: 2¼–3¼ in (6–8.5 cm) long
Number of species: 75

Mayfly

Adult mayflies live for only one day: enough time to mate and lay eggs. Most of the mayfly's life of about a year is spent in water as a nymph.

Mayfly

Nymph

Adult

Family: Lestidae
Size: 1¼–2 in (3–5 cm) long
Number of species: 200

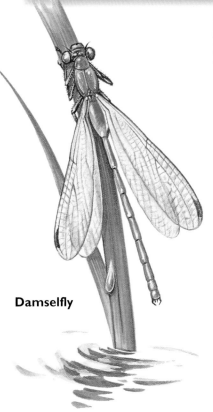

Damselfly

Damselfly

These insects are sometimes known as spread-winged damselflies because they hold their wings partly spread out when at rest. They live around ponds and marshes, where they catch insects such as small flies.

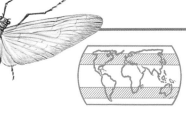

Family: Baetidae
Size: about ⅜ in (1 cm) long
Number of species: 800

210

Clubtail dragonfly

These dragonflies hunt in a different way from many other dragonflies. The clubtail finds a suitable perch and watches for prey. Once it sights the prey, it darts out to seize it, then returns to the perch.

Clubtail dragonfly

Family: Gomphidae
Size: 2–3 in (5–7.5 cm) long
Number of species: 875

Family: Coenagrionidae
Size: 1–2 in (2.5–5 cm) long
Number of species: 1,000

Narrow-winged damselfly

The males of these slender-bodied damselflies are usually brighter in color than the females. The nymphs, like those of all damselflies, live in water and catch small insects to eat.

Narrow-winged damselfly

Family: Libellulidae
Size: ¾–2½ in (2–6 cm) long
Number of species: 1,250

Skimmer

Skimmer

A skimmer is a kind
of dragonfly with a wide
flattened body that is shorter than
its wings. Some have a wingspan of
up to 4 inches (10 cm). Skimmers
are usually seen flying near still or
slow-moving water, such as ponds
and swamps.

Family: Aeschnidae
Size: 2¼–3½ in (6–9 cm) long
Number of species: about 1,000

Darner
dragonfly

Darners are some of the
largest and fastest of all dragonflies.
When hunting, the darner zooms
back and forth with its legs held
ready to seize prey. The male is
very territorial—he has a particular
area that he patrols and defends.
Females are allowed to enter the
territory, but
other male
darners are
chased away.

Family: Libellulidae
Size: ¾–2 ½ in (2–6 cm) long
Number of species: 1,250

Darter

This type of dragonfly gets
its name from its fast,
darting flight. Like all
dragonflies, darters lay
their eggs in or close to
water. The young are
called nymphs or
naiads. They look
quite different
from adults and live
in water, catching prey
such as tadpoles.

Darter

Family: Panorpidae
Size: ½–¾ in (1.2–2 cm) long
Number of species: 400

Scorpionfly

This insect gets its name
from the curving end of the
male's body, which looks
like a scorpion's stinger.
Adults have long, thin legs
and two pairs of wings.
They eat nectar and fruit
as well as insects.

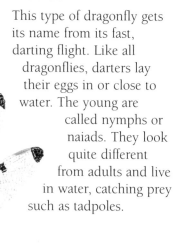

Scorpionfly

Darner
dragonfly

Assassin bug

Family: Reduviidae
Size: ½–2 in (1.2–5 cm) long
Number of species: 5,500

Assassin bug

Fierce-looking assassin bugs attack and kill other insects, such as caterpillars, beetles, and bees. Once the bug has grasped its prey, it injects some spit, or saliva, which paralyzes its victim. The bug then sucks up the prey's body juices. Some assassin bugs also bite large mammals, including humans, and feed on their blood. These bites can be painful and may even carry disease.

Chigoe flea

Like other fleas, chigoes live on the blood of humans and other animals. The flea causes a reaction in the host that makes the skin grow and engulf the insect. The female chigoe lays her eggs while she is embedded.

Chigoe flea

Family: Tungidae
Size: ⅛–¼ in (0.3–0.6 cm) long
Number of species: 20

Family: Pulicidae
Size: up to ¼ in (0.6 cm) long
Number of species: 200

Bark louse

Bark louse

Bark lice are not lice at all but small insects called psocids. There are both winged and wingless species. Most live outdoors on or under the bark of trees and bushes and feed on lichen and algae. Others live indoors, feeding on mold or stored food, and are often called book lice.

Family: Psocidae
Size: ¹⁄₁₆–¼ in (0.15–0.6 cm) long
Number of species: 500

Cat flea

Cat flea

Like most fleas, the cat flea can jump up to 200 times its length. This helps it leap onto cats to feed on their blood. The spiny combs on the flea's head help anchor it in the host's fur. The finer the host's fur, the closer together the comb spines are of the species of flea that feeds on it. The flea also uses its hooklike claws to hold on to the host's skin. Female fleas lay their eggs in the nest or bedding of the host animal.

Feather louse

Feather lice are chewing lice that live on a wide range of birds. They have two claws on each leg that they use to cling to their host's feathers. They feed by biting off pieces of feather with their strong jaws. Females lay up to 100 eggs, which they fix to the feathers of the host with a gluey substance made in their own bodies.

Feather

Feather louse

Family: Philopteridae
Size: ¹⁄₁₆ in (0.15 cm) long
Number of species: 2,700

214

Beetles

More than a quarter of a million species of beetles are known, and there are certainly many more yet to be discovered. They live in almost every type of habitat, from polar lands to rain forests, and feed on almost every type of food with their strong chewing mouthparts. Typically, beetles have two pairs of wings—the front pair are thick and hard and act as covers for the more delicate back wings. When beetles are at rest, their back wings are folded safely away under the front wings, or wing cases.

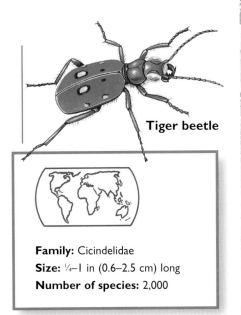

Tiger beetle

Family: Cicindelidae
Size: ¼–1 in (0.6–2.5 cm) long
Number of species: 2,000

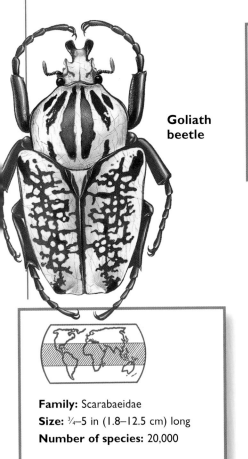

Goliath beetle

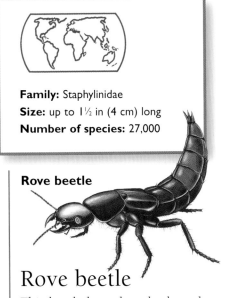

Family: Staphylinidae
Size: up to 1½ in (4 cm) long
Number of species: 27,000

Rove beetle

Tiger beetle

The colorful tiger beetle has long legs and is a fast runner. A fierce, active hunter, it catches smaller insects in its strong jaws. The female beetle lays her eggs in the sand. When the larvae hatch, they dig burrows where they hide, waiting to grab passing prey.

Whirligig beetle

Glossy whirligig beetles swim on the surface of ponds and streams, feeding on insects that fall into the water. Their eyes are divided into two parts so that they can see above and below the water surface at the same time. Larval whirligigs eat aquatic insects, but they also hunt other small creatures such as snails.

Rove beetle

This beetle has a long body and short wing cases that cover only part of the abdomen. When it is disturbed, it holds the back end of its body up, like a scorpion does. Adult rove beetles and their larvae prey on insects and other small creatures such as worms.

Family: Scarabaeidae
Size: ¾–5 in (1.8–12.5 cm) long
Number of species: 20,000

Goliath beetle

One of the largest and heaviest of all insects, the goliath beetle is found in Africa. Males are the giants; females are smaller and less brightly patterned. These beetles have strong front legs and are excellent climbers. They clamber up into trees in search of sap and soft fruit to eat.

Family: Gyrinidae
Size: ⅛–⅝ in (0.3–1.5 cm) long
Number of species: 750

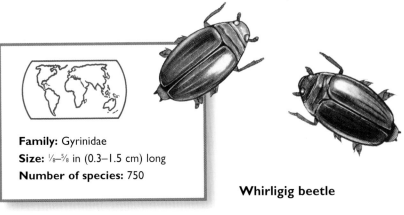

Whirligig beetle

Stag beetles

With their large head and massive jaws, male stag beetles are among the most spectacular of all insects. But despite their fearsome appearance, these insects are harmless to people and feed mostly on tree sap and other liquids, such as honeydew. There are about 1,250 species of stag beetles, some measuring up to 4 inches (10 cm) long. Most stag beetles are black or brownish in color. They usually live in woodlands and are particularly common in tropical areas.

The jaws of the males are branched like the antlers of a stag, and, like stags, these beetles take part in fierce battles with one another to win females. They rarely bite, just use their "antlers." Sometimes they damage each other's wing cases. The beetle with the biggest jaws usually wins the contest.

Female stag beetles lay their eggs in cracks in logs or dead tree stumps. When the larvae hatch, they feed on the juices of the rotting wood.

Larva and pupa

Stag beetle eggs hatch into wormlike, C-shaped larvae called grubs (above). They spend most of their time feeding and grow quickly.

As a larva grows, it molts several times, shedding its skin to allow for the increase in body size. When the larva is full-grown, it becomes a pupa (below)—the stage during which the larva changes into an adult beetle. When the process (called pupation) is complete, a winged adult beetle comes out of the pupa.

Female stag beetle

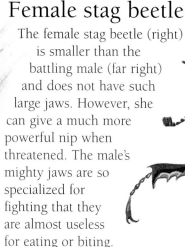

The female stag beetle (right) is smaller than the battling male (far right) and does not have such large jaws. However, she can give a much more powerful nip when threatened. The male's mighty jaws are so specialized for fighting that they are almost useless for eating or biting.

Its wing cases raised, this magnificent **stag beetle** is about to take to the air. When the beetle is not in flight, the tough wing cases (actually the front wings that have been specially adapted) protect the more delicate back wings, which are folded underneath.

The helpless loser

If a stag beetle lands on its back after a battle, it is very hard for it to turn over again. While it struggles, a predator, such as a bird, can easily snap it up.

Battling rivals

When battling for females, males usually meet on the branch of a tree. Each male tries to lock the other in its jaws, which are just the right shape to fit around the top part of a stag beetle's body. Once one competitor succeeds in grabbing the other, he lifts his rival up and tries to throw him off the branch.

Diving beetle

These beetles live in ponds and lakes. They swim by using their back legs as oars. When they dive in search of food, these beetles can stay under for some time, breathing air trapped under the wing cases. Both adults and larvae hunt tadpoles and even small fish.

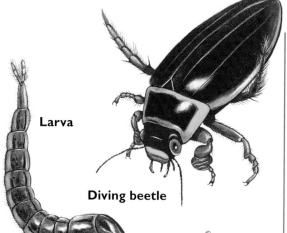

Larva

Diving beetle

Family: Dytiscidae
Size: ¹⁄₁₆–1½ in (0.15–4 cm) long
Number of species: 3,500

Carrion beetle

These brightly colored beetles and their larvae feed on dead animals, such as mice and birds. Some carrion beetles dig under a body, causing it to sink into the ground. These beetles lay their eggs on the decaying creature so that their young have a ready supply of food to eat when they hatch.

Family: Silphidae
Size: up to 1½ in (4 cm) long
Number of species: 250

Carrion beetle

Family: Buprestidae
Size: ¾–2¼ in (2–6 cm) long
Number of species: 14,000

Jewel beetle

Jewel beetle

With their gleaming metallic colors, jewel beetles deserve their name. They live in forests, usually in tropical areas, where the adults feed on flower nectar and leaves. The larvae bore into dead or living wood as they eat and can cause a great deal of damage.

Family: Cerambycidae
Size: up to 7 in (18 cm) long, including antennae
Number of species: 25,000

Longhorn beetle

Longhorn beetle

This beetle has extremely long antennae—up to three times the length of its body. While her mate stands guard, the female longhorn lays her eggs in the crevices of living trees or logs. When the larvae hatch, they tunnel into the wood as they feed and may cause considerable damage to trees. The larvae also eat plant roots. Adult longhorn beetles feed on pollen and nectar.

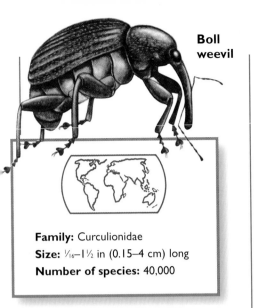

Boll weevil

Family: Curculionidae
Size: 1/16–1 1/2 in (0.15–4 cm) long
Number of species: 40,000

Boll weevil

This insect belongs to the weevil family, all of which eat plants and can cause serious damage. The boll weevil uses its long snout to bore into the seedpods—called bolls—and buds of cotton plants. The female also lays her eggs in holes made in seedpods.

Darkling beetle

Common in dry areas where they lurk under stones, darkling beetles scurry out to feed. They are scavengers and eat many kinds of food, including rotting wood, insect larvae, and stored grain. Some desert-living darklings have long legs and can move quickly as they run from one patch of shade to another.

Family: Tenebrionidae
Size: 3/4–1 3/4 in (2–4.5 cm) long
Number of species: 15,000

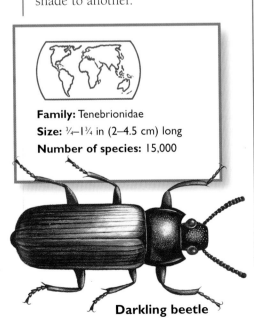

Darkling beetle

Ladybug

The ladybug's round, red-and-black body makes it one of the most easily identifiable of all insects. Adults and larvae feed mainly on aphids, which suck the juices of plants and can be serious pests. Without ladybugs, these insects would be a far greater problem for farmers and gardeners. The ladybug's bright colors warn its enemies that it tastes unpleasant and may be poisonous. Ladybugs often hibernate under logs, bark or piles of leaves, or in attics.

Ladybug

Family: Coccinellidae
Size: up to 3/8 in (0.9 cm) long
Number of species: 5,000

Firefly

Fireflies, also known as glowworms, can produce a yellowish-green light in a special area at the end of the abdomen. Each species of firefly flashes its light in a particular pattern to attract mates of its own kind. Male fireflies have wings, but in some species females are wingless and look like larvae (see p.115). Fireflies usually glow at dusk and can shut off their light when it is not required.

Firefly

Male

Family: Lampyridae
Size: up to 1 in (2.5 cm) long
Number of species: 2,000

Click beetle

The clicking sound made as these beetles leap in the air to turn themselves right side up when they fall on their backs gives them their name. They can jump as high as 1 foot (30 cm). Adult beetles live on the ground or in rotting wood.

Click beetle

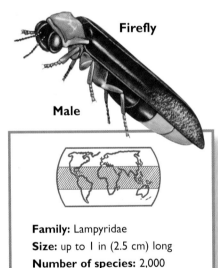

Family: Elateridae
Size: up to 2 1/4 in (6 cm) long
Number of species: 8,500

219

Flies, moths, and butterflies

Robber fly

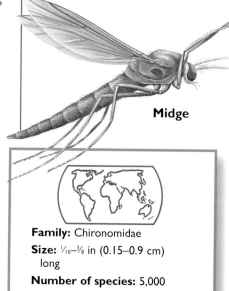

Flies are thought of as dirty and disease carrying, but they do have value. Like bees, they can pollinate flowering plants as they feed, and they are an important source of food for many other creatures, such as birds. Also, their scavenging habits help get rid of dung, dead bodies, and other decaying waste. Butterflies and moths are much more attractive insects. They pollinate plants, too, as they flit from flower to flower, sipping nectar.

Flies

One of the larger groups of insects, with more than 90,000 known species, flies are common almost everywhere. One of the few land-based creatures in Antarctica is a type of fly called a midge. An important feature of flies is that they have only one pair of wings. The hind wings are reduced to small knobbed structures called halteres, which help the fly balance in flight. Flies usually take liquid food. Many feed on nectar and sap from living plants or suck up juices from rotting plants. Some, such as female horseflies, suck blood by biting humans and other animals.

Family: Asilidae
Size: ¼–1¾ in (0.6–4.5 cm) long
Number of species: 5,000

Robber fly

A fast-moving hunter, the robber fly chases and catches other insects in the air or pounces on them on the ground. It has strong, bristly legs for seizing its prey. Once it has caught its food, the robber fly sucks out the body fluids with its sharp mouthparts. Larvae live in soil or rotting wood, where they feed on the larvae of other insects.

Midge

Tiny, delicate insects, midges fly in huge swarms, usually in the evening, and are often seen near ponds and streams. There are two kinds of midges: those that do not bite, and those that bite other animals, including humans.

Midge

Horsefly

These flies have particularly large iridescent (shimmering) eyes. Males feed on pollen and nectar, but female horseflies take blood from mammals, including humans. Their bite can be painful and the flies may carry diseases such as anthrax.

Family: Tabanidae
Size: ¼–1 in (0.6–2.5 cm) long
Number of species: 4,100

Horsefly

Family: Chironomidae
Size: 1/16–3/8 in (0.15–0.9 cm) long
Number of species: 5,000

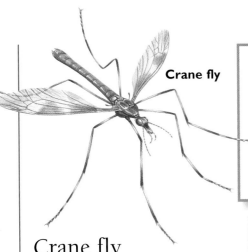

Crane fly

Family: Tipulidae
Size: ¼–2¼ in (0.6–6 cm) long
Number of species: 15,000

Family: Calliphoridae
Size: ¼–⅝ in (0.6–1.5 cm) long
Number of species: 1,500

Crane fly

With their long, thin legs, crane flies look like large mosquitoes, but they do not bite or suck blood. The largest have a wingspan of as much as 2¾ inches (7 cm). Most adults live only a few days and probably do not eat at all. The larvae feed mainly on plant roots and rotting plants, although some do hunt for their food.

Hover fly

Also known as flower flies, adult hover flies feed on pollen and nectar. They are expert fliers and can hover with ease and even fly backward. Many species are brightly colored and look much like bees or wasps. They do not sting, however. Some hover fly larvae hunt insects such as aphids. Others feed on plants or live in the nests of bees or wasps, where they feed on the larvae.

Blowfly

Many blowflies are colored metallic blue or green. Adults feed on pollen and nectar as well as fluids from rotting matter. Many lay their eggs in carrion—the bodies of dead animals—or in dung, so that the larvae, called maggots, have plenty of food to eat when they hatch.

Blowfly

Family: Tephritidae
Size: ⅛–⅜ in (0.3–0.9 cm) long
Number of species: 4,500

Fruit fly

Fruit fly

These little flies are common around flowers and ripening fruit. Their larvae feed on plant matter and some are serious pests, causing great damage to fruit trees and other crops.

Housefly

Found almost everywhere in the world, houseflies suck liquids from decaying matter and from fresh fruit and plants. They also feed on flower nectar. In some places they carry diseases, such as cholera and typhoid fever.

Housefly

Family: Muscidae
Size: ⅛–½ in (0.3–1.2 cm) long
Number of species: 3,000

Family: Syrphidae
Size: ¼–1¼ in (0.6–3 cm) long
Number of species: 6,000

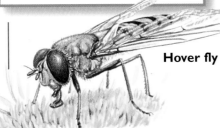

Hover fly

221

Butterflies and moths

Everywhere in the world that plants grow there are butterflies and moths. Known as the Lepidoptera, this is the second largest group of insects, containing about 150,000 species. Generally, butterflies are more brightly colored than moths and fly by day, whereas moths fly by night—but there are exceptions. A butterfly or moth larva is called a caterpillar. It spends most of its life eating plants and growing fast. When it has reached its full size, a caterpillar becomes a pupa. During this stage, it changes from wingless larva to winged adult. Caddis flies form a separate group called the Trichoptera.

Clothes moth

The caterpillar of the clothes moth feeds on hair and feathers in animal nests and on the dried corpses of small mammals and birds. Few creatures, other than some beetle larvae, can digest these difficult foods. Because people use animal wool to make fabric, the caterpillars often come into homes to feed on clothes. The adult moths are small, with narrow front wings that are folded neatly over the body when at rest. They do not usually eat anything.

Geometrid moth

Geometrids have slender bodies and fragile wings. When they are at rest, they spread their wings out flat. Their caterpillars are known as inchworms because they seem to be measuring, inch by inch, as they move. They eat leaves and may cause serious damage to trees.

Family: Tineidae
Size: wingspan ¼–¾ in (0.6–2 cm)
Number of species: 2,500

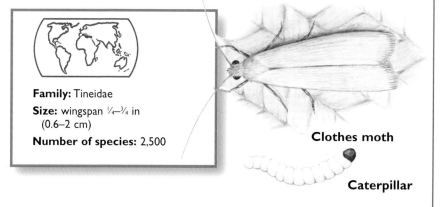

Clothes moth

Caterpillar

Family: Geometridae
Size: wingspan ½–1½ in (1.2–4 cm)
Number of species: 18,000

Family: Sphingidae
Size: wingspan 1¼–6 in (3–15 cm)
Number of species: 1,200

Hummingbird hawkmoth

Hummingbird hawkmoth

This hawkmoth feeds on flower nectar and has a very long proboscis, or feeding tube, that allows it to reach deep into blooms. It hovers as it feeds and looks similar to a hummingbird, from which it takes its name.

Geometrid moth

Caterpillar

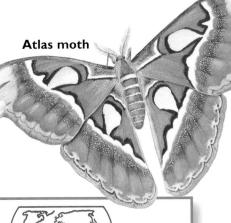

Atlas moth

Atlas moth

These brightly patterned moths are some of the largest in the world. Most have feathery antennae and scaleless, transparent patches on their broad wings. The antennae help male moths pick up the scent signals females give off when looking for mates. Adults have very small mouthparts and do not generally feed during this short stage of their lives.

Family: Saturniidae
Size: wingspan 1–9¾ in (2.5–25 cm)
Number of species: 1,100

Cotton boll moth

This moth belongs to one of the biggest families of moths. Most moths in this family fly at night and are dull in color. The cotton boll caterpillar feeds on cotton seedpods and can damage the plants.

Cotton boll moth

Family: Noctuidae
Size: wingspan ½–3 in (1.2–7.5 cm)
Number of species: 25,000

Larva

Large caddis fly

Family: Phryganeidae
Size: wingspan ½–1 in (1.2–2.5 cm)
Number of species: 500

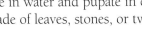

Tiger moth

Tiger moths have broad, hairy bodies and boldly patterned wings. The bright markings of these moths, and of their hairy caterpillars, warn birds and mammals that they are unpleasant to eat. The caterpillars feed on plants that are poisonous to vertebrate animals and store the poison for their own protection.

Large caddis fly

Caddis flies look like moths but have hairs not scales on the body and wings. They have short mouthparts for lapping up food instead of a coiled proboscis. The caterpillar-like larvae usually live in water and pupate in cases made of leaves, stones, or twigs.

Luna moth

This beautiful moth has wings that can measure up to 4 inches (11 cm) across with long, tail-like extensions trailing from them. It lives in forests, and its caterpillars feed on the leaves of trees such as hickory, walnut, and birch. The caterpillars pupate in a cocoon on the ground.

Family: Arctiidae
Size: wingspan ¾–2¾ in (2–7 cm)
Number of species: 2,500

Family: Saturniidae
Size: wingspan 1–9¾ in (2.5–25 cm)
Number of species: 1,100

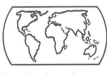

Tiger moth

Luna moth

223

Sphinx moths

O f all butterflies and moths, sphinx moths, also called hawkmoths, are some of the most powerful fliers. Their wings beat so fast that they make a whirring noise. The moths can even hover like hummingbirds in front of flowers as they feed.

Like many moths, adult sphinx moths eat liquid food such as plant nectar. They suck up the food with a special kind of tongue called a proboscis. This structure is hollow in the middle, like a drinking straw, and is kept rolled up under the head when not in use. Sphinx moths have the longest tongues of any moths and can feed on nectar at the bottom of long, tubelike flowers.

There are about 1,200 species of sphinx moths, some with wingspans of up to 6 inches (15 cm). Most have large, heavy bodies and long, narrow front wings. Their caterpillars are fat and smooth, sometimes with a hornlike structure at the end of the abdomen.

Hummingbird clearwing moth

Many scales on this moth's wings fall off after its first flight, leaving large clear areas. It feeds on flower nectar, using its proboscis, or feeding tube, to reach into the flowers. This moth is a strong flier, and its wings beat very fast. It flies by day, not at night.

Poplar sphinx moth

The color and irregular shape of the poplar sphinx moth's wings help it hide on bark as it rests during the day. Its caterpillars feed on the leaves of trees such as poplars and willows.

Egg

Caterpillar

Egg to pupa

As soon as a caterpillar hatches from its egg it starts to feed, devouring plants with its strong chewing mouthparts. It grows fast and sheds its skin several times as it gets bigger. When fully grown, the caterpillar becomes a pupa. The bee sphinx moth pupates on the ground in a cocoon made of silk.

Pupa in cocoon

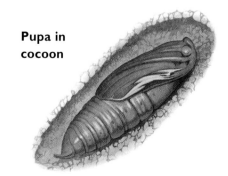

224

Oleander sphinx moth

This is one of the most beautifully patterned of all moths. Its caterpillar feeds on the leaves of oleander and other plants and grows up to 6 inches (15 cm) long. The caterpillar has bold eyespots on its body that can fool a predator into thinking it is a much larger creature than it really is.

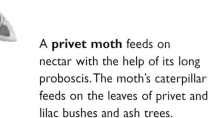

A **privet moth** feeds on nectar with the help of its long proboscis. The moth's caterpillar feeds on the leaves of privet and lilac bushes and ash trees.

White-lined sphinx moth

The white-lined sphinx moth feeds at night on flowers. Like most moths, its antennae are very sensitive to smell as well as touch. By picking up the faintest scents, they help the moth find flowers in the dark.

Fluminense swallowtail butterfly

Fluminense swallowtail butterfly

This beautiful butterfly is one of Brazil's most threatened insects. Drainage of its swampy, bushy habitat to build houses and factories and to plant banana plantations has caused it to die out in many sites. Even the ten or so areas in which it still lives are under threat. Conservationists hope to be able to catch some butterflies and establish new colonies in safer places.

Family: Papilionidae
Size: wingspan 2–11 in (5–28 cm)
Number of species: 700

Swallowtail butterfly

Boldly patterned swallowtail butterflies get their name from the tail-like extensions on the back wings. These may help distract enemies away from the vulnerable head area. Adult swallowtails feed on flower nectar, and their caterpillars usually eat the leaves of trees such as ash and laurel.

Family: Papilionidae
Size: wingspan 2–11 in (5–28 cm)
Number of species: 700

Swallowtail butterfly

Morpho butterfly

Morpho butterflies live in the rain forests of Central and South America. The males are brilliantly colored—the beautiful iridescence of their wings is caused by the arrangement of the rows of scales that reflect the light. Females are much plainer. Like all nymphalid butterflies, morphos walk on only four legs. The front pair are too small to be used for walking.

Morpho butterfly

Family: Nymphalidae
Size: wingspan 1–4¼ in (2.5–11 cm) long
Number of species: 3,500

Cairns birdwing butterfly

Birdwings, which are the biggest butterflies in the world, are highly prized by collectors, so many are now rare. Cairns birdwings, like all birdwing butterflies, are found only in Southeast Asia and northern Australia. Females are bigger than males, but males are more colorful. Adults feed on flower nectar, but caterpillars eat the leaves of plants that are poisonous to most creatures.

Cairns birdwing butterfly

Male

Family: Papilionidae
Size: wingspan 2–11 in (5–28 cm)
Number of species: 700

Caterpillar

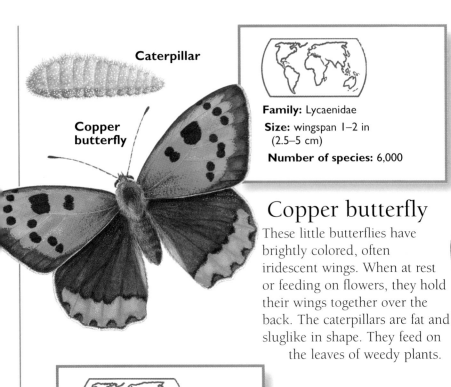

Copper butterfly

Family: Lycaenidae
Size: wingspan 1–2 in (2.5–5 cm)
Number of species: 6,000

Copper butterfly

These little butterflies have brightly colored, often iridescent wings. When at rest or feeding on flowers, they hold their wings together over the back. The caterpillars are fat and sluglike in shape. They feed on the leaves of weedy plants.

Family: Nymphalidae
Size: wingspan 1–4¼ in (2.5–11 cm)
Number of species: 3,500

Monarch butterfly

Every autumn, millions of monarch butterflies fly south from their breeding grounds in Canada and the northern United States to Mexico— a distance of about 2,000 miles (3,200 km). In the spring, the butterflies fly north again. Females stop to lay their eggs along the way.

Monarch butterfly

❶ Queen Alexandra's birdwing butterfly

Family: Papilionidae
Size: wingspan 2–11 in (5–28 cm)
Number of species: 700

Male

Cabbage white butterfly

The cabbage white is a very common butterfly. Unlike many butterflies, cabbage whites have well-developed front legs that are used for walking. Adults feed on nectar. Their caterpillars eat cabbage and other leafy crops and can do great damage.

Cabbage white butterfly

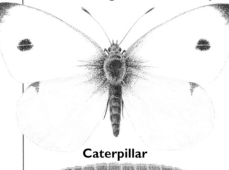

Caterpillar

Family: Pieridae
Size: wingspan ¾–2¾ in (0.9–7 cm) long
Number of species: 1,300

Queen Alexandra's birdwing butterfly

The female of this giant butterfly is the biggest in the world, with a wingspan of up to 11 inches (28 cm), but the male is more colorful. It is very valuable, so local people catch it to sell to traders. It is hoped that if some of the forests in which the butterflies live can be saved in reserves, local people might be able to make money from tourism instead.

227

Bees, wasps, ants, and termites

Bees, wasps, and ants belong to a large group of insects known as the Hymenoptera. Although they vary greatly in appearance, most have a definite "waist" at the front of the abdomen. They have chewing mouthparts and tonguelike structures for sucking liquids such as nectar from flowers. Hymenopterans that do have wings have two pairs, but many worker ants are wingless. Ants and some bees and wasps live in social colonies in elaborate nests. Termites are not related to ants, bees, and wasps, but they do live in huge colonies. They make nests in soil, trees, or specially built mounds.

Family: Megachilidae
Size: ⅜–¾ in (0.9–2 cm) long
Number of species: 3,000

Leafcutter bee

This bee gets its name from its habit of cutting out circular pieces of leaves and flowers with its jaws. It uses these pieces to line larval cells in its tunnel nest, made in soil or rotting wood. Stores of nectar and pollen are put into the cells, and an egg is then laid in each one.

Bees

There are about 22,000 species of bees. They have two pairs of wings, and their bodies are covered with tiny hairs. Some kinds, such as leafcutter bees, live alone and make their own nests for their young. Others, such as honeybees and bumblebees, live in huge colonies that may contain thousands of bees.

Bumblebee

Bumblebees are large, hairy insects, usually black in color with some yellow or orange markings. Queens are the only bumblebees that live through the winter. In spring they look for nest sites. Each queen collects pollen and nectar and makes food called beebread. Later, she lays eggs. When the larvae hatch, they feed on the beebread. These larvae become adult worker bees, and they take over the work of the colony while the queen continues to lay eggs.

Bumblebee

Family: Apidae
Size: ⅛–1 in (0.3–2.5 cm) long
Number of species: 1,000

Plasterer bee

Family: Colletidae
Size: ⅛–¾ in (0.3–2 cm) long
Number of species: 6,000

Plasterer bee

Plasterer bees nest in the ground in burrows with branching tunnels. They line the tunnels with a secretion from glands in the abdomen, which dries to a clear waterproof substance. Cells for larvae are made in the tunnels.

Family: Andrenidae
Size: ⅛–¾ in (0.3–2 cm) long
Number of species: 4,000

Mining bee

Mining bee

Mining bees nest in long, branching tunnels that they dig in the ground. Cells in the tunnels are stocked with nectar and pollen, and an egg is laid in each one. Each bee digs its own nest, but large numbers may live close together.

Orchid bee

Most orchid bees live in tropical areas and are brightly colored. The long proboscis is used for collecting nectar. Males visit orchid flowers to collect scent compounds, which may play a part in their mating rituals.

Orchid bee

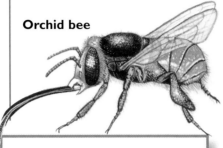

Family: Apidae
Size: ⅛–1 in (0.3–2.5 cm) long
Number of species: 1,000

Stingless bee

Family: Apidae
Size: ⅛–1 in (0.3–2.5 cm) long
Number of species: 1,000

Stingless bee

These bees live in colonies and make nests under the ground in a tree trunk or even in part of a nest of a termite colony. As their name suggests, these bees cannot sting, but they have strong jaws that they use to bite any intruders.

Carpenter bee

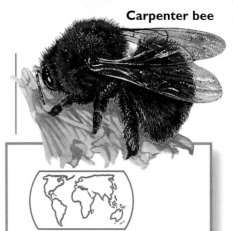

Family: Apidae
Size: ⅛–1 in (0.3–2.5 cm) long
Number of species: 1,000

Carpenter bee

The female carpenter bee chews a tunnel-like nest in wood. She makes a line of cells inside the tunnel, fills each cell with food stores of pollen and nectar, and lays one egg in each cell. She stays nearby and guards the nest against any enemies.

Cuckoo bee

Just as the cuckoo bird lays eggs in the nests of other birds, this wasplike bee lays its eggs in the nests of other bees that have prepared food stores for their own eggs. The cuckoo bee's eggs hatch first, and the larvae eat up all the food intended for the host's larvae.

Cuckoo bee

Family: Anthophoridae
Size: ⅜–½ in (0.9–1.2 cm) long
Number of species: 4,200

Honeybees

Of all the many types of bees, honeybees are probably the best known. They pollinate countless food crops and produce millions of dollars' worth of honey and wax every year.

Many bees lead solitary lives, but honeybees live in huge colonies of thousands of bees, with a complex social organization. The nest is made in a hollow tree or in a hive provided by a beekeeper and consists of a comb—wax sheets of hexagonal (six-sided cells). These cells contain eggs and larvae, or grubs, as well as food stores of pollen and honey. Each colony has a queen. The queen bee is larger than the other bees and lays all the eggs of the colony. Most of the members of the colony are female workers. They care for the larvae, build and repair the nest, and gather food, but they do not lay eggs. There are male bees—called drones—in the colony only at certain times of the year. They do not work in the hive. Their purpose is to mate with the queen at special places outside the colony.

Workers

Most worker honeybees live only about six weeks. For the first week of her adult life a worker cares for the eggs and larvae of the colony. Then she helps build cells and maintain the nest. Finally, she becomes a food gatherer, bringing nectar and pollen back to the nest.

The royal cell

Special cells for future queens hang from the edge of the comb. The larvae in queen cells are fed on royal jelly—a protein-rich substance from glands on the heads of workers. Worker larvae are fed royal jelly for a few days and then given pollen and nectar.

Busy bees

Worker bees always have plenty to do in the nest. When a bee returns from a foraging trip laden with pollen and nectar, the other worker bees gather around to collect the food. They also make the nest cells, building them from wax produced in glands on the undersides of their abdomens. The bees pull out thin flakes of wax and knead them with their mouthparts until the wax is soft enough to use for building.

Equipped for work

All the tools needed by a worker bee are on her own body. On each front leg there are long hairs used for removing pollen from her body and a special notch for cleaning her antennae. On the middle legs there are fringes of hair for removing pollen from the forelegs and a spike for taking wax from glands in the abdomen. On each hind leg there is a pollen basket— a special area lined with hairs, where pollen is carried.

A worker **honeybee** has just returned from a foraging trip, with her pollen baskets full of golden-yellow pollen. Other workers gather round to help her unload the pollen and pack it into cells.

Wasps

Wasps are more useful than they seem. They feed their larvae, or grubs, other insects, such as caterpillars and aphids, that harm garden and food plants. Without wasps there would be many more of these pests. Adult wasps feed mainly on nectar and the juice of ripe fruit. Many kinds of wasps, including mud daubers and spider wasps, live alone and make their own nests for their eggs. Others, such as yellow jackets and hornets, live in large colonies and make communal nests. Wasp colonies do not store food like honeybees do. Only the new queens survive the winter by living in protected places outside the colonies.

Giant hornet

Family: Vespidae
Size: ⅜–1¼ in (1–3 cm) long
Number of species: 3,800

Giant hornet

Adult hornets feed on insects and nectar. They live in colonies in nests built of a papery material they make by mixing saliva with chewed-up plant material. The nest is usually in a tree or attached to an old building. Larvae feed on insects caught by the adults.

Gall wasp

These tiny wasps lay their eggs inside the buds of oak trees. For reasons that are not fully understood the host plant forms a growth, called a gall, around the egg. When the larva hatches it feeds on the gall.

Family: Cynipidae
Size: 1/16–⅜ in (0.15–0.9 cm) long
Number of species: 1,250

Velvet ant

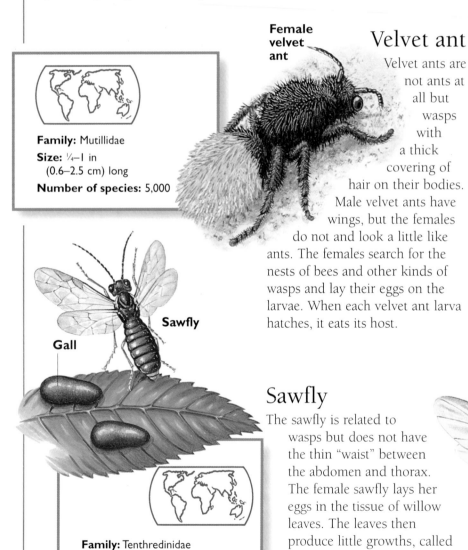

Female velvet ant

Velvet ants are not ants at all but wasps with a thick covering of hair on their bodies. Male velvet ants have wings, but the females do not and look a little like ants. The females search for the nests of bees and other kinds of wasps and lay their eggs on the larvae. When each velvet ant larva hatches, it eats its host.

Family: Mutillidae
Size: ¼–1 in (0.6–2.5 cm) long
Number of species: 5,000

Sawfly

Gall

Sawfly

The sawfly is related to wasps but does not have the thin "waist" between the abdomen and thorax. The female sawfly lays her eggs in the tissue of willow leaves. The leaves then produce little growths, called galls, as soon as the eggs are laid. When the larvae hatch they eat the galls.

Family: Tenthredinidae
Size: ⅛–¾ in (0.3–2 cm) long
Number of species: 4,000

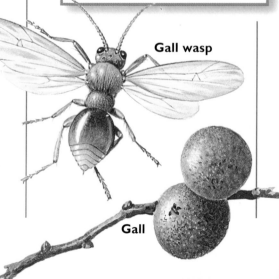

Gall wasp

Gall

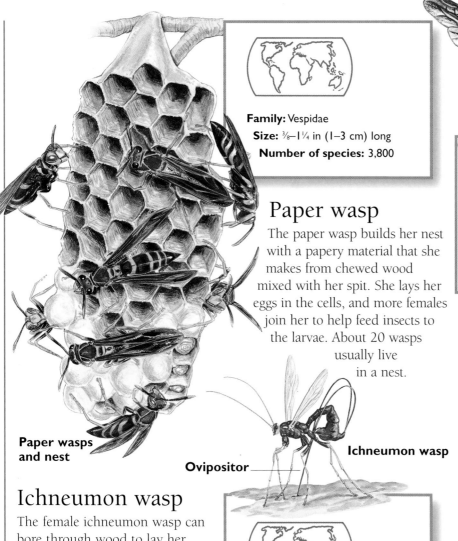

Paper wasps and nest

Family: Vespidae
Size: ⅜–1¼ in (1–3 cm) long
Number of species: 3,800

Paper wasp

The paper wasp builds her nest with a papery material that she makes from chewed wood mixed with her spit. She lays her eggs in the cells, and more females join her to help feed insects to the larvae. About 20 wasps usually live in a nest.

Ichneumon wasp

The female ichneumon wasp can bore through wood to lay her eggs near the larvae of other insects, such as wood wasps. She has a long egg-laying tube, called an ovipositor. When an egg hatches, the ichneumon larva feeds on the host larva.

Ovipositor

Ichneumon wasp

Family: Ichneumonidae
Size: ⅛–2 in (0.3–5 cm) long
Number of species: 20,000

Yellow jacket

Yellow jackets feed on nectar and other sweet things such as ripe fruit. They also catch other insects to feed their young. Wasps are well known for their sting. The pointed stinger is at the end of the abdomen and is linked to a bag of poison. The wasp uses its stinger to kill prey and to defend itself against enemies— including people.

Yellow jacket on an apple

Family: Vespidae
Size: ⅜–1¼ in (1–3 cm) long
Number of species: 3,800

Blue-black spider wasp

Family: Pompilidae
Size: ⅜–2 in (0.9–5 cm) long
Number of species: 4,000

Blue-black spider wasp

Adult spider wasps feed on nectar, but the female catches spiders to feed her young. She paralyzes the spider with her sting and then places it in a nest cell with an egg and seals the top with mud. When the wasp larva hatches, it eats the spider.

Mud dauber

Mud daubers are solitary wasps that feed on other insects and nectar. The female mud dauber wasp makes a nest of damp mud. Into each cell she puts an egg and some paralyzed insects for the larva to eat when it hatches.

Family: Sphecidae
Size: ⅜–2 in (0.9–5 cm) long
Number of species: 8,000

Mud dauber

233

Ants and termites

Ants live in huge well-organized groups, called colonies, of thousands of individuals. Most colonies make nests of interconnecting tunnels in rotting wood or under the ground. Each colony includes at least one queen ant, and she lays all of the eggs. The workers are also females, but they cannot lay eggs. They do all the work of the colony, gathering food and looking after eggs and larvae. Termites are not related to ants, although their habits are similar. They build large nests with special chambers for eggs and larvae and for food storage.

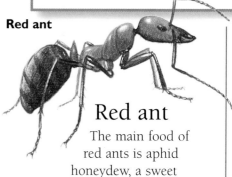

Family: Formicidae
Size: 1/16–1 in (0.15–2.5 cm) long
Number of species: 8,800

Red ant

Red ant

The main food of red ants is aphid honeydew, a sweet liquid that is a by-product of the digestive system of these tiny bugs. The ant strokes the aphid to encourage it to release the sugary liquid from its body. Red ants also feed on flower nectar.

Fire ant

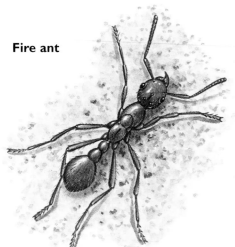

Fire ant

As its name suggests, the fire ant has a powerful bite and sting, which is extremely painful even to humans. It hunts other insects, which it stings to death, but also eats seeds, fruit, and flowers. These ants make nests in the ground or under logs or stones.

Army ant

Unlike other ants, army ants do not build permanent nests. They march in huge numbers in search of prey, overpowering insects or other small creatures in their way. Periodically they stop to lay eggs and remain in one place until the young have developed. The worker ants link their bodies together, making a temporary nest called a bivouac to protect the queen and larvae.

Family: Formicidae
Size: 1/16–1 in (0.15–2.5 cm) long
Number of species: 8,800

Family: Formicidae
Size: 1/16–1 in (0.15–2.5 cm) long
Number of species: 8,800

Harvester ant

Harvester ant

These ants take their name from their habit of feeding on seeds and grain crops. When the ants find a plentiful supply of seeds near their nest, they leave scent trails to lead others in their colony to the food. In times of plenty, the ants collect more seeds than they can eat and store them in special granary areas in the nest.

Family: Formicidae
Size: 1/16–1 in (0.15–2.5 cm) long
Number of species: 8,800

Army ant

Mandible

Carpenter ant

Carpenter ant

Colonies of carpenter ants make their nests in wooden buildings or poles or in rotting tree trunks and often cause a great deal of damage. As with all ants, the queen lays all the eggs for the colony. As she lays, worker ants remove the eggs and take them to special brood chambers, where they are cared for.

Family: Formicidae
Size: 1/16–1 in (0.15–2.5 cm) long
Number of species: 8,800

Leafcutter ant

These ants grow their own food. They cut pieces of leaves with their strong scissorlike jaws and carry them back to their underground nest. Here the leaves are chewed up and mixed with droppings to make compost heaps. The ants eat the special fungus that grows on the compost.

Family: Formicidae
Size: 1/16–1 in (0.15–2.5 cm) long
Number of species: 8,800

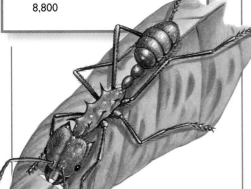

Leafcutter ant

Snouted termite

Most termite colonies have special soldier termites to defend them against enemies, which may attack their nests. The soldiers of this type of termite have long snouts, which they use to spray sticky, bad-smelling fluid at ants and other enemies.

Snouted termite

Soldier

Family: Termitidae
Size: up to 2 1/4 in (6 cm) long
Number of species: 1,650

Drywood termite

These termites attack the wood of buildings, furniture, and even stored timber. Special microscopic organisms in their guts help them digest this tough food. The soldier termites have larger heads and jaws than the others, and their job is to defend the colony against enemies.

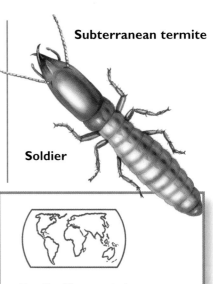

Subterranean termite

Soldier

Family: Rhinotermitidae
Size: 1/4–3/8 in (0.6–0.9 cm) long
Number of species: 200

Subterranean termite

As their name suggests, these termites live in underground nests in warm wooded areas. They eat the wood of rotting trees and roots.

Family: Kalotermitidae
Size: up to 1 in (2.5 cm) long
Number of species: 8,800

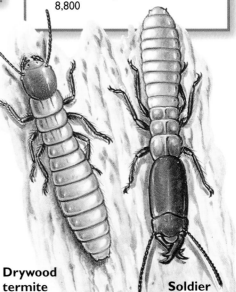

Drywood termite

Soldier

235

BEES, WASPS, ANTS, AND TERMITES

Spiders and scorpions

Arachnids, which include spiders, several types of scorpions, ticks, and mites, are often confused with insects, but they are a separate group of invertebrates. They are a very ancient group of creatures that first lived on land at least 400 million years ago. Today, arachnids include a wide range of body forms, but generally they have four pairs of legs and do not have wings or antennae. Most live on land and hunt other creatures to eat.

Spiders

Most spiders are completely harmless. Only a few, such as the black widow spider, have a venomous bite that is dangerous to people. In fact, spiders do humans a service by keeping the insect population under control—all are hunters, and they feed mostly on small insects. Some of the larger species, such as the bird-eating spider, even catch birds and other small animals. All spiders can make silk with special glands at the end of the abdomen, but not all build webs. Spiders use silk to line their burrows, and some make silken traps that they hold between their legs to snare prey. Young spiders use long strands of silk as parachutes to help them "fly" away and find new territories.

Jumping spider

Unlike most spiders, the jumping spider has good eyesight, which helps it find prey. Once it has spotted something, the spider leaps onto its victim. Before jumping, it attaches a silk thread that it uses as a safety line along which it can return to its hideout.

Jumping spider

Family: Salticidae
Size: ⅛–⅝ in (0.3–1.5 cm) long
Number of species: 4,000

Black widow spider

The female black widow has a red hourglass shape on the underside of her abdomen. Bristles on her back legs help her throw strands of silk over prey caught in her web. She has a venomous bite that is more deadly than a rattlesnake's. Male black widows do not bite.

Family: Theridiidae
Size: up to ½ in (1.2 cm) long
Number of species: 2,500

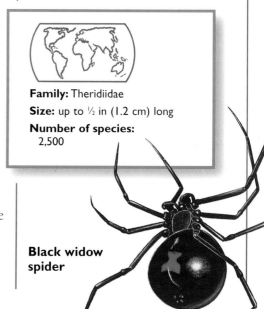

Black widow spider

Wolf spider

Fast-moving hunters like their namesake, wolf spiders creep up on prey and seize it after a final speedy dash. Most do not make webs. Wolf spiders have three sets of eyes that help them find prey.

Family: Lycosidae
Size: ⅛–1½ in (0.3–4 cm) long
Number of species: 2,500

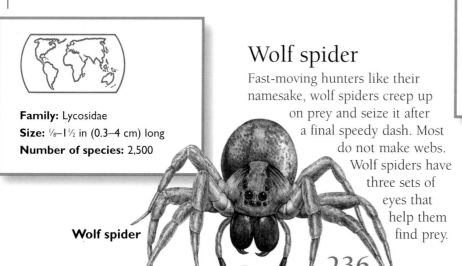

Wolf spider

Fang

236

Trapdoor spider

Family: Ctenizidae
Size: ³⁄₈–2 in (0.9–5 cm) long
Number of species: 700

Red-kneed
tarantula

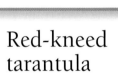

Family: Theraphosidae
Size: up to 3½ in (9 cm) long
Number of species: 300

Trapdoor spider

The burrow of the trapdoor spider has a hinged lid at the top. The spider waits in its burrow until it senses the movement of prey overhead. It then pops out of the door, grabs the prey, and takes it back into its burrow.

Crab spider

Crab spider

This spider moves by scurrying sideways like a crab. It does not make webs, but the smaller males sometimes use their silk to tie the females down before mating. Some crab spiders are dark brown or black, but those that sit on flowers to wait for prey are usually brightly colored to match the petals.

Family: Thomisidae
Size: ¹⁄₁₆–³⁄₈ in (0.15–0.9 cm) long
Number of species: 3,000

Red-kneed tarantula

Tarantulas are some of the largest of all spiders, with legs spanning more than 7¾ inches (20 cm). Most hide during the day and come out at night to hunt insects and small creatures, which they kill with a venomous bite. Harmless to people, they are becoming popular pets. Local people are collecting so many for export that the spiders could soon become scarce in the wild.

Lichen spider

Muted colors help keep this spider well hidden on lichen-covered tree bark. Tufts of tiny hairs on its legs break up any shadows that might otherwise reveal its presence. If the spider suspects an enemy is near, it flattens itself even more against the bark and becomes very difficult to see.

Spitting spider

This unusual hunter approaches its prey and spits out two lines of a sticky substance from glands near its mouth. These fall in a zigzag pattern over the prey, pinning it down. The spider then kills it with a bite.

Family: Sparassidae
Size: ³⁄₈–1¼ in (0.9–3 cm) long
Number of species: 1,000

Family: Scytodidae
Size: ³⁄₈ in (0.9 cm) long
Number of species: 200

Lichen spider 237 **Spitting spider**

SPIDERS AND SCORPIONS

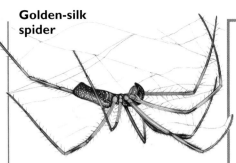

Golden-silk spider

Family: Araneidae
Size: 1/16–1 1/4 in (0.15–3 cm) long
Number of species: 2,500

Golden-silk spider

The female golden-silk spider is eight or nine times the length of the male and may weigh a hundred times as much. The male's size is, in fact, an advantage when he approaches the female to try to mate with her. Like the tiny insects that fly into her web, the male golden-silk spider is too small for her to bother attacking, so he is left alone.

Common house spider

The house spider has long legs covered with strong bristles. It builds its large flat web in any quiet corner of a house, garage, or shed. The spider stays beneath the web, waiting for prey to get tangled in its sticky strands and then removes and eats the prey.

Common house spider

Family: Agelenidae
Size: 1/16–3/4 in (0.15–2 cm) long
Number of species: 1,000

Purse-web spider

This spider builds a silken tube in a sloping burrow in the ground. The top of the tube extends aboveground and is camouflaged with leaves. When an insect lands on the tube, the spider grabs it through the walls of the tube with her sharp fangs and drags it inside.

Purse-web spider

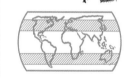

Family: Atypidae
Size: 3/8–1 1/4 in (0.9–3 cm) long
Number of species: 1

Funnel-web spider

This spider makes a funnel-shaped web that leads into an underground burrow. If a creature walks across the web, the spider senses the vibrations and rushes out for the kill. Funnel-webs prey on frogs and lizards as well as insects and have an extremely poisonous bite.

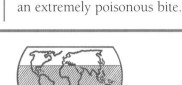

Family: Dipluridae
Size: about 1 1/4 in (3 cm) long
Number of species: about 100

Funnel-web spider

Cell spider

These spiders have only six eyes—most spiders have eight. They spend the day hiding under stones and come out at night to hunt wood lice. Wood lice have strong external skeletons, but this spider can pierce the body armor with its huge, sharp fangs.

Family: Dysderidae
Size: 3/4 in (2 cm) long
Number of species: 2

Fang

Cell spider

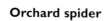

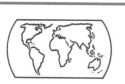

Family: Araneidae
Size: ¹⁄₁₆–1¼ in (0.15–3 cm) long
Number of species: 2,500

Orchard spider

Family: Pisauridae
Size: ¼–1 in (0.6–2.5 cm) long
Number of species: 400

Egg sac

Nursery-web spider

Green lynx spider

Orchard spider

Although a member of the orb weaver family, the orchard spider does not make a web. It simply sits on the branch of a tree and grabs any moth that comes near with its strong front legs. The spider may release a scent that attracts the moths to it.

Water spider

The water spider is the only spider that lives its whole life in water, even though it needs air to breathe. It spins a bell-shaped home of silk attached to an underwater plant and supplies it with bubbles of air collected at the water surface. It then sits inside its bell waiting for prey to come near. It pounces on the prey and takes it back to the bell to eat.

Nursery-web spider

These spiders build webs to protect their young, rather than to catch prey. The female carries her egg sac with her until the eggs are almost ready to hatch. Then she spins a web over the eggs to protect them while they hatch. She stands guard nearby.

Family: Agelenidae
Size: ¹⁄₁₆–¾ in (0.15–2 cm) long
Number of species: 1,000

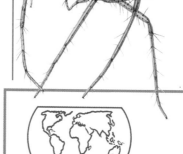

Family: Oxyopidae
Size: ⅛–⅝ in (0.3–1.5 cm) long
Number of species: 500

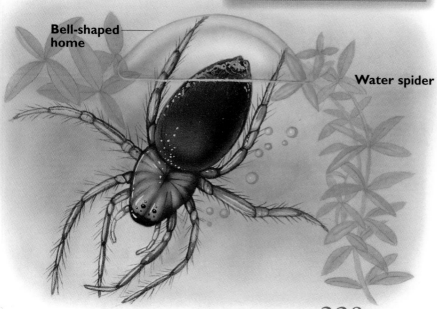

Bell-shaped home

Water spider

Green lynx spider

The lynx spider is a fast-moving, active hunter. It uses its long legs to form a basket-like trap around its prey, which it kills with a venomous bite. It has good eyesight, which helps it spot its prey, and its green color helps keep it hidden when resting on leaves. This spider is used in pest control by farmers.

Orb weavers

Very few creatures build traps to catch their prey. Among the best known are the orb weaver spiders, which build the webs most often seen in our houses and yards. There are more than 2,500 species of these spiders living all over the world.

Spiders build their webs with two types of silk, which comes from glands at the end of the abdomen. The silk is liquid when it comes out of the nozzlelike openings of small structures called spinnerets. One type of silk hardens into extremely tough nonsticky thread; the other type is sticky and is used for the center of the web. Once the web is built, the spider waits near the center or hides nearby, linked to the web by a signal thread. Through this, the spider can sense any movement or disturbance in the web. Once prey is caught in the sticky part of the web, the spider rushes over, bites it, and wraps it in strands of silk to prevent it from escaping.

Ogre-faced spider

This spider (right and above) takes its web to the prey. It makes a small but strong net of very sticky threads in a framework of dry silk. Once the trap is made, the spider hangs from a twig on silken lines, holding the net in its four front legs. When an insect comes near, the spider stretches the net wide so the prey flies into it and becomes entangled. The catch is then bundled up in the net and taken away to eat.

Building a web

First, the orb weaver spider makes a framework of strong nonsticky threads that are firmly attached to surrounding plants or other supports. Spokes are added (2), and the spider spins a widely spaced temporary spiral. With everything locked in place, the spider then moves inward (3), spinning the sticky spiral that will trap the prey and removing the temporary spiral. The whole process takes less than an hour, and the spider may build a new web every night.

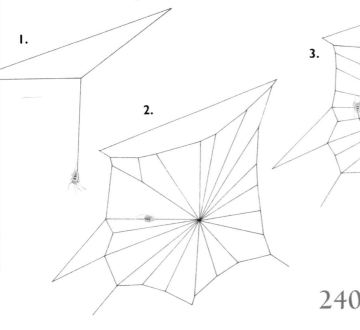

1.

2.

3.

240

Sheet-web spider

Yet another kind of trap is woven by this spider. It makes a flat sheetlike web, which may measure as much as 12 inches (30 cm) across, and lies in wait beneath it. Above the web there are many threads holding it in place. When prey hits these threads, it falls down onto the sheet web, where it is grabbed from below by the spider.

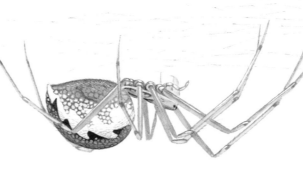

Sheetlike web

This **orb weaver spider** has caught a butterfly in its web and is wrapping the prey in threads of silk so that it cannot escape. It will then carry the butterfly off to eat in a hiding place near the web.

Web

Spider with prey wrapped in silk

Moving on the web

This garden spider has extra clawlike structures on each foot, which help it grip the dry lines of the web while moving around on the web or wrapping up prey. If the spider touches the sticky threads, a special oily covering on its legs prevents the spider from getting trapped in its own web.

241

Scorpions and other arachnids

There are about 1,500 species of scorpions, living everywhere from deserts to rain forests in warm parts of the world. They use the venomous stinger at the end of the body to kill prey and to defend themselves. A few kinds of scorpions have venom so strong that it can kill a human, but the sting of most is no worse than that of a bee or a wasp. Also in the arachnid group are tiny mites and ticks. Mites eat aphid eggs and prey on other small insects. Some also live as parasites on other animals. Ticks feed on the blood of birds, mammals, and reptiles.

Pseudoscorpion

Pedipalp

Family: Chernetidae
Size: up to ¼ in (0.6 cm) long
Number of species: 1,000

Pseudoscorpion

These tiny soil-dwelling relatives of scorpions have venom glands in their pedipalps that they use when attacking prey. They do not have a stinger. Pseudoscorpions have silk glands, and they spin cocoons in which they spend the winter.

Pedipalp

Centruroides scorpion

This scorpion belongs to the family of true scorpions. It comes out at night to seize insects and spiders in its powerful pincers. The female carries her newborn young around on her back for a few weeks while they grow. The scorpion's sting can be deadly to humans.

Wind scorpion

Wind scorpion

Wind scorpions, also known as sun spiders, are related to true scorpions. Common in desert areas, these fast-running hunters come out at night to prey on insects and even small lizards. They use their large leglike pedipalps to catch prey and their front legs as feelers.

Family: Eremobatidae
Size: ⅝–1¾ in (1.5–4.5 cm) long
Number of species: 900

Whip scorpion

Not a true scorpion, the whip scorpion uses its stingless tail as a feeler and its powerful claws for catching prey. The whip scorpion's other common name is vinegarroon because it can spray an acidic, vinegary liquid from glands near the base of its tail when threatened.

Family: Buthidae
Size: 2–2¾ in (5–7 cm) long
Number of species: 700

Whip scorpion

Family: Thelyphonidae
Size: 5¾ in (14.5 cm) long, including tail
Number of species: 100

Centruroides scorpion

242

Velvet mite

Family: Trombiculidae
Size: up to ³⁄₁₆ in (0.5 cm) long
Number of species: 200

Family: Pyroglyphidae
Size: ¹⁄₁₀₀–²⁄₁₀₀ in (0.25–0.5 mm) long
Number of species: 20

Velvet mite

This mite gets its common name from the thick, soft hair that covers its rounded body. Adult velvet mites are not parasites and feed mostly on insect eggs. They lay their own eggs on the ground. When the larvae hatch they live as parasites on insects and spiders, feeding on their body fluids.

House dust mite

These mites are common in houses throughout the world. They feed on scales of skin found in house dust. Their droppings contain material that can cause an allergic reaction or asthma (difficulty in breathing) in some sensitive people.

House dust mite

Scorpion

The scorpion finds prey mostly by its sense of touch. It uses fine hairs attached to nerves on the body, legs, and claws to sense movements. It grabs prey in its huge claws and then swings its stinger forward over its body to inject poison into the creature to paralyze or kill it before eating.

Family: Phalangiidae
Size: ¹⁄₈–³⁄₄ in (0.3–2 cm) long
Number of species: 3,400

Daddy-longlegs

Daddy-longlegs

Also known as the harvestman, this relative of spiders has a rounded body without the narrow waist typical of spiders. All its legs are very long and thin, but the second pair (from the front) are the longest. Usually active at night, it hunts insects. The female lays her eggs in the ground, where they stay through the winter until they hatch in the spring.

Scorpion

Family: Buthidae
Size: 2–2¾ in (5–7 cm) long
Number of species: 700

Family: Ixodidae
Size: ¹⁄₁₆–¹⁄₈ in (0.15–0.3 cm) long
Number of species: 650

Tick, swollen with blood

Tick

Ticks are parasites—they live by feeding on the blood of birds, mammals, and reptiles. They stay on the host for several days while feeding, attached by their strong mouthparts. Some species may pass along diseases as they feed.

243

Snails, slugs, and other land invertebrates

In addition to insects and spiders, there are many other kinds of invertebrate creatures that spend their lives on land. Although most mollusks (see page 203) live in the sea, there are land species such as slugs and snails. Wood lice are related to sea-living crustaceans such as crabs and shrimp. Earthworms spend their lives burrowing through the soil in fields, woodlands, and gardens, but they are relatives of the segmented worms that live in the sea. All of these animals are common worldwide.

Like insects and spiders, millipedes and centipedes are arthropods. Extremely successful creatures, they live everywhere from tropical rain forests to tundra. They may be mistaken for insects, but they have many more legs and do not have wings. Their bodies tend to dry out in the sun, so these creatures usually come out only at night.

Great black slug

The slug is a mollusk, like a snail, but has no external shell. All land mollusks make mucus. This slime helps keep the slug's body from drying out and allows the creature to move more easily. The slug leaves trails of slime wherever it goes, and these help it find its way. It feeds mostly on living and rotting plant and animal material, which it finds by smell.

Size: 6 in (15 cm) long
Range: Europe; introduced into North America
Scientific name:
Arion ater

Great black slug

Earthworm

Earthworms are common in soil all over the world. They spend most of their lives underground and only come to the surface at night or in wet weather. Dead leaves and other plant material are their main food, but they also eat soil, digesting what they can and excreting the rest.

Size: up to 11¾ in (30 cm) long
Range: worldwide
Scientific name:
Lumbricus terrestris

Earthworm

Wood louse

Most crustaceans, such as crabs and shrimp, live in the sea. The wood louse is one of a few that live on land. Like all crustaceans, it has a hard external skeleton that protects a soft body. There are 13 body segments and 7 pairs of legs. The wood louse hides in moist, dark places in the day and comes out at night to feed on rotting plants and tiny dead creatures.

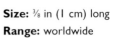

Size: ⅜ in (1 cm) long
Range: worldwide
Scientific name:
Armadillidium vulgare

Wood louse

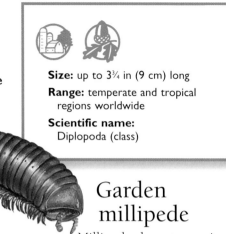

Garden millipede

Armored millipede

Size: up to 3¾ in (9 cm) long
Range: temperate and tropical regions worldwide
Scientific name: Diplopoda (class)

Armored millipede

These millipedes have a particularly hard outer shell and live in forests, where they feed on leaves and other rotting plants on the forest floor. They have poison glands, and some can actually spray poison to defend themselves against enemies.

Garden millipede

Millipedes have two pairs of legs on each body segment. Despite their name (which means "one thousand feet"), they rarely have a thousand legs—most have only a couple hundred. They are slow-moving plant eaters that live under stones or tree bark or hidden inside rotting vegetation.

Centipede

Size: up to 5 in (13 cm) long
Range: temperate and tropical regions worldwide
Scientific name: Diplopoda (class)

Centipede

Unlike millipedes, centipedes only have one pair of legs on each body segment. These animals move fast on their many legs and prey on insects, spiders, and other small creatures. They seize prey in their sharp claws, which can inject a powerful poison to paralyze the food source.

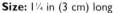

Size: 1¼ in (3 cm) long
Range: temperate and tropical regions worldwide
Scientific name: Chilopoda (class)

Garden snail

Different types of land snails live all over the world. All have a soft sluglike body and a hard shell that is carried on the back. Most snails spend the day resting inside their shell and become active at night. To find food, such as leafy plants, they move along by making rippling movements of the fleshy "foot." They slide on a layer of slime secreted by the foot.

Garden snail

Size: body: 3½ in (9 cm) long
Range: Europe; introduced into North America
Scientific name: *Helix aspersa*

Foot

Sea creatures

In addition to the thousands of kinds of fish that live in the oceans there is also a huge range of invertebrates. About a million species of invertebrate animals, including clams, crabs, and jellyfish, live in every part of the ocean, from the surface waters to the deepest sea. The most highly populated waters are those near the surface. Here, plenty of light penetrates to about 330 feet (100 m), and plant plankton thrives. These microscopic plants are eaten by animal plankton—tiny animals that drift in surface waters and are themselves eaten by larger sea creatures.

Sponges, jellyfish, and their relatives

Sponges have such simple bodies that they look more like plants than animals. Their larvae are free-swimming, but adult sponges remain in one place on a rock or on the seafloor. Sea anemones, too, are plantlike. They belong to a large group of creatures called cnidarians, as do corals and jellyfish. Most have a simple tubelike body and tentacles armed with stinging cells. Comb jellies are a separate group. They are small translucent animals that float in surface waters. Lamp shells are shelled creatures that can anchor themselves to rocks or the seafloor by a fleshy stalk.

Lamp shell

The lamp shell belongs to a group of animals called brachiopods. Brachiopods have lived on Earth for more than 550 million years. The lamp shell has two shells and a short stalk on which it can move around. When the shells open, they expose folded tentacles lined with tiny hairs. These hairs drive water over the tentacles, which trap tiny particles of food.

Size: 1¼ in (3 cm) long
Range: Atlantic Ocean
Scientific name:
 Terebratulina septentrionalis

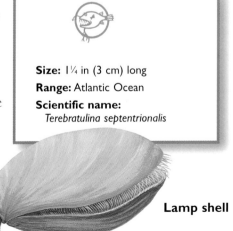

Lamp shell

Common comb jelly

The comb jelly moves with the help of tiny hairs arranged in lines down its baglike body. These hairs are called comb plates, and they beat together to push the comb jelly through the water. It eats shrimp and other small creatures.

Common comb jelly

Size: 6 in (15 cm) long
Range: Arctic and Atlantic Oceans
Scientific name:
 Bolinopsis infundibulum

Vase sponge

Sponges are among the simplest of animals. To feed, they draw water into the chambers of the body, where tiny particles of food are trapped and digested. The water also provides sponges with oxygen and removes carbon dioxide.

Vase sponge

Size: up to 19¾ in (50 cm) long
Range: Caribbean Sea
Scientific name:
 Callyspongia spp.

Brain coral colony

Sea pen

Portuguese man-of-war

The Portuguese man-of-war is not a true jellyfish but a colony of hundreds of individual animals called polyps. They live together under the sail-like, gas-filled float that lies on the ocean's surface. Each kind of polyp performs a different task for the colony, such as capturing food or producing eggs.

Portuguese man-of-war

Size: float: 11¾ in (30 cm) long; tentacles: 60 ft (18 m)

Range: warm and tropical waters in Atlantic, Indian, and Pacific Oceans

Scientific name: *Physalia physalis*

Brain coral

Brain coral is most common in water 20 to 40 feet (6 to 12 m) deep. Colonies of tiny anemone-like creatures called coral polyps create dome-shaped formations that resemble brains. Each of the polyps has a hard skeleton. The skeletons make up the rocky base of the colony.

Size: colony up to 6½ ft (2 m) wide

Range: Indian and Pacific Oceans, Caribbean Sea, and southeastern North Atlantic Ocean

Scientific name: *Meandrina* spp.

Sea pen

The featherlike sea pen is not one animal but a group of many individuals called polyps. One large stemlike polyp stands in the seabed and supports the whole group. On the side branches there are many small feeding polyps. If touched, the sea pen glows with phosphorescence.

Size: up to 15 in (38 cm) tall

Range: North Atlantic Ocean

Scientific name: *Pennatula phosphorea*

Sea anemone

The sea anemone may look like a flower, but it is actually an animal that catches other creatures to eat. At the base of its body is a sucking disk that keeps the anemone attached to a rock. At the top is the mouth, surrounded by stinging tentacles.

Sea anemone

Purple jellyfish

Like most jellyfish, this creature has many stinging cells on its long tentacles. These cells protect it from enemies and help it catch plankton to eat. Although known as the purple jellyfish, it may be yellow, red, or even brown in color.

Purple jellyfish

Size: bell: 1¼ in (3 cm) wide; tentacles: 35½ in (90 cm) long

Range: Atlantic, Indian, and Pacific Oceans

Scientific name: *Pelagia noctiluca*

Size: up to 9¾ in (25 cm) tall

Range: Atlantic and Pacific Oceans

Scientific name: *Tealia* spp.

Crustaceans

There are about 31,000 species of crustaceans, including creatures such as barnacles, crabs, lobsters, and shrimp. Wood lice live on land, and there are some shrimp and other species in fresh water, but most crustaceans live in the sea. Typically, they have a tough outer skeleton that protects the soft body within. The head is made up of six segments, on which there are two pairs of antennae and several different sets of mouthparts. The rest of the body, which may be divided into a thorax and an abdomen, carries the walking legs.

Deep-sea shrimp

The deep-sea shrimp's antennae are longer than its body. It spreads the antennae out in the water to help it find food in the darkness of the deep sea. It eats any dead and decaying matter that it comes across.

Deep-sea shrimp

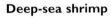

Size: 4 in (10 cm) long
Range: Atlantic Ocean
Scientific name:
  Pasiphaea spp.

Goose barnacles

Goose barnacles live fixed by their stalks to any object floating in the open sea, including logs, buoys, and boats. The barnacle's body is enclosed by a shell made of five plates. These open at the top so that the barnacle can extend its feathery legs and collect tiny particles of food from the water.

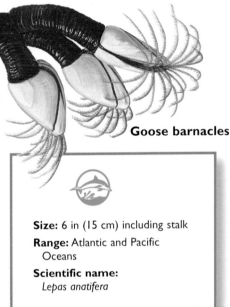

Goose barnacles

Size: 6 in (15 cm) including stalk
Range: Atlantic and Pacific Oceans
Scientific name:
  Lepas anatifera

Giant isopod

A sea-living relative of the wood louse, the giant isopod lives in Antarctic waters, where it catches any food it can find. It also scavenges on the seafloor for dead and dying creatures. Antarctic isopods are among the largest isopods in the world.

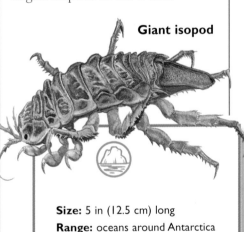

Giant isopod

Size: 5 in (12.5 cm) long
Range: oceans around Antarctica
Scientific name:
  Glyptonotus antarcticus

Size: 11¾ in (30 cm)
Range: North Atlantic coasts
Scientific name:
  Homerus americanus

American lobster

American lobster

During the day this large crustacean hides in rock crevices, but at night it comes out to hunt. It uses its huge pincers to crack and tear apart prey such as mollusks and crabs. In the summer the female lobster lays thousands of eggs, which she carries around with her on the underside of her tail. The eggs hatch into shrimplike larvae that float in surface waters for a few weeks. They then settle on the seafloor and start to develop into adults.

Hermit crab

Unlike other crabs, the hermit crab has no hard shell of its own. It protects its soft body by living in the discarded shell of another creature, such as a snail. The crab has large pincers on its first pair of legs that it uses to grab prey.

Hermit crab

Size: up to 4 in (10 cm) long
Range: North Atlantic coasts
Scientific name:
  Pagurus bernhardus

Montague's shrimp

Shrimp have much thinner shells than crabs or lobsters. The limbs on the abdomen are used for swimming. Some legs on the thorax are for walking, and others are used as mouthparts.

Size: up to 5 in (12.5 cm) long
Range: North Atlantic coasts
Scientific name:
  Pandalus montagui

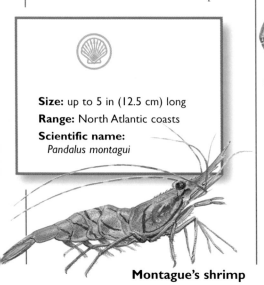

Montague's shrimp

Antarctic krill

Antarctic krill

Shrimplike krill feed on plant and animal plankton that they sieve from the water. In turn, they are the main food of many fish, penguins, and even whales. A blue whale can eat as many as four million krill in a day. Krill are extremely common and sometimes occur in such large numbers that the sea looks red.

Size: up to 2 in (5 cm) long
Range: oceans around Antarctica
Scientific name:
  Euphausia superba

Amphipod

This small crustacean lives on the lower shore under rocks or among seaweed and feeds on tiny pieces of plant and animal matter. On its abdomen are three pairs of jumping legs. The female amphipod holds her developing young in a pouch on the underside of her body.

Amphipod

Size: up to 1 in (2.5 cm) long
Range: Atlantic and Pacific coasts
Scientific name:
  Gammarus locusta

Blue crab

Size: 9¼ in (23 cm) wide
Range: Atlantic and Gulf coasts of North America, South America to Uruguay, West Indies
Scientific name:
  Callinectes sapidus

Blue crab

Most crabs have a strong shell, which protects the body, and five pairs of legs. The first pair have powerful pincers used to break open the shells of mollusks and other prey. The other legs are smaller. The blue crab is an extremely popular edible crab.

Mollusks

There are at least 100,000 living species of mollusks. They are divided into three main groups: gastropods, such as limpets and snails; bivalves, which include clams, mussels, and scallops; and cephalopods, such as squid, cuttlefish, octopuses, and nautiluses. Slugs and some kinds of snails live on land, and there are freshwater snails and clams, but the greatest variety of mollusks is found in the sea. In most mollusks the body is divided into three parts—the head, which contains the mouth and sense organs; the body; and the foot, a fleshy part of the body on which the animal moves along. Most, but not all, mollusks have a tough shell that protects the soft body.

Butternut clam

The usual home of the clam is a burrow deep in a sandy or muddy sea bottom. It digs the burrow with its foot, a fleshy part of its body. Two long tubes can be extended from inside the shell. Water and food (tiny living particles) go in through one tube. The filtered water then goes out the other tube.

Butternut clam

Iceland scallop

Size: 4 in (10 cm) long
Range: Arctic and North Atlantic Oceans
Scientific name: *Chlamys islandicus*

Size: 6 in (15 cm) long
Range: North Pacific Ocean
Scientific name: *Saxidomus nuttalli*

Eye

Atlantic deer cowrie

The cowrie is a type of sea snail with a beautiful shiny shell. Unlike most snails, the cowrie's mantle can be extended to cover the outside of the shell and camouflage the animal. (The mantle is a thin fold of tissue, part of which makes the shell.) The opening of the cowrie's shell is edged with 35 teeth.

Iceland scallop

The scallop has a soft body protected by two shells. A row of well-developed eyes can be seen on each shell when the shells are slightly parted. The scallop moves by pulling its shells together, forcing out jets of water to push itself along.

Eastern oyster

The oyster is a type of bivalve. It has a soft body protected by two hard shells, which are held together by strong muscles. It eats tiny pieces of plant and animal food that it filters from the water. The water is drawn into the partly opened shell, and any food is caught on tiny sticky hairs on the oyster's gills.

Size: up to 4 in (10 cm) long
Range: Atlantic and Gulf coasts of North America
Scientific name: *Crassotrea virginica*

Size: up to 5 in (12.5 cm) long
Range: western Atlantic Ocean, Caribbean Sea
Scientific name: *Cypraea cervus*

Mantle

Atlantic deer cowrie

250

Eastern oyster

Common octopus

The octopus has a pouchlike body and eight long arms lined with two rows of suckers. It pulls itself along with its strong arms and can also swim quickly by shooting jets of water out of its body. It spends much of its time hiding in crevices or under rocks, watching out for prey, such as crabs, clams, and shrimp. The octopus holds its prey in its tentacles and may kill or paralyze it with a poisonous bite.

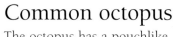
Lightning whelk

Size: up to 39½ in (100 cm) long
Range: Atlantic coasts
Scientific name:
Octopus vulgaris

Size: 15¾ in (40 cm) long
Range: Atlantic Ocean
Scientific name:
Busycon sinistrum

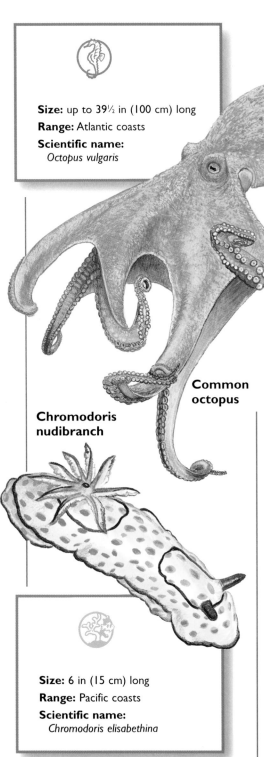
Common octopus

Lightning whelk

This large whelk has a very beautiful spiral shell with brown markings. It lives on sandy or muddy sea bottoms in shallow water and feeds mostly on clams and other mollusks, which it digs out of the seafloor.

Chromodoris nudibranch

Purple sea snail

This little snail cannot swim, but it drifts in the surface waters of the sea, clinging to a raft of bubbles. These are made from mucus the snail secretes, which hardens when it enters the water.

Purple sea snail

Size: 1 in (2.5 cm) in diameter
Range: Atlantic, Indian, and Pacific Oceans
Scientific name:
Janthina janthina

Size: 6 in (15 cm) long
Range: Pacific coasts
Scientific name:
Chromodoris elisabethina

Chromodoris nudibranch

Nudibranchs, or sea slugs, are a group of snails that have no shells. They are often brightly colored. This species has a pair of hornlike projections and a clump of feathery gills on its back. Sponges are its main food.

Longfin inshore squid

The squid has a long torpedo-shaped body, four pairs of arms, and one pair of much longer tentacles. Suckers on the arms and the tips of the tentacles help the squid grasp its prey—mostly fish and crustaceans. A fast swimmer, the squid moves by a type of jet propulsion, shooting water out of its body to force itself backward through the water.

Size: up to 30 in (76 cm) long, including tentacles
Range: Atlantic Ocean and Mediterranean Sea
Scientific name: Loligo pealii

Longfin inshore squid

251

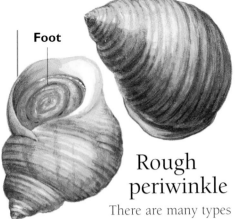

Foot

Rough periwinkle

There are many types of periwinkles, each adapted for life in different parts of the shore. The rough periwinkle lives on stones and rocks higher up the shore than most other species.

Chiton

Unlike other mollusks, the chiton has a shell made up of eight sections held together by muscles. If in danger, the chiton can roll itself up like an armadillo.

Rock clingers

Although most marine creatures swim or float freely in the water, some live firmly attached to rocks or other surfaces. This helps protect them from the water that sweeps over them. Barnacles, one kind of rock clinger, are among the most common creatures on the shore. Huge colonies of them cover rocks and shore debris and even attach themselves to other creatures such as mussels. Barnacles begin life as free-swimming larvae and spend a month or more floating in coastal waters, feeding on plankton. During its final larval stage, each barnacle finds somewhere to settle. It fixes itself to the surface with a cementlike substance that it makes in glands in its body. Once settled, it does not move again.

Limpets, periwinkles, and chitons can all cling to rocks by means of a suckerlike foot, which is so strong that the animals are almost impossible to remove. But these creatures can also move around to graze on algae.

Common limpet

As a limpet moves over rocks feeding on algae, it leaves a sticky trail of mucus behind it. This helps the limpet make its way back to the exact same place on the rock after each feeding trip.

Acorn barnacle

When covered by water at high tide, the barnacle opens its shell at the top and puts out its feathery arms to gather plankton to eat. When the tide is out, the barnacle keeps its trapdoor top firmly closed.

Common mussel

The threads that hold the mussel on to rocks are made as a sticky fluid inside a gland in the mussel's body. One end is attached to the mussel's foot, the other to a rock. The mussel moves around by anchoring some threads to a new rock and then pulling itself along. The shell is in two halves. These are normally held tight together, but they can be partly opened so that the mussel can filter tiny pieces of food from the water.

Inner surface of a mussel shell

Blue-rayed limpet

Not all limpets cling to rocks. The blue-rayed limpet lives attached to seaweed, which is anchored to rock or to the seafloor near the shore. The limpet grazes on the seaweed fronds and on small plants such as algae that grow on the seaweed.

A colorful **painted topshell** clings to rocks on the seashore. It is surrounded by coral polyps, which it eats. Topshells are a kind of snail. Most varieties feed on tiny plants called algae.

253

Worms and echinoderms

There are about 11,500 species of segmented, or annelid, worms. They include earthworms, which live on land, as well as some freshwater worms such as leeches, but most live in the sea. All have a body that is divided into a number of segments. All echinoderms live in the sea. There are four main groups—brittle stars, starfish, sea cucumbers, and sea urchins. Many have a body that is divided into five radiating parts. Most echinoderms move around using tiny stilts called tube feet, each tipped with a sucking disk.

Sea mouse

Despite its plump shape, the sea mouse is actually a kind of worm. Its upper side is covered with lots of grayish brown bristles that give it a furry look and inspire its common name. The sea mouse spends much of its life under mud or sand in shallow water.

Sea mouse

Size: 7 in (18 cm) long
Range: Atlantic and Mediterranean coasts
Scientific name: *Aphrodita aculeata*

Sea lily

Sea lily

This relative of the starfish lives attached to the sea bottom by a stalk. The sea lily's branching arms are lined with suckerlike tube feet. When feeding, the sea lily spreads its arms wide and traps plankton and other tiny particles with its tube feet. The food is then passed down grooves lined with hairs to the mouth, at the center of the body.

Size: up to 23½ in (60 cm) tall
Range: Atlantic Ocean
Scientific name: *Ptilocrinus pinnatus*

Long-spined urchin

Sharp spines protect this sea urchin's rounded body from enemies. The urchin's mouth is on the underside of the body and has five teeth arranged in a circle for chewing food. By day these urchins stay hidden on the reef, but at night they come out to feed on algae.

Size: body: 4 in (10 cm) wide; spines: 4–15¾ in (10–40 cm) long
Range: tropical parts of Atlantic Ocean, Caribbean Sea
Scientific name: *Diadema antillarum*

Long-spined urchin

Brittle star

The brittle star gets its name because its arms are easily broken off, although they grow back again. The animal uses its tube feet to catch small crustaceans and other creatures. Its mouth is on the underside of the central disk.

Brittle star

Tube feet

Size: body: 1 in (2.5 cm) wide; arms: up to 4 in (10 cm) long
Range: Atlantic Ocean
Scientific name: *Ophiothrix fragilis*

Feather duster worm

The body of this spectacular worm usually stays hidden in a flexible tube attached to a reef or the seafloor. The tube is made of fine sand stuck together with a gluey substance made in the worm's body. The worm catches food with its crown of feathery gills.

Tube

Feather duster worm

Size: 5 in (12.5 cm) long
Range: Atlantic Ocean and Caribbean Sea
Scientific name:
  Sabellastarte magnifica

Common sand dollar

The sand dollar, a kind of sea urchin, has a shell covered with short bristles. It uses tube feet on the flat underside of its body to gather food as it moves through the sand.

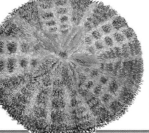

Common sand dollar

Size: 3 in (7.5 cm) wide
Range: North Atlantic and Pacific coasts
Scientific name:
  Echinarachnius parma

Thorny starfish

Large spines cover the body and five arms, or rays, of this starfish. Two rows of tube feet extend down the underside of each arm. They act like suction cups and help the starfish to move and search for food. Some types of starfish are strong enough to pull open mussels or scallops.

Thorny starfish

Size: 4¾ in (12 cm) across
Range: western Atlantic Ocean, Caribbean Sea
Scientific name:
  Echinastur sentus

255

Size: up to 9¾ in (25 cm) long
Range: North Atlantic Ocean
Scientific name:
  Holothuria forskali

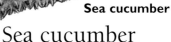

Sea cucumber

Sea cucumber

Sea cucumbers are related to starfish, but they have long, simple bodies. At one end is the anus and at the other is the mouth, which is surrounded by food-gathering tentacles. Rows of tiny tube feet run the length of the body. When threatened, the sea cucumber ejects sticky white threads from its anus. These confuse predators.

Paddle worm

This worm lives under rocks among seaweed, both on the shore and in deeper water. It has four pairs of tentacles on its head and lots of tiny leaflike paddles down each side of its long body. It feeds mainly on other worms.

Size: up to 17¾ in (45 cm) long
Range: Atlantic and Pacific coasts
Scientific name:
  Phyllodoce spp.

Paddle worm

Why do animals build nests?

Although many animals manage without a nest or home of any kind, others build structures that they use for shelter and for rearing their young in safety. This home may be specially built, like a bird's nest, or simply a natural hole or a sheltered spot. Homes may be made in trees, on the ground, or in burrows under the ground. Birds generally only use their nests when breeding. They lay and incubate their eggs in nests and care for their young. The nest is usually abandoned once the baby birds have gone. Some mammals, such as beavers and prairie dogs, spend much of their time in the homes they make. These may contain chambers for sleeping, caring for young, and storing food. Insects such as bees, wasps, ants, and termites also build elaborate homes.

The nest of the **penduline tit** hangs from the end of a slender twig, where it is hard for predators to reach. The nest is woven from plant fibers and has an entrance near the top.

Beavers dam a stream with logs, branches, and mud to create a pond in which to store a winter food supply and build a shelter, or lodge.

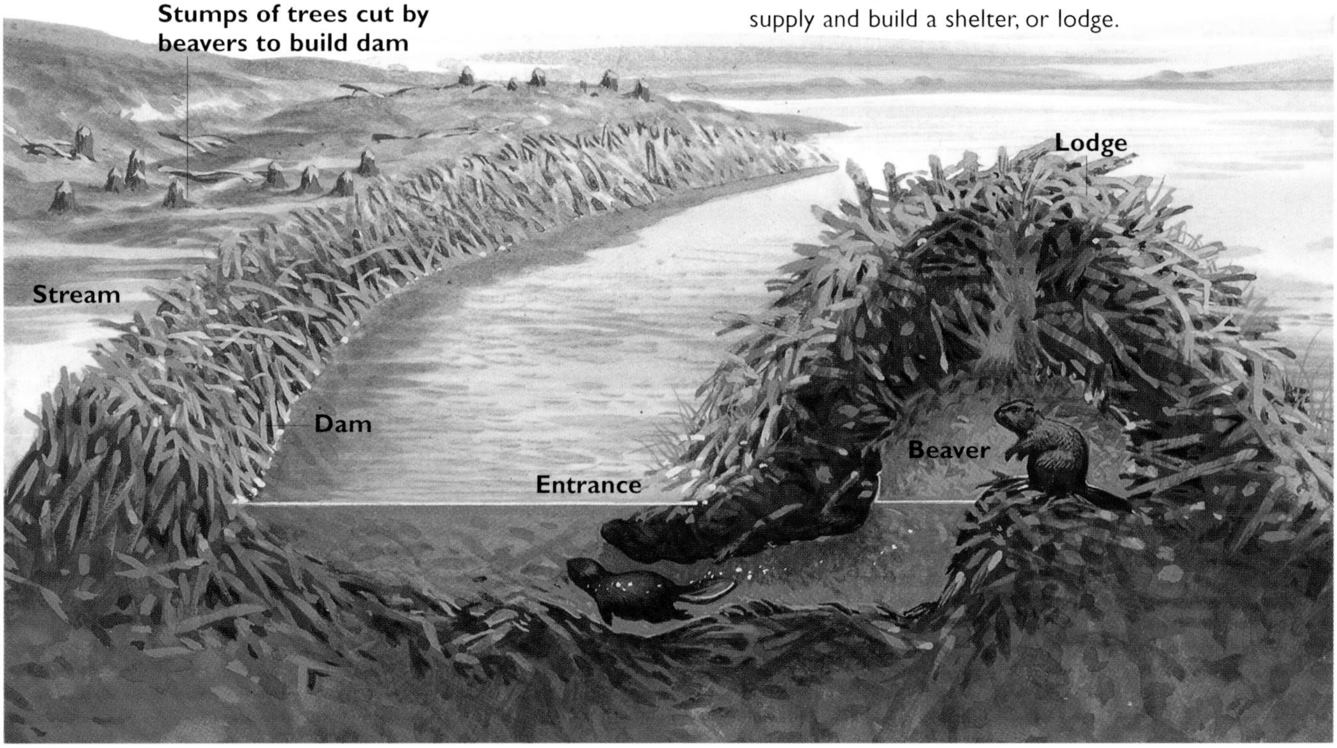

Stumps of trees cut by beavers to build dam

Lodge

Stream

Dam

Entrance

Beaver

The female **harvest mouse** builds a nest as a shelter for her young. She finds some sturdy cereal stems and starts by winding the leaves of one stem around another to make a platform about 20 inches (50 cm) above the ground. She then takes lengths of grass or leaves and uses these to weave a ball-like structure, which measures about 4 inches (10 cm) across.

This large mound is made by small, soft-bodied insects called **termites**. The mound is made of soil mixed with termite waste. Inside is a complex nest: A maze of chambers and tunnels contains special areas for food storage and for eggs and larvae. A chimney inside the mound lets air in and out and helps keep the temperature in the nest comfortable.

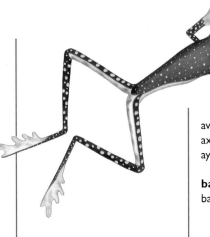

Index

List of abbreviations
Imperial
in = inches
ft = feet
mph = miles per hour
lb = pounds

Metric
cm = centimeters
m = meters
km = kilometers
km/h = kilometers per hour
kg = kilograms

Rainbow lorikeet

Credits

Photographic credits

t = top; b = bottom; l = left; r = right

6–7 Norbert Rosing/Oxford Scientific Films; 20 Haroldo Palo Jr./NHPA; 37 Frank Schneidermeyer/Oxford Scientific Films; 41 Rick Price/Oxford Scientific Films; 49 Martyn Colbeck/Oxford Scientific Films; 66t Alastair Shay/Oxford Scientific Films; 66b Eyal Bartov/Oxford Scientific Films; 66–67 Stan Osolinski/Oxford Scientific Films; 68–69 Amos Nachoum/Corbis; 89 Colin Monteath/Oxford Scientific Films; 95 Lon E. Lauber/Oxford Scientific Films; 103 Michael Fogden/Oxford Scientific Films; 109 Hans Reinhard/Oxford Scientific Films; 114l Jeff Lepore/Oxford Scientific Films; 114r Alastair Shay/Oxford Scientific Films; 115 Jorge Sierra/Oxford Scientific Films; 116–117 Zig Leszczynski/Oxford Scientific Films; 123 David Cayless/Oxford Scientific Films; 133 David Haring/Oxford Scientific Films; 138–139 Zig Leszczynski/Oxford Scientific Films; 153 John Netherton/Oxford Scientific Films; 154 Alastair Shay/Oxford Scientific Films; 154–155 Michael Fogden/Oxford Scientific Films; 155 Marty Cordano/Oxford Scientific Films; 156–157 David B. Fleetham/Oxford Scientific Films; 163 Gary Bell/Planet Earth Pictures; 181 Richard Herrmann/Oxford Scientific Films; 198 Anthony Bannister/Oxford Scientific Films; 198–199 Andrew Plumptre/Oxford Scientific Films; 199t David B. Fleetham/Oxford Scientific Films; 199b Steve Turner/Oxford Scientific Films; 200–201 P.K. Sharpe/Oxford Scientific Films; 217 Stephen Dalton/NHPA; 225 Bob Fredrick/Oxford Scientific Films; 231 David Thompson/Oxford Scientific Films; 241 Oxford Scientific Films; 253 Paul Kay/Oxford Scientific Films; 256 Roland Mayr/Oxford Scientific Films; 257t Roger Hosking/NHPA; 257b Stan Osolinski/Oxford Scientific Films

Artwork credits

Mammals: Graham Allen, John Francis, Elizabeth Gray, Bernard Robinson, Eric Robson, Simon Turvey, Dick Twinney, Michael Woods. **Birds**: Keith Brewer, Hilary Burn, Malcolm Ellis, Steve Kirk, Colin Newman, Denys Ovenden, Peter D. Scott, Ken Wood, Michael Woods. **Reptiles and amphibians**: John Francis, Elizabeth Gray, Steve Kirk, Alan Male, Colin Newman, Eric Robson, Peter D. Scott. **Fish**: Robin Boutell, John Francis, Elizabeth Gray, Elizabeth Kay, Colin Newman, Guy Smith, Michael Woods. **Insects, spiders, and other invertebrates**: Robin Boutell, Joanne Cowne, Sandra Doyle, Bridget James, Steve Kirk, Adrian Lascom, Alan Male, Colin Newman, Steve Roberts, Bernard Robinson, Roger Stewart, Colin Woolf. **Habitat symbols**: Roy Flooks. **Chapter panels**: Michael Woods. **Habitat map**: Eugene Fleury, Carl Mehler. **Cover design**: Holli Rathman.

Status symbols: based on information available on the World Conservation Monitoring Centre's Web site: www.wcmc.org.uk/species/animals/animal_redlist.html

Library of Congress Cataloging-in-Publication Data

Marshall children's animal encyclopedia.
  National Geographic animal encyclopedia.
     p.   cm.
  Originally published: The Marshall children's animal encyclopedia. London : Marshall
     Pub., 1999.
  Summary: A comprehensive look at the world of animals, their features, behavior, and
  life cycles, arranged by the categories "Mammals," "Birds," "Reptiles," "Amphibians,"
  "Fish," and "Insects, Spiders, and Other Invertebrates."
  ISBN 0–7922–7180–7
  1. Animals—Encyclopedias, Juvenile. [1.Animals.] I. Title: Animal encyclopedia. II.
  National Geographic Society (U.S.) III. Title.

QL49 .M29 2000
590'.3—dc21   99-048020

The world's largest nonprofit scientific and educational organization, the National Geographic Society was founded in 1888 "for the increase and diffusion of geographic knowledge." Since then it has supported scientific exploration and spread information to its more than nine million members worldwide.

The National Geographic Society educates and inspires millions every day through magazines, books, television programs, videos, maps and atlases, research grants, the National Geography Bee, teacher workshops, and innovative classroom materials.

The Society is supported through membership dues and income from the sale of its educational products. Members receive NATIONAL GEOGRAPHIC magazine—the Society's official journal—discounts on Society products, and other benefits.

For more information about the National Geographic Society and its educational programs and publications, please call 1-800-NGS-LINE (647-5463), or write to the following address:

National Geographic Society
1145 17th Street N.W.
Washington, D.C. 20036-4688 U.S.A.

Visit the Society's Web site: www.nationalgeographic.com